SAP® Guidelines for
Best-Built Applications
That Integrate with SAP Business Suite

2011 Fall

The SAP Architectural Community
Richard Probst, Series Editor

Terms of Use

You may use this publication for your internal business purposes only. You may make this publication available within your company or to your consultants and subcontractors. However, you are not entitled to distribute this publication to other third parties in electronic or paper form. Any further use of this publication must be expressly approved by SAP in writing.

If you wish to order a printed version of this publication, see the ordering instructions in the Preface.

Please note that this publication is subject to change and may be updated by SAP at any time without notice. The most current version of this publication is published by SAP on http://bestbuiltapps.sap.com or at an alternative location to be designated by SAP. SAP strongly recommends that you always refer to the current version of this publication.

SAP assumes no responsibility for errors or omissions in this publication. SAP does not warrant the accuracy or completeness of the information, text, graphics, links, or other items contained within this publication. This publication is provided without a warranty of any kind, either express or implied, including but not limited to, the implied warranties of merchantability, fitness for a particular purpose, or noninfringement. The only warranties for any SAP products and services are those that are set forth in the express warranty statements accompanying such products and services, if any. Nothing herein should be construed as constituting an additional warranty.

SAP shall have no liability for damages of any kind, including without limitation direct, special, indirect, or consequential damages that may result from the use of this publication. This limitation shall not apply in cases of intent or gross negligence. The statutory liability for personal injury and defective products is not affected.

All statements in this publication with regards to strategies, developments, and functionalities of SAP products represent intentions only and are not intended to be binding upon SAP to any particular course of business, product strategy, or development.

SAP—Copyrights and Trademarks

Writers: Dan Woods and Deb Cameron
Production Editor: Deb Gabriel
Wiki Editors: Deb Cameron, David Penick and Deb Gabriel
Layout and Graphics: Deb Gabriel

Contents

Editorial Credits   i

Foreword   iii

Preface   v

    Reading the Guidelines   v

    Interpreting the Guidelines   vi

    Resources for the Guidelines   vi

    Referring to the Guidelines   vii

    Obtaining Copies of This Document   viii

    A Word about Completeness   viii

1   Introduction   **1**

    Benefits to SAP Customers and Partners   2

    Architectural Concepts for Complementing SAP Business Suite   2

    How SAP Guidelines for Best-Built Applications Are Being Published   3

    Sources for SAP Guidelines for Best-Built Applications   5

    Approaches to Development   6

    Guideline Topics   9

    Detailed How-To Information   10

2   SAP Guidelines for Best-Built Applications, Summarized   **11**

    Overall Goal: Maximize Alignment   11

    Guidelines for Application Lifecycle Management   11

Guidelines for Process Orchestration and Service-Oriented Architecture (SOA)   20

Guidelines for User Interface and User Experience   25

Guidelines for Enterprise Information Management   28

Guidelines for Business Intelligence Tools   31

Guidelines for Application Development   34

Guidelines for Security   37

3 Application Lifecycle Management Guidelines for Best-Built Applications   39

An ITIL-Based Approach to ALM   40

SAP Solution Manager: At the Center of the Lifecycle   42

The Requirements Phase   44

The Design Phase   48

The Build & Test Phase   55

The Deploy Phase   58

The Operate Phase   60

The Optimize Phase   64

Application Lifecycle Management Resources   73

4 Process Orchestration and SOA Guidelines for Best-Built Applications   75

Process Orchestration   76

Composite Applications   78

Loose Coupling Through Web Services   82

A Best Practices Methodology for Designing a Loosely Coupled Composite Application   87

Implementing Process Orchestration   91

SOA   92

Software Migrated to Run in the SAP Environment   99

Software Connected with SAP: Developers Using Microsoft .NET   100

Software Connected with SAP: Developers Using IBM WebSphere   101

Partner-delivered Enterprise Services (PdES)   102

**5 User Interface and User Experience Guidelines for
Best-Built Applications**   **107**

Principles of UI Development   107

The Shell and the Canvas   111

Front-End Client Software   112

UI Technology and Tool Recommendations for Developers Using SAP
Tools   117

Deciding Which SAP UI Technology to Use   119

Guided Procedures and Guided Activities   127

Java UI Technologies for Migrated Software   127

UI Technologies for Rich Internet Applications   128

Mobile User Interfaces Guidelines   128

Output and Forms   128

**6 Enterprise Information Management Guidelines for Best-Built
Applications**   **131**

Database Considerations   133

Data Integration and Data Quality   133

Master Data Management   137

Enterprise Search   144

Enterprise Data Warehousing   145

Information Lifecycle Management   148

Enterprise Content Management   149

Getting Experience with EIM Tools: The SAP Discovery System   151

**7 Business Intelligence Tools Guidelines for Best-Built
Applications**   **153**

SAP BusinessObjects BI Tools at a Glance   156

BI Tools and the BI Platform   157

The BI Toolbox   162

Using BI Tools and Platform SDKs   166

Packaging BI Tools with Applications   168

8 Application Development Guidelines for Best-Built Applications   173

Introduction   173

General Guidance   175

Guidelines for ABAP Development   183

Guidelines for Java Development   186

Guidelines for .NET Development   189

9 Security Guidelines for Best-Built Applications   191

Secure Programming Guidelines   191

Security Guides   193

Authentication, Authorization, and User Management   194

Single Sign-On   195

Identity Management   199

Microsoft .NET Security   199

Security Zones, Security Infrastructure, and Transport Security   200

Conclusion   201

10 NetWeaver Gateway Guidelines for Best-Built Applications   203

Introduction   203

Broader Than Mobility   205

Architecture   206

Deployment Options   207

Service Provisioning   208

Service Consumption   209

The End . . . For Now   210

11 **Mobility Guidelines for Best-Built Applications**   **211**

    Introduction   211

    Note   212

More Guidance for Best-Built Applications   **213**

Editorial Credits

Richard Probst, Series Editor

Joerg Nalik, Technical Editor

Deb Cameron, Managing Editor

Chapter Editors

Richard Probst and Dan Woods: Chapter 1, Introduction

Gordon Muehl and the SAP Architecture & Technology Group: Chapter 2, SAP Guidelines for Best-Built Applications, Summarized

Joerg Nalik: Chapter 3, Application Lifecycle Management Guidelines for Best-Built Applications

Volker Stiehl and Dirk Ammermann: Chapter 4, Process Orchestration and SOA Guidelines for Best-Built Applications

Nis Boy Naeve and Michael Falk: Chapter 5, User Interface and User Experience Guidelines for Best-Built Applications

Markus Ganser: Chapter 6, Enterprise Information Management Guidelines for Best-Built Applications

Stephen Mak and Erica Lailhacar: Chapter 7, BI Tools Guidelines for Best-Built Applications

Olga Dolinskaja and Wolfgang Weiss: Chapter 8, Application Development Guidelines for Best-Built Applications

Martin Raepple: Chapter 9, Security Guidelines for Best-Built Applications

Thomas Meigen: Chapter 10, NetWeaver Gateway Guidelines for Best-Built Applications

Martin LaCasse: Chapter 11, Mobility Guidelines for Best-Built
    Applications

Over 100 SAP architects and experts have contributed their time to compile, discuss, review, and agree on the content of this book. The editors sincerely thank all those involved. Special thanks also to the SAP Mentors, who have provided invaluable feedback.

Foreword

In today's business climate, SAP's customers increasingly look beyond optimizing their internal operations to the opportunity to transform their business networks of customers, suppliers, employees, and partners. Improving end-to-end business processes can be a big challenge, and natural complexity in business processes often leads to increased complexity in IT. Because such end-to-end processes may involve several companies working together, IT also faces the challenge of bringing together different applications, technologies, and platforms, especially across company boundaries, in a world of ever-changing requirements.

For years, SAP has been working with our customers and partners to address these complex business and IT challenges. We've built a world-class ecosystem of solutions that complement the SAP Business Suite. This ecosystem leverages a wide range of technologies, as evidenced by the many SAP partner solutions implemented in Java and in Microsoft's .NET, by developers writing Perl and Ruby scripts that make enterprise service calls to components written in ABAP, and by companies delivering mobile interfaces to SAP on devices such as the iPhone and iPad. And, at the rate that technology is changing, there is much more to come.

But with this pace of change, how are SAP customers and partners going to make informed development decisions? Internally, SAP developers follow SAP architecture guidelines, product standards, best practices, and selected industry standards. After hearing the questions our customers and partners were asking, we decided to provide the same type of developer-focused guidance externally, in an effort to help partners and customers building custom applications to align more closely with SAP solutions.

Several groups within SAP worked together to draft these guidelines, including the Ecosystem & Channels organization, the Office of the CTO, Active Global Support, and the product management and development organizations for the SAP Business Suite and the Technology Innovation Platform. With the cooperation of these groups, we are pleased to offer the SAP guidelines for best-built applications that integrate with SAP Business Suite.

The introduction of these guidelines continues our effort to ensure that developers, at both customers and partners, have solid guidance on how to build their solutions. The more that developers building complementary solutions can follow architectures, standards, and approaches similar to the ones that SAP follows when building its own solutions, the better we can all serve our mutual customers. In a naturally heterogeneous world, together we can do more to improve the experience of our customers.

We welcome your comments, recommendations and ideas on ways to expand and enhance this guidance. You can contribute by visiting the website at http://bestbuiltapps.sap.com where you can find the most up-to-date information, respond to blogs, or add your own thoughts. Or you can email the team at bestbuiltapps@sap.com.

We look forward to your feedback and hope you will join us on this journey.

Dr. Vishal Sikka
Chief Technology Officer,
Member of the Executive Board, SAP AG

November 2011

Preface

This document provides detailed guidance for developers, whether at independent software vendors (ISVs) or at customers, developing applications that integrate with SAP Business Suite.

Chapter 1 provides an overview of the motivation for and scope of this initiative.

Chapter 2 summarizes the specific guidelines in seven areas: application lifecycle management, process orchestration and service-oriented architecture, user interface and user experience, enterprise information management, business intelligence tools, application development, and security.

Chapter 3 covers the important area of application lifecycle management.

Chapter 4 covers process orchestration and service-oriented architecture.

Chapter 5 discusses the guidelines related to the user interface and user experience.

Chapter 6 covers enterprise information management.

Chapter 7 describes guidelines for using business intelligence (BI) tools.

Chapter 8 offers guidelines for application development.

Chapter 9 covers security guidelines.

This edition also includes previews of two new chapters. Chapter 10 covers SAP NetWeaver Gateway and Chapter 11 covers mobility.

Reading the Guidelines

Here is a sample guideline.

> ***ALM-PRD-7. SAP recommends that developers name software components uniquely to avoid name collisions with SAP software and with software components from SAP partner companies.***

Namespaces
In Java, use package names to specify the namespace. You can either request a unique namespace from SAP or use a namespace that is very

unlikely to be used by another company, such as com.mycompany. myapplication (assuming that the company owns the domain name mycompany.com). To get an ABAP namespace, you first request the namespace from SAP, then reserve it. To request a development namespace, you need a valid development license and the name for the namespace must refer to the name of your company. The namespace itself consists of three to eight capital letters bounded by slashes (for example, /MYCOMP/).

To Learn More

To request and register namespaces and for more information: http://service.sap.com/namespaces

The number in the front of the guideline is for reference purposes only, enabling us to easily link to guidelines in the wiki, for example. These numbers do not change over time and are not necessarily sequentially described in their respective chapters.

The specific guideline itself is in **bold, *italic*** font.

If a bulleted list is part of a guideline, it will also be shown in **bold**, ***italic*** font.

Many guidelines are accompanied by some explanatory text, in normal font. This explanation may provide further details, examples, or the reasoning and motivation behind a certain guideline.

Most guidelines also provide a link to additional resources, as described later.

Interpreting the Guidelines

The guidelines are meant to be helpful, clear, and actionable. Please bear in mind what the guidelines are not. They are:

- **Not mandates:** SAP recognizes and honors the independence of customers and ISVs

- **Not guarantees:** The guidelines provided here have been rigorously reviewed and are solid and stable. However, the world of technology is subject to continual change. As a result, the guidelines are under a strong disclaimer, similar to disclaimers found with other materials from technology companies and publishers

- **Not necessarily tied to certification:** If a particular guideline relates to an aspect of a software solution that can be certified by SAP, then certification is recommended. Simply following the guidelines is not equivalent to certification by SAP, but may ease the path to SAP certification, which is a separate process

Resources for the Guidelines

The guidelines explain what to do (for example, which UI technologies are recommended), not how to do it (how to create a UI using that technology).

As a result, most guidelines provide one or more references to how-to information.

This additional information might be found at:

- http://help.sap.com
- http://sdn.sap.com
- http://service.sap.com
- http://sapdesignguild.org

Here are some details about these sites.

SAP Help, at http://help.sap.com, provides official documentation from SAP. It is structured help that is indexed and includes diagrams to illustrate key points. This site is open to the public; no login information is required.

The **SAP Developer Network** is found at http://sdn.sap.com. This site is chock full of blogs, wikis, articles, webcasts, elearning, and forums. You need to register to use all of the features of SDN, although many resources can be accessed without registration. Registration on SDN is free and highly recommended.

The **SAP Service Marketplace** is located at http://service.sap.com. Access to the Service Marketplace requires a special username referred to as an S-user. All SAP customers have S-users and can access this site. Partners may gain access by joining SAP's PartnerEdge program. For more information about PartnerEdge, visit http://www.sdn.sap.com/irj/sdn/pe-ssp. To join PartnerEdge, go to http://www.partnerwithsap.com/get_started.php.

The SAP Design Guild, at http://sapdesignguild.org, is a public site offered by the SAP User Experience group. The Design Guild provides information about building effective user interfaces and about SAP's research into this important area. No registration is required to access this site.

Some of the links in the guidelines are redirects provided by TinyURL.com, a free service for abbreviating long links. This measure was taken for the convenience of readers of the printed document, who would otherwise be forced to type URLs as long as 100 characters in some cases.

Referring to the Guidelines

These guidelines are not a new certification or program that SAP is making available to partners. They represent developer-focused guidance being offered to customers and ISVs who want to technically align their solutions with SAP's.

You may not refer to applications developed following the guidelines as being "best-built applications" or "best-built" in any way. You can refer to your use of the guidelines during your development effort, as in:

We developed our application in accordance with SAP guidelines for best-built applications that integrate with SAP Business Suite.

There are no certifications specifically for these guidelines, so although the guidelines may influence the development of solutions, applications developed using the guidelines cannot be referred to by partners as being "best-built." You can and should use the guidelines to improve integration with the SAP Business Suite, but do not refer to the resulting applications as "best-built apps."

Obtaining Copies of This Document

A PDF and an ePub version of this document are freely available online at http://bestbuiltapps.sap.com. Printed copies are available from Amazon.com and can also be ordered in bulk by sending an email to books@evolvedmedia. com.

A Word about Completeness

This is a living document. SAP intends to add guidelines and additional chapters to augment these materials over time. For the latest information or to provide feedback, visit:

bestbuiltapps.sap.com

Chapter 1

Introduction

The purpose of this document, SAP® Guidelines for Best-Built Applications That Integrate with SAP Business Suite, is to offer development recommendations to partners and customers building complementary applications that extend the value of the SAP Business Suite. This will help SAP's ecosystem partners to create higher-quality software for our mutual customers and will also help SAP customers with developers on staff who build their own (custom) complementary applications. Many of the recommendations are based on guidelines that SAP considers in building its own applications.

When this document was initially published, it stated that independent software vendors (ISVs) were the primary audience for these guidelines—and ISVs are still a very important audience. But the clear feedback from customers with their own staff of SAP developers was that they also needed such guidance, and so ISVs are no longer the sole audience. Both ISVs and customers building their own complementary applications must make significant investment commitments in the software they develop and can benefit from knowing what SAP recommends.

Note that these guidelines explain what to do, not how to do it—and then provide links to the how-to technical documents needed to follow the guidelines.

SAP guidelines for best-built applications that integrate with SAP Business Suite is a set of recommendations to help developers, whether working for ISVs or for customers, build applications that work well with SAP's on-premise software. By adhering to these guidelines, you can create applications that deliver greater tangible value by reducing the total cost of ownership (including costs for integration, training, administration, and upgrades) while increasing security, usability, scalability, and other factors supporting governance and compliance policies.

Benefits to SAP Customers and Partners

The ultimate beneficiaries of these guidelines will be SAP customers, who enjoy the following benefits from complementary applications (whether from SAP partners or built in-house) that adhere to these SAP guidelines:

- **Consistent product experience:** SAP is committed to delivering products that work well together to create a consistent product experience—with these guidelines, complementary applications will contribute to (and benefit from) that consistent experience

- **Integration:** Complementary applications built using these guidelines should result in lower integration costs

- **Support:** Products that use standard components and work according to well-understood and proven patterns are easier to support. For ISVs, leveraging SAP's support infrastructure can reduce support costs

- **Familiarity:** Customers have invested substantial amounts of time in learning to operate SAP solutions—software that deploys and runs like SAP solutions lowers both operating and user training costs

- **Capability:** Faster adoption of new SAP technologies by developers results in more powerful products for SAP customers

Architectural Concepts for Complementing SAP Business Suite

SAP products have always been guided by our vision of providing the best business solutions. Adopting new generations of technology has enabled SAP and its partner ecosystem to meet the evolving business requirements of customers in new ways.

Understanding three key architectural concepts that underlie SAP's vision and approach to developing the SAP Business Suite can help your company extend the functionality of SAP applications with complementary solutions.

Timeless Software

The first concept is **timeless software**. Enterprise software solves fundamental business problems, and it must do so over generations of business and technological change. Vishal Sikka, Chief Technology Officer of SAP, has commented on the similarities between urban planning and managing enterprise software. Cities and enterprise systems both have longer lifetimes than the careers of the people who build and manage them. In both cases, valuable assets must be preserved and sometimes renovated, and new development must be thoughtfully integrated. Both have a mix of centralized and decentralized decision-making—in cities, decentralized decisions can be guided by a comprehensive plan and zoning ordinances; in enterprise systems, architectural guidelines serve the same purpose.

Sikka believes the architectural principles of timeless software can enable a constant cycle of renovation for business solutions, preserving still-valuable assets while introducing new functionality and new technology.

To Learn More

Timeless software: http://tinyurl.com/timeless-software

End-to-End Business Processes

The second concept is **end-to-end business processes** supported by componentized software. Rather than focusing on separate product categories like enterprise resource planning (ERP), customer relationship management (CRM), product lifecycle management (PLM), supply chain management (SCM), and so forth, end-to-end business processes shift the focus to the value that enterprise software helps provide in such broad "themes" as operational excellence, product leadership, organizational change management, and sustainability. In this approach, applications by themselves become less important, and how applications work together to deliver value becomes more important.

SAP guidelines for best-built applications help developers build applications that complement the end-to-end process support from the SAP Business Suite.

To Learn More

End-to-end business processes:
http://www.sdn.sap.com/irj/bpx/business-suite

Business Networks

The third concept is SAP's focus on **business networks**. SAP customers have processes that require increasingly complex management and integration within their own dynamic network of suppliers, customers, and partners. In a business network, IT systems are necessarily distributed and much more likely to be heterogeneous.

How SAP Guidelines for Best-Built Applications Are Being Published

To be useful, SAP guidelines must cover many topics. They must also be clear to be actionable. Finally, the guidelines must be updated to reflect changes in technology, the IT industry, and the evolution of SAP solutions. This section summarizes key principles for how the guidelines are being published to meet these requirements.

SAP guidelines for best-built applications assume a working knowledge of SAP technologies and partnering with SAP. This document is written for customers and ISVs ready to make key architecture and design choices.

The guidelines explain what to do, not how to do it. As an example, the guidelines may explain that the preferred user interface technology for a certain situation is Web Dynpro. But when it comes to how to use Web Dynpro to implement that user interface, you should look to the SAP Developer Network (SDN), the SAP Service Marketplace, SAP Press books, and other resources that explain the details of Web Dynpro and how to use it. Where applicable, this document provides links to such resources.

Think of it this way: SAP guidelines for best-built applications are "the what." SAP Developer Network and other resources are "the how."

The publication of SAP guidelines for best-built applications will be incremental and iterative. The first version of the guidelines, published in October 2009, provided an initial set of recommendations to begin the conversation. This edition and future versions will address new technologies and changes introduced in SAP technologies, platforms, and business solutions.

Because the guidelines are evolving, the authoritative version is located at the "best-built applications" website (http://bestbuiltapps. sap.com). You can get a bound copy of this book, print out a PDF, or download the ePub version of the guidelines, but the online version on the website is the canonical version of these guidelines.

The guidelines deal with currently available SAP solutions and technologies. The goal of these guidelines is to help developers make choices about technologies and integration options based on functionality currently available from SAP. Recommendations are based on the latest releases because those releases typify the way SAP is currently building its own solutions and reflect our current technical direction.

It is not appropriate for SAP to use a document like this to communicate about what might or might not happen to a particular technology or about the company's roadmap. Therefore, if you are considering making decisions based on these guidelines, pay special attention and understand the terms of use included at the beginning of this document. As mentioned previously, the ultimate architecture and implementation decisions are based on many factors; technology considerations are only one aspect.

The guidelines describe what is recommended as well as what is not recommended. SAP software is continually evolving, and SAP and its customers need to move forward incrementally. This reality is reflected in the guidelines. The guidelines use the following terminology:

- **SAP recommends:** This represents the safe way to do something, and it likely fits into the long-term SAP product direction
- **SAP does not encourage:** This represents an acceptable way to do something that may be altered in the future
- **SAP does not recommend:** This represents a technique or product that should be avoided for new development

It is neither possible nor desirable for SAP to attempt to control every development decision made by developers. These guidelines are meant to help you understand how your software can be compatible with SAP's, best serve SAP customers, and be intuitive for them to use. In some cases, business concerns or other factors may mean that you cannot follow the guidelines. However, following these guidelines is likely to be your best option to minimize disruption and costs moving forward.

Sources for SAP Guidelines for Best-Built Applications

SAP has formally addressed many architecture and design questions in building its solutions. The SAP guidelines for best-built applications draw upon the following sources of information used inside SAP, making relevant content available to our partner ecosystem.

SAP Architecture Guidelines

SAP architecture guidelines are SAP's internal recommendations for how to build software components; SAP's own developers use these guidelines. SAP guidelines for best-built applications incorporate selected content from SAP architecture guidelines.

SAP Product Standards

SAP product standards define quality characteristics that are required for SAP products. SAP follows standards for developing its applications in 15 areas (see Table 1-1). SAP guidelines for best-built applications incorporate selected content from SAP product standards.

Table 1-1: SAP Product Standards

Area	Description
Accessibility	Software accessible to persons with disabilities
Application integration and interfaces	Integration between applications
Business solution configuration	Adaptability to customer-specific business processes
Development environments	Use of development environments and programming languages
Documentation	Documentation for consultants, developers, and administrators
Functional correctness	Elimination of software bugs as much as possible
Globalization	Multilingual capability and internationalization
Information lifecycle management	Managing the lifecycle of business data, including archiving and retention
IT service and application management	Efficient operation at the customer site
Multitenancy	Enables the implementation of multiple SAP systems in one system instance
Open source	Controlled use of open source software
Performance	System performance, scalability, and hardware capacity sizing
Security	High level of product security
Technical implementation and change management	Simple implementation and upgrades
Usability	User friendliness

Product Availability Matrix

The SAP product availability matrix describes which platforms and specific technologies are supported for each SAP product. The product availability matrix is available in SAP Service Marketplace at http://service.sap.com/pam. Note that advance registration is required for access to SAP Service Marketplace.

The product availability matrix includes some partner products that SAP resells as part of its portfolio. Following SAP guidelines may simplify certifying a solution for resale, but it does not qualify a solution to be listed in the matrix.

Industry Best Practices and Standards

SAP is committed to open standards and follows a wide variety of technology standards and business semantic standards. To a large extent, SAP guidelines for best-built applications are informed by SAP's commitment to industry standards. For example, the guidelines recommend using Business Process Modeling Notation (BPMN), a standard maintained by the Object Management Group (OMG).

To Learn More

Standards: http://www.sdn.sap.com/irj/sdn/standards

Approaches to Development

There are many processes and mechanisms to meet common requirements when creating products for a global customer base that deploys software on heterogeneous platforms. Ultimately, you must decide how closely to align your architecture with SAP's and how much SAP technology to leverage in your solution. SAP guidelines for best-built applications describe three approaches you can take when developing or deploying software in an SAP environment.

SAP has encapsulated decades of learning into its design and development practices and the tools and technology it makes available to customers and partners. Every software company has to grapple with choosing which databases to support, which operating systems to run on, which languages to use for development, and so forth. In addition, customers such as governments may add requirements for other aspects of software such as accessibility, security, and privacy. And there is always the task of integration.

SAP has developed ways to systematically manage this complexity and to meet many development challenges. Perhaps the simplest way to think of the SAP guidelines for best-built applications is as a guide to using the technology, processes, tips, and tricks that SAP has come up with over the past 30-plus years.

We understand that developers, whether at customers or at partners, will have different starting points when building software that fits into the SAP universe. For example, the degree to which an ISV wants to adhere to SAP guidelines is a business decision. Not every company will want to or be able to follow all SAP guidelines.

With this complexity in mind, we have identified three basic development choices you can make when developing and deploying products to complement SAP, as outlined in Table 1-2.

Table 1-2. Approaches to Developing Complementary Applications

Software designed with SAP tools to run in the SAP environment	Software migrated to run in the SAP environment	Software connected to an SAP solution
These applications are built using SAP design and development tools, and they are naturally deployed on the SAP technology platform	These applications are developed using non-SAP design tools and are later migrated to run on the SAP technology platform	These applications are developed using non-SAP design tools and run on non-SAP platforms while connecting with SAP Business Suite solutions

It's important to note that even in one company, different solutions may follow different approaches. Even a single solution with multiple components can have elements that follow different approaches—one part built with SAP tools, another part loosely connected. Also, these approaches are not "categories" of ISVs or even ISV products. Instead they describe development decisions that are made at the level of individual software components.

A more detailed discussion of each approach follows. Where relevant, SAP guidelines for best-built applications identify the approach to which each guideline applies. If there is no indication, the guideline applies to all three approaches.

Products Developed with SAP Tools for the SAP Environment

From a technical perspective, this approach provides guidance for using SAP design tools and runtime functions to create products that are as similar as possible to SAP Business Suite solutions.

The guidelines answer questions like the following:

- Which user interface framework is recommended?
- How could an application be affected by the switch framework?
- What standard data models should be used?

Applications that are developed with SAP design tools and built for the SAP environment are the closest that a company can come to creating software that is designed, developed, deployed, and operated like an SAP solution. Essentially, they are built like SAP solutions.

Products Migrated to Run in the SAP Environment

From a technical perspective, this approach provides guidance for software components built using non-SAP design tools that are migrated to operate in the SAP runtime environment.

There are two main advantages to migrating an application to run in the SAP environment. First, solutions that operate on the SAP runtime may be able to leverage more operational features and lifecycle management functionality of SAP software. Second, by running an application on the SAP NetWeaver

Application Server (SAP NetWeaver AS) component, a customer can reduce the total cost of operation (TCO), and an ISV can reduce the cost of acquisition of their product for SAP customers.

Because SAP NetWeaver supports two development environments—ABAP™ and Java—a product to be deployed on SAP's runtime must be written for one of these environments. Only SAP provides design tools for ABAP, so software products that are migrated to SAP will in practice be applications written in Java.

The guidelines for software migrated to the SAP environment help you answer questions like:

- What version of Java EE does SAP NetWeaver support?
- What mechanisms, like the system landscape directory, must an application running on SAP NetWeaver use?
- How should an application running on SAP NetWeaver interface with the SAP Solution Manager?

Guidelines for products that are migrated to the SAP environment explain which SAP technologies and practices to use to make a product written with non-SAP design tools look and act as much like an SAP solution as possible.

Products That Are Connected to SAP Solutions

From a technical perspective, this type of guidance is for a software component that was not developed using SAP design tools and that does not operate in an SAP runtime environment.

Software that is connected to SAP solutions could be developed on Microsoft .NET, IBM WebSphere, another Java platform, or any number of other application environments such as Ruby, Python, PHP, and so on. In practical terms, the diversity of development platforms means that the product is a discrete collection of business logic that may have various integration points with the SAP Business Suite. The guidelines for software that is connected to SAP solutions answer the following types of questions:

- How can your software use the data and functionality of SAP Business Suite?
- How can your software present its data and functionality for use by SAP solutions?
- What computing platforms, operating systems, and databases should ISVs support to align their products with the SAP customer base?

These are just a few of dozens of questions that you may seek to answer, either as an SAP customer building an in-house solution with optimal return on investment, or as part of an ISV's business strategy to make a product easier to use for SAP customers.

Assessing an ISV's Commitment to SAP Customers

The development approaches described here do not imply that an ISV using one approach is more committed to delivering value to SAP's customers than other ISVs. An ISV with an application that merely connects to SAP solutions might be very committed to SAP's vision of end-to-end process orchestration, for example, while another ISV that develops applications using SAP tools might not be quite as committed to that vision. These categories indicate the degree of proximity to the SAP Business Suite and the platforms being used for development and runtime and do not imply that one approach is inherently better or worse than another. However, all else being equal, using SAP design tools should result in the best integration and lowest cost of ownership.

Guideline Topics

Because so much information is involved and the process of creating software is so complex, SAP guidelines for best-built applications are organized into the following topics:

- **Application lifecycle management:** Encompasses the requirements, design, build and test, deployment, operation, and optimization phases as well as support

- **Process orchestration and service-oriented architecture (SOA):** Explains topics related to process orchestration, business process management, business rules, and the usage of enterprise services

- **User interface and user experience:** Describes how to build user interfaces so that the user experience is as pleasing and productive as possible

- **Enterprise information management:** Describes the six pillars of enterprise information management, including data integration and data quality, master data management, enterprise search, enterprise data warehousing, information lifecycle management, and enterprise content management

- **BI tools:** Recommends techniques and tools for making information more accessible and understandable

- **Application development:** Covers topics related to general programming guidelines as well as guidelines specific to ABAP, Java, and .NET

- **Security:** Provides recommendations about secure programming, identity management, single sign-on, security zones, security Infrastructure, and transport security

- Guidelines regarding NetWeaver Gateway and mobility are coming in a future edition of this document

Detailed How-To Information

The guidelines describe what to do, not how to do it. Most guidelines are followed by links to material that explains the technical topics in more detail.

In all cases, SAP documentation is the authoritative source of information about SAP software. These guidelines are designed to help you find your way to that authoritative information.

Changes in This Release

This is version 2.3 of these guidelines. Chapters 1 through 5 as well as Chapter 7 have now been updated to address developers at customers as well as at ISVs. Chapter 7 was substantially revised and expanded to provide updated guidance that reflects SAP BusinessObjects BI 4.0. Chapter 2 has been changed to reflect the modified or new guidelines in Chapter 7. Chapters 6, 8, and 9 have not yet been updated and so continue to address only developers at ISVs, but this will be fixed as the revision cycle continues. The decision to provide guidance for developers at customers applies to all chapters, but edits to implement this decision need to be made carefully.

This edition includes a preview of chapters 10 and 11, which cover SAP NetWeaver Gateway and mobility respectively.

See http://bestbuiltapps.sap.com for updates to this book.

Chapter 2

SAP Guidelines for Best-Built Applications, Summarized

This chapter summarizes the SAP guidelines for best-built applications that integrate with SAP Business Suite and provides links to additional information. In some cases, these links take you to SAP Service Marketplace (http://service.sap.com). Note that advance registration is required for access to SAP Service Marketplace.

Overall Goal: Maximize Alignment

SAP-BBA-1. SAP recommends developing software components with SAP design tools and deploying on an SAP runtime to deliver the best value for SAP customers. If that is not possible, migrate existing software components to run on the SAP runtime. If that is not possible, develop software components for non-SAP runtimes that connect to SAP systems using web services. If appropriate, divide a complex application into parts and develop some of the components using SAP design tools for tightest integration.

Guidelines for Application Lifecycle Management

SAP's approach to application lifecycle management is based on the IT Infrastructure Library (ITIL) lifecycle.

To Learn More

Application lifecycle management: http://service.sap.com/alm

ALM-PRD-1. SAP recommends adopting an ITIL-based approach to application lifecycle management.

Product-Related Recommendations

Product-related recommendations covered in this section include release strategy, software version recommendations, versioning, namespaces, software logistics, and documentation.

Release Strategy

> ***ALM-PRD-2. SAP recommends that development organizations understand the SAP strategy of releases, enhancement packages, and support packages and consider adopting a release strategy that follows the same model.***

To Learn More

SAP's release strategy: http://service.sap.com/releasestrategy

SAP's maintenance strategy: http://service.sap.com/maintenance

The Enhancement and Switch Framework

The switch framework allows customers to install an enhancement package and turn on only the business functions they desire, thus reducing the cost of deploying enhancements in a complex enterprise software environment.

> ***ALM-PRD-3. SAP recommends that developers understand how the Switch Framework could affect their applications.***

The functioning of an application that integrates with the SAP Business Suite may be affected by the particular functionality the customer has turned on via the switch framework. You may need to understand this dependency when testing and supporting your applications.

Sometimes it is necessary or desirable to add specific business functionality to SAP software. Adapting SAP software should be approached carefully.

> ***ALM-ADAPT-1. SAP recommends building add-ons that connect to SAP software via SAP supported interfaces rather than modifying SAP software.***

> ***ALM-ADAPT-2. SAP recommends that developers who need to adapt SAP development objects use an SAP enhancement technology rather than modify the SAP software development objects.***

> ***ALM-ADAPT-3. SAP recommends making your enhancement add-on projects switchable by using reversible business functions of the Switch Framework.***

For more on the Enhancement and Switch Framework, see Chapter 3.

SAP Releases

ALM-PRD-4. SAP recommends that ISVs develop for the latest release of SAP products since these releases provide the most functionality for smooth integration with partner products.

For more information, review the Product Availability Matrix (PAM), which provides all necessary hardware, operating system, and platform details for SAP software.

ALM-PRD-5. SAP recommends consulting the Product Availability Matrix when making platform decisions.

To Learn More

Product Availability Matrix (PAM): http://service.sap.com/pam

Versioning

ALM-PRD-6. SAP recommends that all application development objects be accompanied by versioning metadata.

ABAP applications developed using SAP tools are provided with versioning metadata automatically. Java applications that are developed on SAP NetWeaver with SAP tools or whose components are imported into the SAP NetWeaver development infrastructure during migration to the SAP runtime receive versioning information from SAP NetWeaver. However, applications that are only migrated onto the SAP NetWeaver Java infrastructure without using the development infrastructure as well as applications that simply connect to SAP solutions should provide equivalent versioning metadata. Such metadata should either be updated automatically using a tool or be updated manually by developers.

To Learn More

SAP NetWeaver development infrastructure:
http://www.sdn.sap.com/irj/sdn/nw-di

SAP Help: http://tinyurl.com/helpnwdi

Miigrating Java applications to SAP NetWeaver:
http://wiki.sdn.sap.com/wiki/x/KoO1Bw

Miigrating Java applications to SAP NetWeaver:
http://tinyurl.com/scn-java-ee-migration

Namespaces

> **ALM-PRD-7. SAP recommends that developers name software components uniquely to avoid name collisions with SAP software and with software components from other SAP partner companies.**

In Java, use package names to specify the namespace. You can either request a unique namespace from SAP, or you can use a namespace that is very unlikely to be used by another company, such as com.*mycompany*.myapplication (assuming that your company owns the domain name *mycompany*.com). An ABAP namespace, which must be registered with SAP, is three to eight capital letters bounded by slashes (for example, */MYCOMP/*).

To Learn More

To request and register namespaces and for more information:
http://service.sap.com/namespaces

Software Logistics

Customers need to maintain multiple systems, such as development systems, test systems, and production systems, and therefore need a way to transport changes from one system to the next.

> **ALM-REL-3. SAP recommends using the SAP Change and Transport System (SAP CTS) to transport changes from one system to another.**

CTS tools are part of SAP NetWeaver, so they are easy to use for ISVs that use SAP development tools or migrate their software to the SAP environment. It is very important to SAP's customers that ISVs merely connecting their software to SAP solutions provide equivalent tools for handling software logistics.

To Learn More

Software logistics: http://www.sdn.sap.com/irj/sdn/cts

Software logistics: http://www.sdn.sap.com/irj/sdn/softwarelogistics

Software logistics wiki: http://wiki.sdn.sap.com/wiki/display/SL/Home

Country Specific Legal Changes

> **ALM-SL-1. SAP recommends that developers whose applications complement or adapt SAP HCM keep up to date with Country-specific Legal Changes, which must be applied on a regular basis.**

Documentation

> *ALM-PRD-8. SAP recommends that developers create a complete set of documentation. A complete set of documentation includes at minimum the following:*
>
> - *Terms and definitions*
> - *Documentation of external technical interfaces released to the customers, for example, web services or application programming interfaces (APIs)*
> - *Customizing and configuration documentation*
> - *Release notes*
> - *Application documentation*
> - *Installation information*
> - *Upgrade information*
> - *A master guide that provides a starting point for navigating the documentation*
> - *An operations guide that includes information on backup and online backup*
> - *A security guide*

Documentation about how to implement software can be kept in SAP Solution Manager. For further details, see Chapter 3.

> *ALM-PRD-9. For implementation documentation, SAP recommends using SAP's documentation format so that documentation can be incorporated into SAP management tools.*

Certification-Related Guidelines

> *ALM-CERT-1. SAP strongly recommends that ISVs obtain SAP certification of their applications and integration solutions.*

SAP certification tests check for proper use of SAP integration methods and APIs as well as basic integration into SAP support tools.

To Learn More

SAP Integration and Certification Center:
http://www.sdn.sap.com/irj/sdn/icc

SDN section on certification and partnership:
http://www.sdn.sap.com/irj/sdn/certification-and-partnership

Software Dependencies and Registration

> **ALM-CERT-2. SAP recommends that SAP-certified ISV software document all development and runtime platform dependencies in the product and production management system (PPMS).**

This information is invaluable to customers who plan component software upgrades and need to evaluate dependencies on platforms.

To Learn More

Product and production management system: http://tinyurl.com/ppmshelp

Article on SDN describing how to view a customer's product and production management system: http://tinyurl.com/ppmsarticle

Deploying applications should also include registering them in the customer's system landscape directory (SLD).

> **ALM-REL-6. SAP recommends that all application components be registered in the customer's System Landscape Directory.**

See Chapter 3 for further details about the SLD.

Logging and Tracing

> **ALM-CERT-3. SAP recommends that all log, trace, and similar files created or maintained by your applications be stored only in documented locations in a human-readable format.**

Support personnel should be able to read these files, so they should not be in binary format, for example. Following this recommendation enables customers to more easily use general operational and support tools with ISV solutions. It also integrates ISV solutions into SAP's support infrastructure for customers.

Readability of log and other files is a requirement of the SAP Solution Manager ready program.

To Learn More

Logging: http://tinyurl.com/logging-sdn

Readability of log and other files: http://tinyurl.com/solutionmanagerready

Solution Reliability

For overall reliability of a business software solution, all elements need to be optimized for performance and availability.

Application Performance

> **ALM-REL-1. SAP recommends that you familiarize yourself with SAP's approach to optimizing the performance of applications.**

To Learn More

> Performance and SAP guidelines on database performance, scalability, and optimizing response time:
> http://www.sdn.sap.com/irj/sdn/performance-analysis

> SAP Service Marketplace at http://service.sap.com/performance

Optimizing Response Time

ALM-REL-2. SAP recommends that you design user interface implementations to allow optimal user interaction with the shortest possible application response time, especially when these applications are deployed over a wide-area network. The user interface implementation should optimize:

- *The number of synchronous communication steps between the user interface and the application layer or between two servers*

- *The amount of data transferred between the user interface and the application layer. (Transferring large amounts of data can cause performance problems. Always strive to transfer the right amount of data in the fewest number of trips.)*

- *The application's processing time inside the application server*

Scalability and Capacity Planning

ALM-REL-4. SAP recommends that development groups provide hardware sizing information to facilitate capacity planning for productive use of customer systems.

A capacity planning (or sizing) procedure should be available for all hardware resources such as disk space, CPU, memory, and network bandwidth. Providing accurate sizing information for products is vitally important for customers to plan and build reliable and high-performing application landscapes.

To Learn More

> Sizing: http://service.sap.com/sizing

High Availability

ALM-REL-5. SAP recommends that applications intended to be part of a mission-critical business process be architected for high availability to allow customers to deploy their application instances in a high-availability configuration as needed.

The documentation should include instructions on how to set up high availability for an application.

To Learn More

High availability: http://www.sdn.sap.com/irj/sdn/ha

Output Management

Output management refers to printing, emailing, and generating documents and faxes. It also encompasses form design, both interactive forms and static PDF forms.

ALM-OM-1. SAP recommends that developers design their applications to provide alternatives to printing.

SAP has three output management related technologies:

* SAP Interactive Forms by Adobe
* SAPscript forms
* SAP Smart Forms

See "Guidelines for User Interface and User Experience" for recommendations about SAP Interactive Forms by Adobe and SAPscript forms.

ALM-OM-2. SAP recommends use of SAP Smart Forms for high-volume printing needs.

Support-Related Guidelines

ALM-SUP-1. SAP recommends that you follow SAP's support–related guidelines.

Support spans the application lifecycle. SAP Solution Manager adds value to many phases; think of it as occupying the center of this lifecycle. As a result, the SAP support standards encompass best practices at all phases of the lifecycle to improve the supportability of applications for enterprise customers.

To Learn More

Support standards, click on the Media Library link at:
http://service.sap.com/supportstandards

SAP Solution Manager

ALM-SUP-2. SAP strongly recommends that developers integrate their complementary applications with SAP Solution Manager to align their application lifecycle management and support infrastructure with that of SAP.

For applications integrated with SAP Solution Manager, depending on the level of integration, support staff can gain access to log files, check performance data, and perform root-cause analysis using the customer's installation of SAP Solution Manager.

To Learn More

SAP Solution Manager: http://service.sap.com/solutionmanager

SAP Solution Manager: http://tinyurl.com/solutionmgr

Testing with SAP Solution Manager: http://tinyurl.com/sm-testing

Secure Remote Support Access

ALM-SUP-3. SAP recommends using support tools that provide secure remote access to customer landscapes.

You can implement SAP Solution Manager to follow this recommendation. If you use other support tools, access should be secure. The software should not pass sensitive credentials in clear text to achieve access, and communication traffic should be encrypted. Support personnel should be able to see the problem, but not make changes to the application or to application data.

To Learn More

Remote support access: http://service.sap.com/access-support

Monitoring and Alerting

ALM-SUP-4. SAP recommends that applications provide alerts for all relevant situations (heartbeat, performance, resource utilization, and business-critical situations). You should also provide alerts for resources that your application manages, such as caching and queues, as well as documentation with information about monitoring.

SAP-certified solutions must provide monitoring and alerting integration with SAP Solution Manager, including its business process monitoring functionality.

To Learn More

SAP EarlyWatch® Alert: http://service.sap.com/

System Management/Reliable Operations:
http://service.sap.com/systemmanagement

SDN Monitoring page: http://www.sdn.sap.com/irj/sdn/monitoring

SAP Standards for System Monitoring (paper):
http://tinyurl.com/monitoringarticle

Guidelines for Process Orchestration and Service-Oriented Architecture (SOA)

Guidelines for process orchestration and SOA cover BPM, BPMN, SOA governance, web services, enterprise services, service metering, and more.

Process Orchestration

> ***SOA-BPM-1. SAP recommends that developers consider architecting an application as a set of components that can be orchestrated using business process modeling techniques.***

SAP follows this approach to give customers increased business agility with stable, high-quality components. An ISV application that follows this approach will enable an SAP customer to integrate the ISV application into its unique, differentiating business processes that are based on SAP software.

Business Process Modeling

> ***SOA-BPM-2. SAP recommends using SAP NetWeaver BPM for business process modeling. SAP also recommends using the SAP Business Workflow tool for workflows within a pure, ABAP single-instance application. SAP does not recommend using:***
>
> - ***SAP Business Connector, which has been retired and replaced with functionality in SAP NetWeaver***
> - ***Workflow Modeler, except for applications that enhance SAP CRM***
> - ***SAP NetWeaver Business Warehouse process chains (process chains are recommended for loading but not for workflow)***
> - ***SAP NetWeaver MDM workflow***
> - ***Java ad-hoc workflows***

To Learn More

Business process modeling:
http://www.sdn.sap.com/irj/sdn/nw-processmodeling

BPMN

> ***SOA-BPM-3. SAP recommends using Business Process Modeling Notation (BPMN) to create process models.***

To Learn More

BPMN: http://tinyurl.com/sdnbpmn

SOA Governance

SOA-MGMT-1. SAP recommends implementing a SOA governance process to drive clear decisions about the use of service-oriented architecture in software products and to align its use with business goals and strategy.

Web Services

SOA-WS-1. SAP recommends implementing remote consumption of business functionality using loosely coupled, asynchronous, stateless communication using web services. If you develop your own web services, SAP recommends that you:

- *Use WS standards WSDL 1.1, WS-Policy 1.2, XSD 1.0, SOAP 1.1, and WSRM 1.1*

- *Keep XSD structures simple*

- *Publish services to the Services Registry*

Enterprise Services

SOA-WS-2. SAP recommends using enterprise services to integrate with SAP applications if at all possible.

Enterprise services are web services that share a common data model and specific communications patterns to support higher reliability.

SOA-WS-3. If access is needed to SAP application functionality that has not yet been service-enabled, SAP recommends wrapping remote function calls (RFCs) or BAPI® programming interfaces as web services. Direct access to RFCs or BAPIs is possible, but it is not encouraged.

In some special cases, using RFCs or BAPIs directly may offer better performance. However, you should balance this approach against the greater flexibility gained by using enterprise services.

Service Metering

To measure usage patterns, SAP NetWeaver meters all web service and enterprise service calls.

SOA-MGMT-2. SAP recommends that developers who connect their applications to SAP solutions from non-SAP platforms should add application-specific and customer-specific information to the SOAP header of all web service calls to SAP solutions to improve the measurement of usage patterns.

To Learn More

SAP note 1358528: http://service.sap.com/sap/support/notes/1358528 and specifically the PDF document in the note

Characteristics of Well-Designed Web Services

ISVs developing web services should design the services to support asynchronous, stateless, loosely coupled communication between applications. Enterprise services are designed to have these characteristics.

SOA-WS-4. SAP recommends that services:

- *Be self-contained. A consumer of a service should send all the data necessary to the service provider to continue the business process asynchronously. The provider should not have to "call back" the consumer for additional information*

- *Be robust in the case of accidental double calling. Implement services so that they ignore any duplicate calls (that is, they are idempotent)*

- *Use compensating transactions to reestablish consistency. Have pairs of write operations: a modifying service and a second service for undoing the business outcome of the modifying service, to be called when needed*

- *Practice forward error recovery. The receiving system must not send an error to the calling system if that error could be handled closer to the receiving system*

- *Combine remote calls where possible. Combine and orchestrate multiple calls into one coarse-grained service rather than make many fine-grained calls*

To Learn More

Detailed introduction to SOA, see "The SOA Handbook:" http://tinyurl.com/sdn-soa-handbook

Partner-Delivered Enterprise Services

SOA-WS-5. SAP recommends that ISVs service-enable the functionality of their applications according to SAP's SOA methodology and certify these applications under the ESR Content certification.

SAP internal developers use SOA methodology to develop web services with clear interface patterns and naming rules based on business objects that are semantically aligned with SAP Business Suite and global data types based on the UN/CEFACT CCTS standard. (Web services developed this way are called enterprise services.)

You can use this methodology to simplify the integration of your software components into end-to-end business processes supported by SAP Business Suite.

The SAP education course SOA300 ("Design Time Governance in SOA"), part of the enterprise service development curriculum, enables ISVs to build SAP methodology-compliant interfaces that can then be certified under the ESR Content certification (certification interface ESR-CNT). Note that ISVs retain full control of selling their service-enabled components.

To Learn More

SAP Enterprise Service Development curriculum:
http://tinyurl.com/nwgmp5

Partner-delivered Enterprise Services (PdES) central page:
http://www.sdn.sap.com/irj/sdn/pdes

Integration and Certification Center central page:
http://www.sdn.sap.com/irj/sdn/icc

Why Partner-delivered Enterprise Services?: http://tinyurl.com/l7o8fo

SAP Co-Innovation Lab Architecture Series: Partner-delivered Enterprise Services:
http://www.sdn.sap.com/irj/scn/weblogs?blog=/pubwlg/13693

Global Data Types

SOA-GDT-1. SAP recommends modeling business objects based on global data types.

SAP global data types are based on UN/CEFACT's Core Component Technical Specification for global data types.

To Learn More

CCTS: http://www.unece.org/cefact/ebxml/CCTS_V2-01_Final.pdf

A no-cost license for the global data types is available to partners that certify their applications under the ESR Content certification. (Customers are licensed to use global data types under normal customer licenses.)

To Learn More

Catalog of global data types: http://tinyurl.com/sdngdtcatalog

Business Rules

SOA-BRM-1. SAP recommends that business logic be expressed as business rules where appropriate. ABAP applications should use Business Rules Framework plus (BRFplus) to define rules. Other applications developed with SAP design tools should use SAP NetWeaver Business Rules Management to define rules.

To Learn More

Business rules management:
http://www.sdn.sap.com/irj/sdn/nw-rules-management

.NET Tools

SOA-NET-1. SAP recommends that .NET developers use the SAP Enterprise Services Explorer tool for Microsoft .NET. SAP does not recommend using .NET connector.

To Learn More

SAP Enterprise Services Explorer: http://tinyurl.com/esefordotnet

.NET and SAP: http://www.sdn.sap.com/irj/sdn/dotnet

Microsoft's SAP page: http://www.microsoft.com/isv/sap/

Integration with IBM WebSphere

SOA-IBM-1. SAP recommends that developers working with IBM WebSphere review the efforts of IBM and SAP to achieve interoperability between their Java EE application servers.

Recently, IBM and SAP worked together to achieve bidirectional synchronization between IBM's WebSphere Service Registry and Repository and SAP's Enterprise Services Repository. Details on how to set up this bidirectional synchronization are available in an article published on SDN at http://tinyurl.com/registry-interop.

To Learn More

IBM WebSphere page on SDN: http://tinyurl.com/sdn-websphere

IBM and SAP Alliance page: http://tinyurl.com/ibmsapalliance

Guidelines for User Interface and User Experience

User interface and user experience guidelines encompass areas such as user-centered design, separating the business logic from the UI, and UI governance as well as recommendations about specific UI technologies, output and online forms, and accessibility.

User-Centered Design

UI-UCD-1. SAP recommends adopting the philosophy and methodology that SAP has adopted for developing user interfaces: user-centered design.

An important resource from SAP for learning about user-centered design is the SAP Design Guild Website at http://www.sapdesignguild.org/. The Website is published by the User Experience group at SAP.

To Learn More

Summary of all available resources:
http://www.sapdesignguild.org/resources/resources.asp

User-centered design:
http://www.sapdesignguild.org/resources/ucd_process.asp
http://www.sapdesignguild.org/resources/ucd_paper.asp

Separating Business Logic from the UI

UI-PROG-1. SAP recommends that business logic be separated from UI coding.

UI Governance

UI-GOV-1. SAP recommends implementing a user interface governance process to ensure harmonization, to drive clear user interface decisions that are aligned with business goals and strategy, and to effectively implement those goals.

Recommended UI Technologies for Software Built with SAP Development Tools

> **UI-TECH-1. SAP recommends that developers using SAP tools select one of the following user interface technologies:**
> - **Web Dynpro ABAP with the Floorplan Manager**
> - **Web Dynpro Java for development on the SAP NetWeaver Java stack**
> - **WebClient UI Framework for development of applications that complement SAP CRM**

Applications developed with these user interface technologies can run in the SAP NetWeaver Enterprise Portal. Applications developed with either version of Web Dynpro can run in the SAP NetWeaver Business Client, a desktop UI client.

To Learn More

SAP NetWeaver Business Client and the UI Client for SAP NetWeaver Enterprise Portal: http://tinyurl.com/faq-clients

An article that compares the functionality of Web Dynpro Java and Web Dynpro ABAP: http://tinyurl.com/webdynproabapjava

WebClient UI Framework: http://tinyurl.com/webclientui

WebClient UI Framework: http://tinyurl.com/wcuif-scn

Recommended UI Frameworks for Software Built with SAP Development Tools

> **UI-TECH-2.1. For development of new applications via Web Dynpro ABAP, SAP recommends using the Floorplan Manager to increase consistency among user interfaces.**

The Floorplan Manager is a tool on top of Web Dynpro ABAP that allows user interface designers to select from a number of preset "floor plans" that provide uniformity to the user interface.

To Learn More

Floorplan Manager: http://tinyurl.com/floorplanmanager

> **UI-TECH-2.2. For development of new applications that should be strongly integrated with SAP CRM or other applications that use the WebClient UI Framework, SAP recommends using the WebClient UI Framework to increase consistency among user interfaces.**

The WebClient UI Framework supports the configuration of user interfaces for SAP CRM and other applications that use this framework (SAP for Utilities is one such example).

To Learn More

WebClient UI Framework: http://tinyurl.com/webclientui

WebClient UI Framework: http://tinyurl.com/wcuif-scn

UI-TECH-10. For Java UIs, SAP recommends either Web Dynpro Java or standards-based development using JavaServer Faces (JSF).

Recommended UI Technologies for Migrated Software

UI-TECH-3. SAP recommends that Java applications that are migrated to run on SAP NetWeaver use JavaServer Faces (JSF) technology.

SAP provides support for rendering JSF applications with unified rendering libraries to achieve a consistent look with SAP-developed applications.

Recommended UI Technologies for Rich Internet Applications

UI-TECH-5. SAP recommends using Adobe Flash or Microsoft Silverlight in Web Dynpro Islands or WebClient UIF Islands.

To Learn More

Flash Islands, see http://tinyurl.com/flash-scn

Silverlight Islands tutorial: http://tinyurl.com/silverlight-tutorial

Both Adobe Flash Islands and Silverlight Islands can be used with the Floorplan Manager and with the WebClient UI Framework.

UI Technologies That Are Not Encouraged

UI-TECH-6. SAP does not encourage use of the following user interface technologies:

- *Business Server Pages (BSP)*
- *HTMLB*
- *Portal Framework*
- *XHTML or plain HTML*
- *ITS flow logic*
- *ABAP Dynpro*

Guided Procedures

UI-FLOW-1. SAP does not recommend using Guided Procedures for new development efforts.

Using SAP NetWeaver BPM is the preferred approach, as explained on SDN at http://tinyurl.com/workflow-netweaver.

Output and Offline Forms

UI-TECH-8. SAP recommends using SAP Interactive Forms by Adobe for forms that are printed or used online or offline. SAP does not recommend that developers use SAPscript.

To Learn More

Forms: http://www.sdn.sap.com/irj/sdn/adobe

SAP's form strategy: http://tinyurl.com/sap-forms

SAP GUI

UI-TECH-9. SAP does not recommend developing new applications in SAP GUI.

Accessibility

UI-STD-1. SAP recommends making applications accessible by ensuring that all user interface elements and relevant information in an application are available to and usable by users with disabilities.

To Learn More

Accessibility resources on SAP Design Guild:
http://www.sapdesignguild.org/resources/acc.asp

Legal requirements in the US: http://www.section508.gov

W3C's Web Content Accessibility Guidelines: http://www.w3.org/WAI

Guidelines for Enterprise Information Management

Guidelines for enterprise information management cover databases, data integration and data quality, master data management, enterprise search, enterprise data warehousing, and information lifecycle management.

Databases

EIM-DB-1. SAP recommends that ISV applications that use a relational database support at least two databases listed on the product availability matrix, for example, Oracle __and__ IBM DB2 or DB2 __and__ Microsoft SQL Server. SAP also recommends making applications agnostic concerning the underlying database and operating system wherever possible.

Data Integration and Data Quality

EIM-DIDQ-1. SAP recommends using the Data Quality features of SAP BusinessObjects Data Services to support customers in improving the quality of existing and incoming data.

Master Data Management

EIM-MDM-1. SAP recommends that partners gain expertise in using both SAP NetWeaver Master Data Management and SAP BusinessObjects Data Services because of their complementary nature.

EIM-MDM-2. SAP recommends using SAP NetWeaver MDM openness (for example, MDM Enrichment Architecture, APIs, and web services) to add ISV integration content (for example, system connections to automated translation engines or third-party data enrichment services).

EIM-MDM-3. SAP recommends an architecture with a process layer, a UI layer, and a services layer for centrally governed data creation processes (i.e., globally relevant master data information) in heterogeneous landscapes with:

- *MDM, Data Services and SAP Business Suite application services*
- *WebDynpro based user interfaces*
- *BPM as a process orchestration layer*

Enterprise Search

EIM-ES-1. SAP recommends using SAP NetWeaver Enterprise Search to collect structured and unstructured data that is dispersed across heterogeneous landscapes into a single work environment.

Enterprise Data Warehousing

EIM-BW-1. SAP recommends that source system data be replicated into the SAP NetWeaver Business Warehouse component and stored there persistently if any of the following data integration requirements need to be fulfilled:

- **Consolidating data from heterogeneous transactional systems in one location (if necessary, leverage SAP BusinessObjects Data Services tools to cleanse or qualify external data for analytical purposes in the Business Warehouse)**
- **Organizing and integrating high volumes of data**
- **Merging, standardizing, and cleaning historical data**
- **Providing high availability and performance data for analysis**
- **Isolating high-performance transactional systems from analytical queries**

EIM-EDW-1. SAP recommends using SAP BusinessObjects Metadata Management to analyze metadata coming from SAP NetWeaver Business Warehouse and combine it with metadata from other models (BI, SAP BusinessObjects Data Services, RDBMS, and third-party tools) to see impact analysis and data lineage for the end-to-end BI to data source environment.

EIM-EDW-2. SAP recommends that ISVs who want to ease the integration of data from their applications into SAP Business Warehouse use naming conventions that ease the process and, when possible, reuse SAP business objects.

Information Lifecycle Management (ILM)

EIM-ILM-1. SAP recommends that ISVs enable information lifecycle management best practices for their products to ensure that ISV and SAP applications conform to a complete and uniform ILM solution.

ISVs using SAP development tools or that have migrated their software to the SAP environment should enable customers to relocate retention-relevant data from an application database to an archive using the standard SAP data archiving function in accordance with relevant governance.

EIM-ILM-2. SAP recommends that every ISV application component support the major ILM cornerstones:

- *Data volume management—supports system load reduction and compliance with relevant internal and external governance*

- *Retention management—provides tools and methods for retention of information based on relevant governance*

- *Retention warehousing—provides a standardized solution for legacy system decommissioning*

To Learn More

ILM: http://www.sdn.sap.com/irj/sdn/ilm

Information Management:
http://www.sdn.sap.com/irj/sdn/nw-informationmanagement

Guidelines for Business Intelligence Tools

BI tools guidelines cover areas such as analytics, the BI platform, the semantic layer, specific BI tools and their SDKs, and issues around packaging and deployment.

Analytics

BT-BO-1. SAP recommends using SAP BusinessObjects™ BI tools for analytics.

BT-SAP-1. SAP does not encourage use of SAP Business Explorer business user tools BEx Report Designer, BEx Analyzer and BEx Web Analyzer for new development.

BT-CI-1. To help end users gain immediate insight into their businesses, SAP recommends that ISVs create SAP BusinessObjects BI content (such as reports, and visualizations) that is specific to their enterprise applications and data.

BI Tools and the BI Platform

> **BT-BO-2. SAP recommends that ISVs incorporate SAP BusinessObjects software into their applications to provide data visualization and analysis.**

The Semantic Layer

> **BT-META-1. SAP recommends using the SAP BusinessObjects semantic layer as an intermediate layer between reports, analytics, queries, analysis and dashboards and the underlying database.**

> **BT-UNIV-2. For new development, SAP recommends using the information design tool for universes.**

> **BT-UNIV-3. SAP does not encourage using the universe design tool for creating universes.**

> **BT-META-2. SAP does not recommend using SAP BusinessObjects Business Views as the semantic layer.**

Query as a Web Service

> **BI-DASHBOARDS-1. SAP does not recommend using Query as a Web Service as a data connectivity method for dashboards.**

SAP BusinessObjects Web Intelligence

> **BT-QUERY-1. SAP recommends using Web Intelligence as an ad-hoc query and reporting tool.**

> **BT-QUERY-2. SAP does not recommend using Desktop Intelligence as a query and analysis tool.**

SAP BusinessObjects Analysis

> **BT-ANALYSIS-1. SAP recommends using SAP BusinessObjects Analysis to interact with multi-dimensional data.**

Crystal Reports SDKs

BT-BO-3. **SAP recommends using functionality from any of the following products when developing using the component deployment model:**

- *Crystal Reports 2011*
- *Crystal Reports 2008*
- *Crystal Reports XI Developer*
- *Microsoft Visual Studio*
- *Crystal Reports for Visual Studio .NET*
- *Crystal Reports for Eclipse*
- *Rational Application Developer*

BT-BO-3a. **SAP does not recommend using the Crystal Reports report designer component (RDC), which is an older COM-based solution.**

BT-BO-4. **SAP recommends using the component deployment model for the following situations:**

- *Small, self-contained component desktop applications*
- *Small Web applications that will be accessed by a department or work group in a company*
- *Reports that are run on demand*
- *A reporting engine embedded in the application process*

SAP recommends using the server deployment model rather than the component deployment model in more demanding situations like the following:

- *For mission-critical Web applications that need report processing failover*
- *For reports that need to run at specific times or are based on specific events or the successful completion of a third-party business process*
- *For reports that share objects like formulas, SQL commands, text objects, and images in an object-oriented repository*
- *For managing shared reports*
- *For providing access to enterprise data via web services*
- *For situations with a complex semantic data layer*

> - *Where robust security options for user, group, object, and folder levels are required*
> - *For batch report processing*

Authentication and Authorization

BI-SEC-1. *To enable federated identity management, SAP recommends using Trusted Authentication. This technique allows a developer to leverage their own security model to provide single sign-on from their application to SAP BusinessObjects BI.*

Managing Users

BI-USER-1. When embedding the BI platform, SAP recommends that developers follow up any user management tasks in their applications with a corresponding user maintenance action in the BI platform.

Packaging Applications: Deploying Content

BI-PKG-1. When delivering a BI solution, SAP recommends packaging the content as LCMBIAR files.

BI-PKG-2. When deploying a BI solution, SAP recommends using the lifecycle management console for importing and exporting objects.

BI-PKG-3. SAP does not recommend using the Import Wizard tool for importing and exporting objects.

Installation

BT-INST-1. When silent installation is required, SAP recommends the use of response files to silently install SAP BusinessObjects BI.

Guidelines for Application Development

Guidelines for application development are broken into general guidelines, ABAP guidelines, Java guidelines, and .NET guidelines.

General Guidelines

General guidelines described in Chapter 8 include recommendations regarding componentization, running on a single stack, creating composite applications, data handling, functional correctness, and open source.

Componentization

DEV-COMP-1. SAP recommends componentization of business application solutions.

Single Stack

DEV-AS-1. SAP recommends developing components built on a single stack, whether ABAP, Java, or a third-party platform.

Composite Applications

DEV-COMPOSITE-1. SAP recommends creating composite applications to support new business processes or scenarios without the need to modify or enhance SAP Business Suite components.

Extensibility

DEV-COMP-2. SAP recommends that business solutions allow customizations and extensions of their functionality.

Data Handling

DEV-DATA-1. SAP strongly recommends that data in SAP applications be accessed only via interfaces supplied by SAP.

DEV-DB-1. SAP recommends that the persistency layer should be free of application logic.

Functional Correctness

DEV-QA-1. SAP recommends creating test plans and using state-of-the-art testing tools to ensure functional correctness before releasing software.

SAP customers have complex system landscapes, and applying changes and fixes to enterprise software requires a particular methodology (see "Change Management" in Chapter 3). As a result, ISVs should follow a high standard for functional correctness and include rigorous quality assurance testing to eliminate as many problems as possible before software is released.

Open Source

DEV-OS-1. SAP recommends that ISVs keep track of any open source software that is integrated into their products. SAP also recommends that ISVs carefully analyze the terms of the license of any open source software that is integrated into their products, considering license terms from a business perspective.

To Learn More

Open source integration:
http://www.sdn.sap.com/irj/sdn/opensource-integration

Guidelines for ABAP Development

DEV-ABAP-1. SAP recommends using the version of ABAP released in SAP NetWeaver 7.0 and beyond.

DEV-ABAP-2. SAP recommends using ABAP Objects for new programming initiatives and for significant refactoring of older programs.

DEV-ABAP-3. SAP recommends the SAP Press book, Official ABAP Programming Guidelines, to learn more about effective ABAP programming.

To Learn More

ABAP: http://www.sdn.sap.com/irj/sdn/abap

Guidelines for Java Development

Like ABAP, Java is a key development platform for SAP and its partners.

DEV-JAVA-1. SAP recommends that Java developers use the version of Java and Java EE supported in the latest version of SAP NetWeaver.

DEV-JAVA-2. SAP recommends using SAP NetWeaver Developer Studio if you develop for and run on SAP NetWeaver AS Java.

To Learn More

Java: http://www.sdn.sap.com/irj/sdn/java

Guidelines for .NET Development

SAP and Microsoft have worked jointly on ensuring interoperability between the SAP Business Suite and .NET.

DEV-NET-1. SAP recommends that .NET developers use one of the following versions, all of which have been tested by SAP for interoperability:

- *.NET 2.0 with Web service enhancements 3.0*
- *.NET 3.0*
- *.NET 3.5*

To Learn More

.NET: http://www.sdn.sap.com/irj/sdn/dotnet

Guidelines for Security

Guidelines for security cover security guides, the Security Assertion Markup Language (SAML), single sign-on, identity management, and security zones.

Security Guides

SEC-STD-1. SAP recommends that ISVs follow secure programming guidelines, read the SAP security guides, and adhere to relevant industry standards and SAP product standards to ensure security of customer's business-critical applications.

To Learn More

Security area of SAP Service Marketplace:
http://service.sap.com/security

Security section of SDN: http://www.sdn.sap.com/irj/sdn/security

SAML

SEC-STD-3. SAP recommends Security Assertion Markup Language (SAML) version 2.0 for central authentication and single sign-on when integrating homogeneous SAP landscapes as well as heterogeneous landscapes.

Web Browser Single Sign-On

SEC-SSO-1. SAP does not recommend using SAP Logon Tickets for single sign-on in heterogeneous landscapes, outside the corporate firewall or in an environment with high security requirements.

SOA Single Sign-On

SEC-STD-4. SAP recommends that web service calls be authenticated with SAML tokens that use the SAML Holder of Key confirmation method to ensure auditability and interoperability.

Identity Management

SEC-STD-2. SAP recommends that ISVs delegate authentication and role management to SAP NetWeaver Identity Management. Solutions built on SAP and non-SAP platforms can continue to use platform-specific authorization concepts, but SAP recommends delivering identity-related development artifacts (such as authorizations and roles) as an integral part of the solution and centralizing the management of this data by integrating with SAP NetWeaver Identity Management.

Security Zones, Security Infrastructure, and Transport Security

SEC-ZONE-1. SAP recommends that ISVs advise customers about which security zone is most appropriate for deploying the ISV's application

Chapter 3

Application Lifecycle Management Guidelines for Best-Built Applications

Application lifecycle management (ALM) comprises support for building and assembling software, the installation, patching, and upgrading of systems, transporting changes between systems in the system landscape, and operations such as technical configuration, administration, and monitoring. In this chapter, we look at what ALM means from a developer perspective.

SAP has been writing, deploying, and supporting enterprise software for over 30 years. In that process, there have been many lessons learned, standards adopted, and best practices formulated that SAP asks its internal developers to adhere to.

SAP customers use ALM to run their often-extensive SAP landscapes and many customers have dedicated IT teams for operating SAP solutions. Some SAP customers also have developers of custom SAP extensions, who are one target audience for the guidelines in this book. The other audience is developers who work for ISVs, developing software that will complement the SAP Business Suite. In order to support enterprise customers, ISVs need a deep understanding of the way that the application lifecycle is managed at large companies. By considering SAP customers at various points in the lifecycle, ISVs can make life easier for their customers, reducing customers' total cost of operations (TCO) and reducing ISVs' total cost of development (TCD).

Current trends such as cloud computing, software-as-a-service (SaaS), and virtualization create a blended environment of on-demand solutions; this can present additional challenges since remote resources represent new areas to manage. Whether you are a developer at a large SAP customer or a developer at a partner company creating a product that fills the need of a particular industry, proper understanding of and attention to application lifecycle management issues are a must.

An ITIL-Based Approach to ALM

SAP bases its approach to ALM on industry standards: using the phases for application lifecycle management specified by the IT Infrastructure Library standards (ITIL). This approach is designed to ensure a disciplined, best-practices approach to managing applications throughout their lifecycle, from requirements gathering to optimization. According to ITIL, application lifecycle management encompasses six phases:

- Requirements
- Design
- Build & Test
- Deploy
- Operate
- Optimize

ALM-PRD-1. SAP recommends adopting an ITIL-based approach to application lifecycle management.

Adoption of this guideline simply means structuring one's own approach to ALM according to the six phases outlined in ITIL and then following the guidelines laid out in this chapter for each phase.

These phases are surrounded by ALM processes, tools (SAP Solution Manager and its extensions provide much of the tooling needed by SAP customers), services (such as consulting and education to get help where needed), and organization (to ensure that applications are managed in a consistent and productive manner).

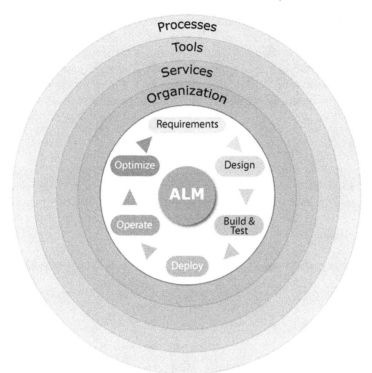

Figure 3-1. Application Lifecycle Management

Processes, tools, services, and organization can augment the ALM lifecycle as follows:

- **Processes:** Solutions can plug into existing ALM processes if ISVs and internal developers follow the guideline from earlier in this section, ALM-PRD-1, making their processes compatible with SAP's

- **Tools:** ISVs can use SAP Solution Manager features both for supporting customers and for internal product development. Customers always have SAP Solution Manager installed, so internal developers should be aware of its capabilities

- **Services:** Offerings from SAP's SI partners and the SAP Services organization can help developers approach their projects in the most efficient way possible. To give just one example, the SAP Modification Justification Check is a service offered by SAP Enterprise Support that provides expert evaluation of planned modifications to see if your requirements can be met in another way, whether through standard functionality, business process reengineering, or a workaround

- **Organization:** Following ALM best practices enables solutions you develop to fit right into the existing organization for running SAP solutions

A disciplined approach to ALM facilitates alignment between business and IT stakeholders, offers the possibility for continuous improvement, and can accelerate business innovation. The cycle includes gathering business requirements from all stakeholders and ensuring business continuity at all phases in the way that software is built, tested, deployed, and operated. By optimizing the application and cycling those optimizations back into requirements, SAP customers can gain a larger view of the way that software serves business requirements, enabling business innovation.

SAP Solution Manager: At the Center of the Lifecycle

A comprehensive approach to ALM is challenging, a problem of not only knowing what to do but how to do it in practice. SAP has literally decades of experience in supporting enterprise customers and has developed processes and tools to reduce the support effort for customers and for SAP. When partners use the same processes and tools, this further reduces the support effort for all parties.

ALM- SUP-1. SAP recommends that you follow SAP's support-related guidelines.

Developers need:

- To provide support for reported issues
- To have their solutions integrated into a common diagnostic framework
- To have their solutions integrated into the ALM processes in the customer's SAP Solution Manager
- To have transparency on the customer's SAP application landscape
- To have access to knowledge hubs in SAP's Service Infrastructure
- To share knowledge (such as tips and tricks and known issues) in a standardized way within the SAP ecosystem

By adopting SAP Solution Manager, developers can meet all of these requirements within a common framework and satisfy the expectations of enterprise customers. As a result, the guideline for SAP Solution Manager states:

ALM-SUP-2. SAP strongly recommends that developers integrate their complementary applications with SAP Solution Manager to align their application lifecycle management and support infrastructure with that of SAP.

SAP Solution Manager provides the following benefits:

- There is no need to invest in other support tools and processes
- Developers can easily share and access knowledge within the SAP support infrastructure

- Any existing investments in support tools can be leveraged

- It is integrated into SAP Global Support

How specifically can SAP Solution Manager help with each phase of ALM? SAP Solution Manager supports ALM as summarized in Table 3-1.

Table 3-1. Capabilities of SAP Solution Manager by ALM Lifecycle Phase

ALM Phase	SAP Solution Manager Capabilities
Requirements	Solution Documentation. Central documentation of processes, system landscape, custom code, and partner applications
Design	Templates allow multi-site SAP installations to efficiently manage their business processes across geographical distances, such as part of a global rollout approach. Partners can deliver partner templates
Build & Test	Test capabilities in SAP Solution Manager include: • Risk-based Test Planning. Identification of business processes affected by SAP solution changes • End-to-End Integration Testing. Methodology and capabilities to test business processes from start to finish • Testing capabilities ranging from functional and regression testing to root-cause analysis • Test Management tools. Documentation of business processes and assignment of manual and automated test cases
Deploy	Change control management capabilities, including: • Integrated quality management • Improved central software logistics • Integration of quality gate management and change request management • Synchronized transports of various components • Controlled and documented adjustment of business processes including approval process
Operate	Technical operations functionality, including: • Central monitoring and alerting infrastructure • End-user experience monitoring • Central administration tools • Support tools, including, application incident management, which provides integrated service desk, involvement of partners in problem resolution, and root-cause analysis for complex landscapes with diverse technology stacks
Optimize	Capabilities for the Optimize phase include: • Business process operations that help ensure business continuity, provide business KPIs, and offer business process benchmarking • Maintenance management, including management of corrective software packages • Upgrade management: Project support for release transitions • Performance optimization through usage of Solution Manager diagnostics tools

If a developer codes and deploys on SAP platforms, SAP Solution Manager provides diagnostic capabilities that can be helpful with code development and quality assurance (QA). Developers who code on other platforms and port to the SAP runtime can be helped during QA. Developers who connect their applications with SAP via web services may find some of the SAP Solution Manager third-party extensions helpful for their product development efforts.

It is through SAP Solution Manager that SAP supports its customers. Therefore, SAP customers are familiar with support provided through SAP Solution Manager.

With this background in place, this chapter now examines the phases of the application lifecycle, starting with the Requirements phase.

The Requirements Phase

The requirements phase of the application lifecycle is informed by the platforms, databases, and operating systems SAP software runs on.

The Product Availability Matrix: Supported Platforms, Databases, and Operating Systems

A cornerstone of SAP's product strategy is allowing customers to run SAP Business Suite products on a wide variety of hardware, operating systems, databases, and other technology platforms. This strategy helps customers to reduce costs by encouraging a competitive market for such infrastructure, while enabling them to consolidate their IT (including SAP products) on a small number of technology platforms of their choice. Such consolidation is a great cost saver in comparison to operating overly heterogeneous IT environments. At the same time, SAP increases its addressable market by supporting many platforms for its products because different customers select different platforms. ISVs can benefit from this extended market reach and attract customers through low TCO of their solution by aligning with SAP's multiplatform strategy. To find out what platforms are supported for each SAP product, developers can consult a repository called the Product Availability Matrix (PAM).

> **ALM-PRD-5. SAP recommends consulting the Product Availability Matrix when making platform decisions.**

Available in the Service Marketplace at http://service.sap.com/pam,[1] the Product Availability Matrix bundles technical and release information on SAP components for quick reference. It provides product-level details about precisely which operating system and database combinations are supported (such as Linux/MaxDB or MS Windows Server/SQL Server) as well as which web browsers, web servers, and JEE, JSE, and JDBC versions are supported.

---

1   Prospective partners need to join SAP PartnerEdge to get access to the PAM as well as to all the other resources in the SAP Service Marketplace. SAP customers get access to Service Marketplace automatically.

It provides per-product information about the availability of SAP component releases and maintenance end dates. The guidelines recommend developing for the latest release.

ALM-PRD-4. SAP recommends that ISVs develop for the latest release of SAP products since these releases provide the most functionality for smooth integration with partner products.

Since your solution might integrate only with a particular SAP product or sub-component, the PAM can help you to focus on platforms released by SAP for that product.

Here are some things to know about using the PAM:

- The release restrictions noted in SAP's support knowledge base for an SAP component release supplements the information given in the PAM
- Anything not listed in the PAM is not supported
- Comments contain important information

System Management and Virtualization Support

Virtualization is increasingly popular with SAP customers, both for their on-premise solutions as well as for their hosting partners using virtualization. Customers use virtualization to consolidate their IT landscapes and achieve better utilization of hardware and increased operational efficiency through IT process automation in order to lower their TCO.

Information about SAP's support for virtualization is not currently part of the PAM, but the latest details about virtualization and the SAP Adaptive Computing Controller (SAP ACC, a tool to manage SAP systems on virtual and physical IT infrastructure landscapes) are available at http://www.sdn.sap.com/irj/sdn/virtualization and http://www.sdn.sap.com/irj/sdn/adaptive. Note that when developing applications that you want to work with SAP ACC, make sure that your applications and components reference logical host names rather than IP addresses.

To Learn More

Partner virtualization supported by SAP:
http://tinyurl.com/partner-virtualization

Certification Planning

ISVs should get their applications certified by the SAP Integration & Certification Center (SAP ICC, see http://www.sap.com/icc). During the certification process, SAP certification experts will help ISVs make their software more supportable and also aid in testing it with SAP applications.

> ### ALM-CERT-1. SAP strongly recommends that ISVs obtain SAP certification of their applications and integration solutions.

Certification offers a number of benefits for partners. Certification shows customers that the ISV and SAP worked together to ensure proper integration. Additionally, consider the go-to-market value of certification. Certification logos and taglines make ISV products attractive to SAP customers. Certification also includes support integration via SAP Solution Manager. Further, certification is a prerequisite for becoming a member of SAP PartnerEdge and obtaining a listing in the SAP EcoHub.

SAP Solution Manager Ready

Partner solutions are also certified to ensure the entire solution is capable of operating well in tandem with SAP systems (as opposed to just being integrated with them). This coordination happens through SAP Solution Manager, which collects operational data from all managed systems and keeps it up to date. For this reason, SAP launched the SAP Solution Manager Ready program, an obligatory part of the certification carried out by the SAP ICC. Making a product "Solution Manager Ready" means that information about installed partner products is automatically available in the customer's SAP Solution Manager system.

To Learn More

SAP Solution Manager Ready: http://tinyurl.com/solmanready

Documentation

Another key aspect of the ALM requirements phase is providing complete documentation. SAP recommends that partners provide documentation to customers to help them implement and operate their products. Documentation is critical for enabling solutions to be operated in tandem with SAP software. Effective documentation can reduce implementation and support costs.

Documentation should be checked for accuracy of content and technical correctness (the hyperlinks should all work, for example). The documentation in question here is aimed not so much at end users—although clearly that is important to customers—but is for consultants, administrators, and IT staff.

> ### ALM-PRD-8. SAP recommends that developers create a complete set of documentation. A complete set of documentation includes at minimum the following:
> - Terms and definitions
> - Documentation of external technical interfaces released to the customers, for example, web services or application programming interfaces (APIs)
> - Customizing and configuration documentation
> - Release notes

- *Application documentation*
- *Installation information*
- *Upgrade information*
- *A master guide that provides a starting point for navigating the documentation*
- *An operations guide that includes information on backup and online backup*
- *A security guide*

Implementation Documentation

An important adjunct to providing the standard documentation set described above is implementation documentation that helps smooth the implementation process for customers. This documentation should follow SAP's format for documentation so that customers can access it using SAP management tools. SAP has provided an "implementation suitcase"[2] to help partners create implementation documentation that fits in seamlessly with SAP's. The implementation suitcase includes how-to documents, information, and templates for creating documentation such as a best practices document, a frequently asked questions document, and more.

Developers can enter relevant information into Solution Manager's Business Process Repository (BPR) and provide an Implementation Roadmap. The Business Process Repository lists the business processes that the solution covers. An Implementation Roadmap describes the implementation process; each part of the process includes pointers to documents that customers will need at that stage in the implementation. The implementation suitcase includes a document that helps you determine what to put in the BPR and the implementation roadmap. It is a very helpful toolkit for partners creating documentation for their solutions.

Documentation can be transported via SAP transport systems into SAP Solution Manager.

ALM-PRD-9. For implementation documentation, SAP recommends using SAP's documentation format so that documentation can be incorporated into SAP management tools.

In order to distribute their documentation in this way, partners must have SAP Solution Manager installed and use it to produce and export their documentation. In other words, the partner is still in charge of distributing the documentation to their customers, whether through an ABAP transport via Solution Manager or through some other method. SAP does not distribute documentation for partner products

---

2   Partners can request a copy of the implementation suitcase by contacting e2esolutionoperations@sap.com

The Design Phase

The Design phase naturally involves designing the application or component itself (see Chapter 8). In terms of the application lifecycle, the Design phase encompasses designing effective ALM processes and a system landscape that can handle the demands of the application, both now and in the future.

Developers should focus on understanding how their solution helps solve business problems and fits into existing business processes. Important ALM aspects to consider during the Design phase include:

- Landscape design and architecture
- Technical infrastructure as it relates to performance, scalability, and high availability requirements
- Information lifecycle management: the effective management of data's lifecycle
- Output management: Management of printing versus electronic document creation
- Template Management: Helping ensure consistent rollout of software across locations in a way that is repeatable

One key consideration that applies across much of the Design phase is the need to strive for "Green IT." The way you design your system landscape and technical infrastructure can use resources efficiently or inefficiently.

Here are two examples.

- **Archiving:** Information lifecycle management should be informed by an approach that retains data for legal requirements but archives infrequently used information to storage that requires little or no power on an ongoing basis.
- **Printing:** The approach to output management (printing) should ensure that, where possible, users have the option to generate an electronic document such as a PDF or other file format rather than printing on paper.

All of these factors help reduce IT costs, as well as being good for the environment.

To Learn More

Green IT: http://www.sdn.sap.com/irj/bpx/green-it

Landscape Design and Architecture

ISVs should think about system landscapes in two ways. First, customers design and run their SAP landscapes for productive use by their business units and ISVs need to understand customers' SAP solution deployment options for seamless integration of their product into customer landscapes. Second, ISVs need to operate a system landscape for supporting their own product development, delivery, and support processes. While customer landscapes (see Figure 3-2) include development, QA, and production systems, ISV landscapes include development, QA, and software assembly systems that they use to package their application for shipment to and installation by their customers.

This section briefly summarizes considerations to be aware of when thinking about system landscapes for either purpose.

Types of Systems

Most SAP documentation about landscape design is written for customers. Their minimal system landscape for an enterprise software component includes:

* **A development system (DEV):** A system on which all customizing and development work is done. All maintenance changes will also be done on this system

* **A quality assurance system (QAS):** After unit testing on the development system takes place, the changes are transported to the quality assurance system. Only after extensive testing are these changes then transported to the production environment

* **A production system (PRD):** A system where business is conducted and the company's live data resides

Many SAP customers also deploy a so-called sandbox system (SBX) where more experimental changes can be attempted. Changes to the sandbox system are isolated from the other systems, as shown in Figure 3-2.

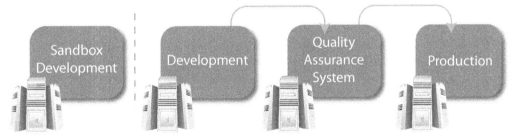

Figure 3-2. System Landscape with Four Systems

What is important to note for an ISV is that, typically, multiple systems for one component are needed to support and structure an efficient development process. An ISV would likely need a development and QA system as well. A production system is specific to customers while an ISV might instead have a final software assembly system (FSAS).

The term horizontal system landscape refers to how changes are propagated from one system to another (for more information on this topic, see "The Optimize Phase" later in this chapter). Another aspect of system landscape planning is to decide how software components, databases, and physical hosts will relate to each other.

In terms of physical hosts, SAP customers have several deployment options. ISVs should be aware that these options exist and design their software in such a way that it can fit into the following deployment scenarios. An SAP application may be deployed in one of several ways:

- **One SAP component and one database per host:** This is the most straightforward setup, but it requires a considerable investment in hardware and administration

- **Server virtualization:** This involves running several systems on the same physical host, with each SAP application having its own database

- **Multiple components on one database (MCOD):** This involves several SAP components sharing a single database. Each NetWeaver ABAP or NetWeaver Java SAP system in this scenario is identified by a unique system ID (SID), which allows the use of different database schemas for different SIDs

- **Bundling usage types:** Multiple SAP software components can be bundled into a single system ID and served by one database. This requires an understanding of which usage types can be run on a single system

Exactly how SAP system landscapes are designed depends on many factors. Can multiple QA systems be placed on a single host? Is it necessary to refresh test systems from backup to an initial state often? (In such cases, using virtualized system images is very helpful.) Many factors influence the development of the system landscape in terms of the relationships between types of systems (DEV, QAS, and FSAS) as well as the deployment of systems, databases, and physical hosts. Because of the ability to customize the landscape for business and development needs, ISVs should ensure that their applications do not make assumptions about the underlying system landscape in their product design. Customers might have integration problems with ISV applications if strict landscape assumptions are made.

To Learn More

How to Design an SAP NetWeaver System Landscape:
http://tinyurl.com/nwlandscape

Landscape design resources and guidelines:
http://www.sdn.sap.com/irj/sdn/landscapedesign

Technical Infrastructure

Customers demand reliability from their technical infrastructure for running SAP systems, and this strong requirement extends to complementary solutions. If the technical infrastructure fails, customers are losing business, which is a worst-case scenario. While many factors influence reliability, consider the following:

- Server-side computing performance
- Client-side response time performance
- Scalability and capacity planning
- High availability

Some of this might appear obvious. However, the practice at customer sites shows that these four points are of major concern and a significant source of calls to support hotlines. Ensuring reliability also means making investments in testing reliability as part of product development quality assurance. Some tools for performance testing will be described later in this chapter under the Build & Test phase.

As a result, this section provides some explicit guidelines that can influence the reliability of business application software. To narrow the scope, the section focuses on reliability factors that can be influenced by application software product quality. Other technical infrastructure considerations, such as network performance, reliability, and availability, are outside the scope of this section.

Server-Side Performance

Server-side performance defines the combined performance of a database, the application servers, and their underlying hardware. Server-side performance influences hardware resources needed for processing in business applications, which in turn represent a significant part of the TCO of a solution as well as impacting application response times for end users. Good server-side performance depends on efficient coding, efficient use of interfaces for integration of software components, efficient database schema designs, and more. For the various aspects of server-side performance, the SAP NetWeaver platform and SAP Solution Manager offer various test tools.

ALM-REL-1. SAP recommends that you familiarize yourself with SAP's approach to optimizing the performance of applications.

To Learn More

Performance Analysis on SDN:
http://www.sdn.sap.com/irj/sdn/performance-analysis

Performance on SAP Service Marketplace:
http://service.sap.com/performance

Next-generation ABAP runtime analysis tool:
http://tinyurl.com/abapruntime

Client-Side Response Time Performance

Client-side response time performance defines the combined performance of the application running on a server, the network time for connecting clients to a server, and client software processing times.

The server response time is covered in the previous section on server-side performance. In particular, in regard to integration of software with SAP software, it should be pointed out that synchronous calls between server components tend to increase server response times since all server component response times add up (the guidelines in Chapter 4, specifically SOA-WS-1, recommend using asynchronous calls wherever possible for this reason). If synchronous calls must be used, such calls should be specially optimized.

The network times depend on the amount of data delivered to a client and the number of network roundtrips needed to deliver that data. Therefore, simply strive to transfer the right amount of data in the fewest number of trips.

In summary:

ALM-REL-2. SAP recommends that you design user interface implementations to allow optimal user interaction with the shortest possible application response time, especially when these applications are deployed over a wide-area network. The user interface implementation should optimize:

- *The number of synchronous communication steps between the user interface and the application layer or between two servers*

- *The amount of data transferred between the user interface and the application layer. (Transferring large amounts of data can cause performance problems. Always strive to transfer the right amount of data in the fewest number of trips.)*

- *The application's processing time inside the application server*

Scalability and Capacity Planning

Scalability is the notion that the hardware resource consumption of an application is linearly proportional to the amount of business application processing. Capacity planning, referred to in SAP terminology as "sizing," is the process of determining how many hardware resources will be needed for a certain amount of application processing. In this way, capacity planning assumes scalability of an application. An application that does not scale might not be able to support a higher processing load on any amount of hardware, and therefore might not be usable for customers.

Mostly, server-side performance factors determine how much hardware (in terms of storage, servers, and networking) is needed for a given processing load. This ratio strongly impacts application TCO for customers since hardware must not only be provided but also operated and maintained over time. Customers need information on the hardware requirements of an application in order to size their technical infrastructure properly for a reliable productive use of an application.

Therefore:

ALM-REL-4. SAP recommends that development groups provide hardware sizing information to facilitate capacity planning for productive use of customer systems.

To Learn More

Hardware sizing: http://service.sap.com/sizing (See the Build & Test phase for details on testing tools that can aid in formulating such guidelines)

High Availability

High availability addresses the critical business need to avoid downtime. For most customers, high availability is an essential feature and a strong business requirement.

> ***ALM-REL-5. SAP recommends that applications intended to be part of a mission-critical business process be architected for high availability to allow customers to deploy their application instances in a high-availability configuration as needed.***

The goal for high availability is to minimize planned and unplanned downtime. Unplanned system outages are of course most disruptive to businesses, but planned downtimes, for example for patching, should also be minimized to help customers achieve 24/7 business operations.

Achieving high availability requires an analysis of the system landscape that eliminates single points of failure (SPOF). For instance, this requires clustering application server instances and using load balancing.

You should provide documentation on how to set up high availability for your applications.

To Learn More

High availability on SDN: https://www.sdn.sap.com/irj/sdn/ha

Information Lifecycle Management (ILM)

When using business applications, business data accumulates over time at a high rate. This is problematic because storage costs money and consumes power. Further, the performance of very large databases can degrade. As a result, the seemingly infinite growth of data volumes must be controlled. Therefore, just as applications have a lifecycle, so does information (data). Information is created, stored, updated, archived, and eventually deleted. You should follow best practices for ILM as described in Chapter 6 (specifically, see EIM-ILM-1).

Developers using SAP development tools or who have migrated their software to the SAP environment should enable customers to relocate retention-relevant data from an application database to an archive using the standard SAP data archiving function in accordance with relevant governance (see EIM-ILM-2).

To Learn More

ILM section of Chapter 6, Enterprise Information Management Guidelines

Information Lifecycle Management on SDN:
http://www.sdn.sap.com/irj/sdn/ilm

Information Management on SDN:
http://www.sdn.sap.com/irj/sdn/nw-informationmanagement

Information Lifecycle Management on the Service Marketplace (see
especially the Media Library link): http://service.sap.com/ilm

Output Management

Output management refers to printing, emailing, and generating documents
and faxes. It also encompasses form design, both interactive forms and static
PDF forms.

Although printing is just one aspect of output management, it is the aspect most
frequently discussed. Like cars that fly through the air, the paperless office
was hyped long before the amount of paper on our desks began to decline. The
ability to view documents and presentations and read books on convenient
screens, along with greater awareness about the cost and environmental
impact of printing, is reducing the amount of printed material in offices.

> ***ALM-OM-1. SAP recommends that developers design their
> applications to provide alternatives to printing.***

SAP provides a printing and output management infrastructure as part of its
SAP NetWeaver Platform to ensure the enterprise readiness of its customers.
SAP's printing infrastructure enables customers to administer the printing
landscape and print documents and forms from an SAP system.

As an extension to its print and output management capabilities and to meet
the high-end printing solution needs of our customers, like high-volume
printing, printing cost management, and the like, SAP collaborates with
multiple output management solution partners. SAP relies on its printing and
output management partner ecosystem to meet customers' broader output
management needs.

SAP has three output management related technologies:

- SAP Interactive Forms by Adobe
- SAPscript forms
- SAP Smart Forms

SAP Interactive Forms by Adobe was introduced in SAP Web AS 6.4. For
designing interactive forms, forms that can be used to save data to backend
systems, or PDF forms for noninteractive use, SAP Interactive Forms by Adobe
is the preferred technology (see Chapter 5, UI-TECH-8).

The oldest of these technologies is SAPscript forms. SAPscript is limited in
its capabilities compared with Smart Forms (introduced by SAP in 4.6): it
does not support color printing, cannot be generated into XML or HTML for
web viewing, and is generally less capable and slower from a development

perspective. SAPscript forms represent a legacy technology and SAP does not recommend using it for new development (see Chapter 5, UI-TECH-8).

SAP Smart Forms do not have many of these limitations and remain a good option for some scenarios. Although no additional development is underway for SAP Smart Forms, but they are suitable for certain use cases, such as high-volume printing.

> ### ALM-OM-2. SAP recommends use of SAP Smart Forms for high-volume printing needs.

To Learn More

Output Management on SDN: http://www.sdn.sap.com/irj/sdn/printing

Comparison of SAPscript forms and SAP Smart Forms: http://wiki.sdn.sap.com/wiki/x/wAY

Template Management

Template management is a feature of SAP Solution Manager that is relevant to the Design phase. Template management enables standardizing configurations for global software rollouts. The template management approach allows multi-site SAP installations to efficiently manage their business processes across geographical distances—from initial template definition to template implementation and template optimization. Customers can use templates to ease the process of rolling out software across multiple locations. ISVs can create templates and deliver them to their customers as partner templates.

To Learn More

SAP Help on Using Templates: http://tinyurl.com/solmantemplates

Template Management on SDN: http://www.sdn.sap.com/irj/sdn/alm-template-management

The Build & Test Phase

In the Build & Test phase, developers implement the system, conduct testing, and release the system to customers (in the case of ISV developers) or to production (in the case of in-house custom development).

Building Software

Ensuring that software components use unique namespaces and that each software component can be identified with versioning information are two important considerations for the Build portion of the Build & Test phase.

Namespaces

Naming collisions can cause problems for customers deploying software from a variety of vendors. As a result, having a unique namespace is an important consideration for developers who want their software to interoperate effectively with SAP software.

> **ALM-PRD-7. SAP recommends that developers name software components uniquely to avoid name collisions with SAP software and with software components from SAP partner companies.**

In Java, use package names to specify the namespace. You can either request a unique namespace from SAP or use a namespace that is very unlikely to be used by another company, such as com.mycompany.myapplication (assuming that the company owns the domain name mycompany.com).

To get an ABAP namespace, you first request the namespace from SAP, then reserve it. To request a development namespace, you need a valid development license and the name for the namespace must refer to the name of your company. The namespace itself consists of three to eight capital letters bounded by slashes (for example, /MYCOMP/).

To Learn More

Namespaces on the Service Marketplace:
http://service.sap.com/namespaces

Versioning

Another important consideration for the Build portion of the Build & Test phase is versioning information. The versioning data included in software is an important key for ALM and for support. An upgrade can work only when installed components are versioned (so it knows what component is an older version and what is newer). In terms of support, frequently, the first question that must be asked is what version of the software the customer is running. SAP support personnel must be able to find out the version of the application and associated source code versions. This is the rationale behind the following guideline:

> **ALM-PRD-6. SAP recommends that all application development objects be accompanied by versioning metadata.**

Developers must ensure that all their application development objects include versioning metadata. In some cases, tools take care of this for the developer. (Product version information, on the other hand, is stored in the PPMS; the versioning in question here is at the application development level.)

ABAP applications developed on SAP tools are updated with versioning metadata automatically.

For Java applications, the SAP NetWeaver Development Infrastructure (SAP NWDI) provides versioning information automatically in two cases:

- If a Java EE application is developed on SAP NetWeaver and deployed on SAP NetWeaver

- If a Java EE application is migrated to run on SAP NetWeaver and its components are imported into NWDI

To Learn More

NWDI on SDN: https://www.sdn.sap.com/irj/sdn/nw-di

NWDI on SAP Help: http://tinyurl.com/helpnwdi

Developers of other types of applications that are connected to SAP applications should either use a tool that provides equivalent versioning data automatically or enter and update this information manually.

Testing Tools

Testing tools can be used to aid in testing software. Here is a quick tour of some of the testing capabilities available via SAP NetWeaver, SAP Solution Manager, and partners such as HP:

- **SAP Solution Manager Business Blueprint:** Enables documentation of business processes and assignment of manual and automated test cases

- **SAP Solution Manager Test Workbench:** Enables management of functional tests from test planning to test execution to test status reporting and signoff

- **SAP Solution Manager Business Process Change Analyzer:** Provides impact analysis prior to changing a business process to see what areas would be affected by the proposed change

- **SAP Quality Center by HP:** Supports role-specific testing and covers the complete testing process from requirements gathering to test case definitions and reporting

- **SAP LoadRunner by HP:** Helps to simulate running software under high loads and checking its performance

- **SAP eCATT:** Allows creation of automated functional test cases for applications running in SAP GUI for Windows/Java/HTML or Web Dynpro environments. For more information on eCATT, see http://www.sdn.sap.com/irj/sdn/ecatt

- **SAP Test Data Migration System (SAP TDMS):** Quickly populates a QA system with a snapshot of data from the production environment to use when testing

- **SAP Test Acceleration and Optimization (SAP TAO):** Supports automating business process tests by generating test components for SAPGUI-based SAP transactions. It helps QA professionals break down business processes into components for unit testing

Figure 3-3 illustrates how SAP Solution Manager extensions dovetail with the testing capabilities of SAP Solution Manager.

TEST CAPABILITIES

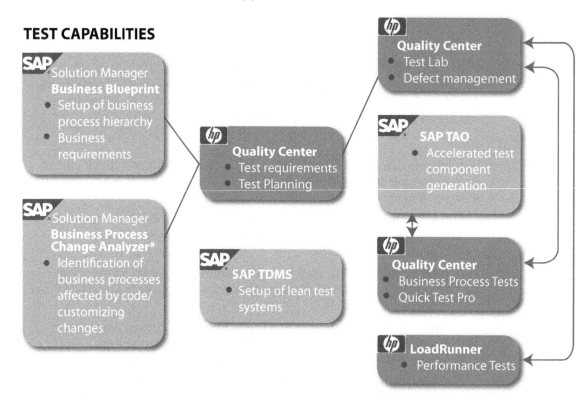

Figure 3-3. SAP Solution Manager Testing Capabilities and Extensions

To Learn More

SAP Solution Manager testing capabilities: http://tinyurl.com/sm-testing

The Deploy Phase

The Deploy phase is handled by SAP customers' operational teams. Development groups move their work from a development system (DEV) to a quality assurance system (QA) using the Change and Transport System (CTS). A customer would use CTS again to make the final move of developments from QA to a productive system instance (PRD) while an ISV could use CTS to move and consolidate developments.

Two important aspects for all development groups are:

- Upon deployment, applications need to be registered in the System Landscape Directory (SLD) (see the following section)

- Providing hardware capacity planning information for the hardware and software requirements of the application (see "The Design Phase" earlier in this chapter

For ISV software packaging, developers that deliver their products on the SAP NetWeaver platform might consider using the ABAP Add-on tool for ABAP-based products (see "SAP Integration and Certification Center (SAP

ICC)—Integration Scenario—ABAP Add-Ons" at
http://tinyurl.com/abap-addons) and NWDI (http://www.sdn.sap.com/irj/sdn/
nw-di) for Java-based products.

Registering in the Customer's System Landscape Directory

The customer's System Landscape Directory (SLD) contains a comprehensive
view of all software that is installed at the customer site. The SLD is the central
information repository for SAP system landscapes. The SLD's architecture is
based on the Distributed Management Task Force's Common Information
Model (CIM) standards.

When an ISV application is deployed, it can register in the customer's SLD
if the application and relevant dependencies have been documented in the
product and production management system (PPMS) as outlined in the next
section. That way, when SAP support is called, the support personnel can
tell what third-party applications are registered in the customer's system
landscape and the versions of those applications. This speeds up support
because customers need not be asked for this information; it is available to
support personnel automatically.

***ALM-REL-6. SAP recommends that all application components be
registered in the customer's System Landscape Directory.***

Details about how to register in the customer's SLD as well as example code
are available.

To Learn More

System Landscape Directory on SAP Help: http://tinyurl.com/saphelp-sld

System Landscape Directory on SDN (see section on registering third-
party systems): http://tinyurl.com/sdn-sld

SAP Solution Manager Integration Documentation (see especially
SLDREG_QuickGuide_for_SSPs.pdf): http://tinyurl.com/sm-ssp

Defining Software Dependencies

Enterprise software includes dependencies in which one component depends
on the installation of another component. SAP tracks all its products and
their dependencies on each other and with partner products in a software
catalog known as the Product and Production Management System (PPMS).
Customers need this information for making proper technical deployment
decisions. Since the PPMS is very important for smooth, low TCO deployment
activities, inclusion in the PPMS is part of the partner product certification
process. A PPMS entry is required for ISV products to show up in SAP Solution
Manager.

***ALM-CERT-2. SAP recommends that SAP-certified ISV software
document all development and runtime platform dependencies in
the product and production management system (PPMS).***

The Operate Phase

This phase encompasses the tasks involved in operating software on a day-to-day basis. This includes managing the system landscape, databases, portals, and application instances. It also encompasses monitoring applications and troubleshooting any problems that come up.

Database Management

Managing databases largely entails data reorganizing and archiving, log file archiving, and monitoring table space and backup space. Beyond these activities, it is important that ISVs ensure that customers are provided with a backup and recovery procedure for their product.

SAP-recommended backup/recovery procedures can be used as an example. Descriptions of the type of data that SAP stores in each kind of table space can be found at http://tinyurl.com/databaseadminhelp.

To Learn More

Best practices for backing up and restoring databases:
http://tinyurl.com/backuprestorehelp

Instance Management

Instance management is a key activity in the administrative stage of the Operate phase. Tasks are performed regularly, often daily, and include starting and stopping system instances, scheduling jobs, creating technical and central configurations, and establishing and comparing profile parameters.

Developers with Java applications that run on SAP NetWeaver will want to leverage the NetWeaver Administrator (NWA). The Configuration Wizard of NWA saves time and reduces errors by enabling administrators to perform typically repetitive activities just once. For instance, rather than performing the initial technical configuration of a newly installed system manually, administrators start the Configuration Wizard, which prompts for required parameters and executes the configuration faster, with less expertise required and fewer errors. In this way, the Configuration Wizard helps administrators save time and effort when setting up and operating SAP systems.

To Learn More

Technical configuration on SDN:
http://www.sdn.sap.com/irj/sdn/technicalconfiguration

Wizard-Based Configuration of the SAP NetWeaver Administrator SAP help page: http://tinyurl.com/nwa-help

Monitoring

The complexity of modern enterprise software makes the ability to monitor the system on various levels a critical task. A typical SAP solution such as CRM or ERP is complex, comprising many hardware and software components, interfaces, and business processes that span multiple components. Monitoring the entire deployment is important to ensuring that all components are available, that transactions are performed with sufficient timeliness and accuracy, that each interface is working properly, and that yesterday's backups are complete and usable. If a problem occurs, both its source and its resolution must be quickly determined.

> ***ALM-SUP-4. SAP recommends that applications provide alerts for all relevant situations (heartbeat, performance, resource utilization, and business-critical situations). You should also provide alerts for resources that your application manages, such as caching and queues, as well as documentation with information about monitoring.***

Monitoring happens at two levels, business and technical. Both levels require unique tools, including SAP Solution Manager, NWA, and the Computing Center Management System (CCMS). This last is vital to successful monitoring and is included in every ABAP system. It monitors all of the alerts, for single and integrated systems, and can be configured to send particular notifications.

Monitoring operations at the business level entails observing the state of business processes at runtime. Administrators deploy timely notifications to push business-critical events to users and offer resolutions. Monitoring at this level also includes reporting on business KPIs.

The technical level is concerned with similar details, only here, administrators monitor the technical state of business processes and technical components at runtime, deploying timely notifications about technical events and resolution capabilities, manual or automated. Technical KPIs are also reported.

SAP Solution Manager can help with monitoring applications. If an application is built using SAP tools and run on SAP or simply migrated and run on SAP NetWeaver, it can take advantage of these monitoring and reporting capabilities.

Applications that are merely connected to SAP do not run on the SAP platform and therefore need additional integration in order to be monitored using SAP Solution Manager.

Another capability of SAP Solution Manager, SAP EarlyWatch Alert is a proactive service that informs a customer when there is a problem in their system landscape. SAP Solution Manager can also generate alerts for ISV applications.

To Learn More

Monitoring on SDN: http://tinyurl.com/lcmoperations

Log Files

Reviewing log files for errors or anomalies is another important activity related to operations.

Developers must ensure that all log, trace, and similar files created or maintained by their applications can be easily found by support personnel.

> *ALM-CERT-3. SAP recommends that all log, trace, and similar files created or maintained by your applications be stored only in documented locations in a human-readable format.*

Problem Management

Problem management entails monitoring both manually and automatically triggered problem alerts. When an alert is received, administrators must analyze the problem, then determine the best solution in the knowledge/ solution databases. On locating a solution, they must apply it to the problem and monitor it to ensure its durability. Beyond the solution database, the primary toolkit for problem management includes SAP Solution Manager and the service desk.

Service Desk

Service Desk functionality includes the ability for SAP to pass trouble tickets between SAP and its customers as well as forwarding customers' trouble tickets to SAP's partners when needed. This is referred to as incident management (see Figure 3-4).

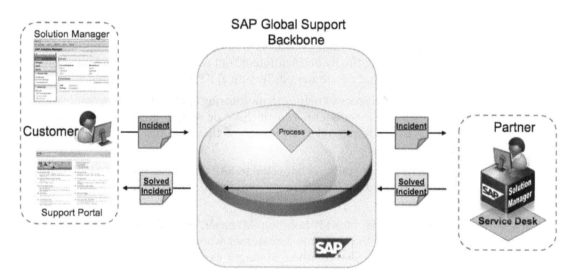

Figure 3-4. Incident Management

In the event of a problem, the ISV's support organization can gain rapid access to an SAP knowledge network from a range of sources, for example SAP Notes, online documentation, how-to guides, forums, wikis, and so on.

If the problem relates to an error in the partner software, SAP transfers the message to the partner. The message is then received in the partner's SAP Solution Manager, which is connected to the SAP global support backbone and checks whether new messages have arrived. The customer can tell that a message has been forwarded to the partner from the message status. The partner can now start working on a solution to the problem and communicate directly with the customer.

An important standard for ISVs to know about in the area of Service Desk is the Open Service Desk Interface. This interface allows ISV software to communicate with the Service Desk functionality of SAP Solution Manager via web services. Detailed information about the web services involved in using this interface can be found at http://tinyurl.com/open-service-desk-interface. Note that although this SDN page currently says that the document refers to SAP Solution Manager 4.0, in fact it refers to web services for communicating with Service Desk functionality in SAP Solution Manager 7.0.

Root Cause Analysis

Getting to the root of the problem in multitier application environments is what Root Cause Analysis is about. Solution Manager Diagnostics can be used to perform a root cause analysis on certified partner products (since Solution Manager integration is part of the certification process). The tools provided in Solution Manager Diagnostics enable problems that arise in a distributed customer solution with critical business processes to be systematically analyzed and resolved. Solution Manager Diagnostics has direct access to the error, log, and trace files for the partner product. This means the root cause analysis for partner products takes place in a familiar environment in exactly the same way as it is done for SAP products. Tools such as CA Wily Introscope are integrated with SAP Solution Manager, which assists in identifying any performance issue in non-ABAP environments, such as Java, .NET, C, and C++.

Safe Remote Access

Customers' business data is highly confidential. Since it is in the nature of providing support to customers to get certain access to their data, it is important to secure such access.

ALM-SUP-3. SAP recommends using support tools that provide secure remote access to customer landscapes.

The best way for partners to establish such secured support connections to customers is collaborative use of SAP's support infrastructure. This enables problem solving on behalf of the customer and obviates the need for the customer to act as a bridge between the two support organizations. The customer needs to open an incident report only once. When tickets are forwarded and worked on by the ISV or SAP, using this collaborative infrastructure, communication delays and errors are kept to a minimum. From the customer's perspective, support looks like it comes from a single source, whether it comes from SAP or the ISV.

ISVs using SAP Solution Manager can also log onto the customer system remotely if required (and if customers give permission for them to do so).

SAP Solution Manager must be installed on premise at the ISV for this feature to work; being certified as SAP Solution Manager Ready is not enough.

End-to-End (E2E) Diagnostics

End-to-end diagnostics entail cross-component and component-specific, root-cause analysis and problem solution for clients, systems, networks, and databases, including exception, workload, trace, and change analysis. SAP Solution Manager is used for E2E diagnostics. E2E diagnostics helps point out problems wherever they occur across the landscape.Root cause analysis is then used to find out what the exact problem is. E2E can help ISVs during their own product development and when a customer problem involving their solution needs to be analyzed. For example, the test tools incorporated in SAP Solution Manager and described earlier in this chapter can, in many instances, also be used for customer on-site problem diagnostics. The SAP Solution Manager operations tools are helpful in customer support as well.

Note Access and Creation for Partners

SAP Notes describe known problems and their solutions and are accessible to all customers online. SAP Notes may also contain FAQs and tips and tricks about installing and configuring a solution. Some notes also amend printed documentation, like installation and upgrade guides, with last-minute information. (Problems discovered past the release date of an SAP application are found in release and upgrade notes. For release notes, see http://service.sap.com/releasenotes.)

Through SAP Solution Manager, software partners are given access to the SAP Notes database and can create Partner Notes for their enhancements. Partner Notes can be located using the Notes search and can help customers solve problems efficiently.

The Optimize Phase

The Optimize phase of ALM involves upgrading and adding components and system landscape elements, importing corrections such as notes and support packages, and tuning performance. Since customers want to ensure that optimization procedures are fast, simple, and reliable, with a minimum of downtime and manual effort and low costs, ISVs may want to model their software logistic tools, processes, and platforms on SAP's. Such uniformity can contribute to smoother system updates for customers.

A particular strength of SAP solutions is their adaptability to individual customer requirements. Customers may add to and adapt their SAP applications and some ISV developments do the same. Optimizations of customers' productive systems may originate from SAP, the customers' own developments, or from ISVs. This adaptability creates the need to control potential conflicts of changes from different origins. Understanding the procedures and guidelines laid out in this section helps to manage optimization changes in a safe way.

Customers do not want to disturb their business processes to install frequent upgrades. SAP's release management strategy takes this into account. It includes Enhancement Packages that enable new functionality without disturbing core business processes (a concept referred to as innovation without disruption).

This section covers the following areas:

- Release architecture: How SAP releases software
- Enhancement Packages
- Support Packages
- Maintenance
- The Change and Transport System
- The Enhancement and Switch Framework
- Adapting SAP Software

Release Architecture: Understanding How SAP Releases Software

When deciding how to release changes to software, it can help to understand how SAP handles its software releases and therefore how SAP customers are used to dealing with releases and updates.

SAP follows a strategy for releasing software that has three aspects:

- Major releases
- Enhancement Packages
- Support Packages and Note Corrections, which provide corrections and legal changes

ALM-PRD-2. SAP recommends that development organizations understand the SAP strategy of releases, enhancement packages, and support packages and consider adopting a release strategy that follows the same model.

SAP's strategy for releasing software enhancements and support updates has been designed with the needs of SAP customers in mind. Enterprise customers may stay on a release for a decade or even longer because their business is critically dependent on their SAP systems and they do not make changes lightly. ISVs should keep these horizons in mind when considering the needs of their enterprise customers.

Enhancement Packages

SAP is dedicated to innovation without disruption for its customers and has created mechanisms, such as SAP Enhancement Packages, to reduce the need for system upgrades. Enhancement Packages allow customers to install and enable new functionality with less effort.

SAP releases updates to Business Suite components via SAP Enhancement Packages. SAP Enhancement Packages are a significantly improved methodology for implementing new functionality. Customers expressed a desire for new functionality but also made it clear that upgrading Business Suite components, such as ERP, entailed significant effort. SAP responded with its enhancement packages as a way to deliver new functionality to customers and partners, including service-enablement of key functionality, while allowing the release level of the software to remain stable.

Two major characteristics comprise the key difference between SAP Enhancement Packages and previous technologies:

- Selective installation of software components
- Selective activation of new functionality via the Switch Framework (described later in this section)

New functionality is added in enhancement packages. This is particularly true in the area of enterprise services. Enhancement packages may include many new enterprise services, and these enterprise services are the primary way that ISVs integrate their solutions with SAP's (see Chapter 4 for details). If an application depends on a service or other component in a given enhancement package, it is critical to ensure that customers have installed that enhancement package and activated it.

A further distinction about Enhancement Packages must be made at this point. SAP NetWeaver is the underlying technology platform for the SAP Business Suite, and developers can also build applications directly on the SAP NetWeaver platform. There are Enhancement Packages for the SAP Business Suite and for SAP NetWeaver. When an SAP NetWeaver Enhancement Package is applied, all of the functionality is activated. When an SAP Business Suite Enhancement Package is applied, functionality can be activated selectively.

To Learn More

Enhancement Packages: http://service.sap.com/erp-ehp (Service Marketplace User required)

Using the Enhancement and Switch Framework as a means to adapt SAP software, see the section on this topic later in this chapter

Support Packages

Support packages provide fixes to existing components. Those customers who are not interested in enhancement packages have the clear expectation that support packages contain only code corrections or legal changes and not any new or hidden functionality.

Individual changes are included in Notes. Such fixes might be applied because a customer is having a particular issue solved by the Note.

Note fixes and other corrections are included in Support Packages (SPs), which are released periodically. Support packages are in turn grouped into Support Releases (SRs), which are used only on new installations to bring them up to the current fix level.

An SR is a bundle of SPs. For instance, if six months have gone by since a customer last installed the most recent SR, and seven SPs have been created in the interim, the latest SR will include those SPs and automatically install them when the customer installs the new SR. In short, an SR is a fresh install while an SP is applied to an existing system. An SP will include fixes to any known bugs, but will not include new functionality. An SR is typically integrated into an installation package to enhance a system with the latest patch sets and usually includes the latest version of the installation tools.

Maintenance

This portion of the optimization stage of ALM entails implementing any SAP notes, installing support packages, working with hot news, and implementing needed corrections. Customers may also enhance their systems according to their own needs using CTS.

SAP Solution Manager's Maintenance Optimizer is one tool that applies to this phase of application lifecycle management.

Change and Transport System

Since SAP customers run business-critical functionality on the SAP platform, they apply all changes, including support packages, in a particular way, across the various systems in their system landscape, as described in "The Design Phase" earlier in this chapter. Changes are applied from development to QA to production and are moved using the Change and Transport System.

> ***ALM-REL-3. SAP recommends using the SAP Change and Transport System (SAP CTS) to transport changes from one system to another.***

CTS tools are part of SAP NetWeaver, so they are easy to use for ISVs that use SAP development tools or migrate their software to the SAP environment. It is very important to SAP's customers that ISVs merely connecting their software to SAP solutions provide equivalent tools or procedures for handling software logistics.

To Learn More

Software logistics: http://www.sdn.sap.com/irj/sdn/cts

Software logistics: http://www.sdn.sap.com/irj/sdn/softwarelogistics

Software logistics wiki: http://wiki.sdn.sap.com/wiki/display/SL/Home

Change Management for Non-ABAP Objects

The Enhanced Change and Transport System (CTS+) is an add-on to CTS that enables non-ABAP objects to be transported between systems.

To Learn More

Resources page on SDN: http://tinyurl.com/cts-plus

Change Management and BusinessObjects

SAP BusinessObjects has its own ALM features with which both ISVs and customers should be familiar (see the "Lifecycle Management for SAP Business Objects Enterprise 4.0 User Guide" at http://tinyurl.com/bobj-user).

This user guide includes a chapter on using CTS+ with SAP BusinessObjects. Figure 3-5 shows one possible configuration that includes both an SAP BusinessObjects system landscape as well as an SAP NetWeaver Business Warehouse system landscape.

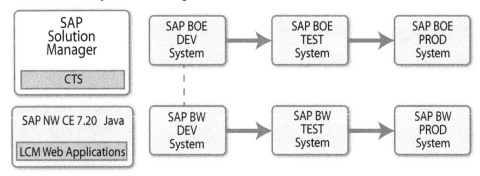

Figure 3-5. Software Logistics for SAP BusinessObjects

The SAP BusinessObjects Enterprise 4.0 Admin Guide includes information specifically related to transporting Crystal Reports 2008 or Crystal Reports 2011. This guide provides information about configuring the BW publisher so that Crystal Reports can be saved into BW and can then be transported like any other BW object.

SAP BW can also help with transporting SAP BusinessObjects Dashboards (formerly called Xcelsius).

To Learn More

Admin Guide: http://tinyurl.com/bobj-admin

Transporting dashboards: http://tinyurl.com/dashboard-transport

Country Specific Legal Changes

For human resources applications in particular, year-end brings many changes related to how payroll deductions and taxes should be handled. SAP supplies update packages called Country-specific Legal Changes (CLC). These CLC packages must be imported for continued compliance with local tax laws in a timely manner.

ALM-SL-1. SAP recommends that developers whose applications complement or adapt SAP HCM keep up to date with Country-specific Legal Changes, which must be applied on a regular basis.

To Learn More

SAP Country Legal Change packages:
http://service.sap.com/hrlegalchanges

Audio book on this topic available in the SAP Service Marketplace:
http://tinyurl.com/clc-ebook (Service Marketplace user required)

The Enhancement and Switch Framework

The Enhancement and Switch Framework is a mechanism by which customers can activate business features of ABAP-based SAP solutions. Because of the framework, all functionality, including Industry Solutions, is now delivered on one set of DVDs and you can switch on the functionality you need. This has important advantages for partners and customers. They don't have to turn on all the functionality included in their software but can turn on just the functionality they need. See the wiki on this topic on SDN (http://wiki.sdn. sap.com/wiki/x/rBE) for a collection of articles and resources that explain the Enhancement and Switch Framework in detail.

The Switch Framework allows partners and customers to install an Enhancement Package and to turn on only the business functions they desire, thus reducing the cost of adopting enhancements in a complex enterprise software environment. For the time being, most of the business functions of the SAP Industry Solutions and the SAP Business Suite are not reversible, so, in general, partners and customers should be aware that once business functionality is turned on via the Switch Framework, it cannot be turned off again. To check in your system whether a particular business function can be switched off, look in the transaction SFW2 or SFW5 to see if it is reversible.

To find out whether you might benefit from the functionality of a particular business function of SAP ERP, access the information on the different enhancement packages of SAP ERP in the SAP Service Marketplace at http:// service.sap.com/erp-ehp. If you are still not sure whether the functionality provided by a particular business function fits your needs, it is generally recommended to activate and test this business function in a separate sandbox system.

ALM-PRD-3. SAP recommends that developers understand how the Switch Framework could affect their applications.

With an understanding of the Switch Framework, ISVs can determine, when applicable, what particular functionality each specific customer has turned on. An ISV application needs this information in order to interoperate effectively with SAP applications. Furthermore, as described in the next section, developers can use the Enhancement and Switch Framework as a better way to adapt or supplement functionality of SAP software than changing SAP development objects by using classic modification technology.

Adapting SAP Software

Partners and customers sometimes need to adapt SAP software to provide extensions or customizations to various areas to meet unique business requirements. Since SAP products include all their source code, partners and customers have a number of approaches to adapt SAP software:

* Creating an ABAP or Java add-on, which runs inside an SAP system

- Using web services to call functionality in the SAP application from an independent component, for instance a composite application (for details, see Chapter 4)

- Using SAP enhancement technologies (Enhancement Framework, classic BAdIs or customer exits) and the Switch Framework to create an enhancement application project that can be activated (and deactivated if encapsulated by a reversible business function) when needed

- Modifying SAP development objects directly (classic modification technology)

The following sections discuss this important area and provide recommendations related to adaptations of SAP development objects.

Decouple by Creating an Add-On

The preferred approach is not to adapt SAP software at all, but to build add-ons that access SAP software via SAP supported interfaces (see Chapter 4 for details).

> **ALM-ADAPT-1. SAP recommends building add-ons that connect to SAP software via SAP-supported interfaces rather than modifying SAP software.**

There are times, however, that you need a closer integration into the code of an existing application. For example, you may need to: enhance existing business logic by adding some steps, access more variables of an ABAP program than are currently available via web services, include additional accounting steps within an existing ABAP program, or add more steps to an existing database transaction to meet business requirements.

Closer integration comes with additional costs in terms of long-term maintenance, however. The lifecycle of your application will be linked to the lifecycle of the application you modify. Further, the integration might have side effects. It might interfere with the business logic of the SAP application. To avoid such unwanted side effects, you need in-depth knowledge of the application you enhance, both on the business and on the technical level. In addition, you should also make sure that you have a suitable package structure for your enhancement application project that takes into account dependencies between different parts of your enhancement application project. As for possible dependencies of your enhancement application project on parts of an enhancement package, see the following sections.

Verify the Need for Adapting SAP Development Objects

SAP business software has been developed to meet the needs of many of the world's largest companies. This can create the challenge that it is difficult to understand all its capabilities. Therefore, before you adapt SAP development objects or Web Dynpro ABAP components, make sure it's really necessary (in other words, don't reinvent the wheel). An easy way to find out whether an existing capability can meet your needs is to use the SAP Modification Justification Check. Available to SAP Enterprise Support customers, this service checks whether the functionality you need is already available either through SAP software or through business process reengineering.

To Learn More

SAP Enterprise Support: http://www.sap.com/enterprisesupport

Enhancing SAP Software

If you determine that your adaptations are really necessary and that there isn't another suitable approach, the next step is to decide how to approach your changes.

ALM-ADAPT-2. SAP recommends that developers who need to adapt SAP development objects use an SAP enhancement technology rather than modify the SAP software development objects.

If you modify SAP software development objects directly (using classic modification technology), then when the software is upgraded all your modifications to SAP development objects are overwritten, and you have to reapply every modification.

If instead you use an enhancement technology supported by the Enhancement Framework or you implement classic BAdIs and customer exits, your enhancements of SAP development objects exist in your own namespace and are only merged with the SAP software at compile time. Since your enhancements are transport objects of their own, they are not overwritten during an upgrade. You only have to adjust an enhancement if the underlying SAP development object has been deleted or changed in an incompatible way by an upgrade. The Enhancement Framework provides the transaction SPAU_ENH to show which enhancements you have to adjust and help you adjust them. It covers all enhancements supported by the Enhancement Framework.

The preferred enhancement technology to use is (in order of preference):

1. Kernel-based BAdI

2. Classic BAdI and customer exits

3. Other enhancement technologies that are part of the Enhancement Framework such as class enhancements. (Do not use source code enhancements unless it is the only way to achieve what you need to develop)

To Learn More

Enhancement technologies:
http://www.sdn.sap.com/irj/scn/weblogs?blog=/pub/wlg/12225
(Note especially the section on "how to enhance business logic" which contains information on how to implement classic BAdIs and customer exits so that the implementation is switchable)

ALM-ADAPT-3. SAP recommends making your enhancement add-on projects switchable by using reversible business functions of the Switch Framework.

The next step is to make these enhancements switchable using the Switch Framework. If your enhancements are properly assigned to switches and reversible business functions (this is important because you can only deactivate reversible business functions), you can use the Switch Framework transaction SFW5 to turn your enhancements on or off or allow the customer to do so. There are many ways you may benefit from making your enhancement application projects switchable:

- It is helpful when tracking down bugs. If the bug is gone when you switch off your enhancement, it is on your side

- If you have different switchable deactivatible enhancement application projects, you can keep them isolated from each other in the same test system. Simply activate the business functions for the enhancement application project you want to test and deactivate all other enhancement application projects

- Using switchable business functions of the Switch Framework, you can easily model and implement dependencies between your enhancement application project and the enhancement packages of the SAP Business Suite. For example, suppose SAP delivers the functionality SAP-FI+ on top of a solution SAP-FI in an Enhancement Package. The functionality SAP-FI+ is switchable. An ISV develops an add-on enhancement ISV-FI+ to the switchable functionality SAP-FI+. It should only be possible to switch on ISV-FI+ if SAP-FI+ is activated. You can easily achieve this by implementing a dependency between the relevant business functions. In that case, the Switch Framework makes sure that you cannot switch on ISV-FI+ unless SAP-FI+ is switched on

Of course, it is also possible to use enhancements of the Enhancement Framework without the Switch Framework, that is, without assigning them to switches and business functions, because, in principle, the Enhancement Framework and the Switch Framework are different frameworks. But in this case, you cannot profit from the advantages of switchable enhancements listed above. You can use this approach if you are sure that that your enhancement application project will not benefit from these advantages.

Note that use of the Enhancement and Switch Framework does not alleviate the need for testing. Clearly a new release of the SAP software could change the way the business logic works and thus impact the way your enhancement interacts with the SAP software. Testing is necessary after any upgrade.

The way you approach adaptations of SAP development objects (both enhancements and modifications) can make supporting your application over time considerably easier. A complete discussion of this critical topic is beyond the scope of this chapter, and there are many more considerations.

To Learn More

Enhancement and Switch Framework blogs:
http://tinyurl.com/switchframework-blog

Enhancement and Switch Framework wiki:
http://wiki.sdn.sap.com/wiki/x/rBE

Switch Framework help: http://tinyurl.com/switchframework-help

Application Lifecycle Management Resources

Extensive resources are available online for learning more about all areas of application lifecycle management.

To Learn More

SDN page on ALM: http://www.sdn.sap.com/irj/sdn/alm

Landscape Design: http://www.sdn.sap.com/irj/sdn/landscapedesign

SAP NetWeaver Developer's Guide on SDN:
http://www.sdn.sap.com/irj/sdn/devguide

Help: SAP NetWeaver Developer's Guide:
http://tinyurl.com/help-nw-dev-guide

ABAP Add-Ons: http://tinyurl.com/abap-addons

ICC Step-by-Step Guide for Certification of Third-Party ABAP Add-On Integration: http://tinyurl.com/abap-addon-cert

Integration and Certification Center (ICC):
https://www.sdn.sap.com/irj/sdn/icc

Technical Configuration:
http://www.sdn.sap.com/irj/sdn/technicalconfiguration

Configuration Wizard: http://tinyurl.com/nwa-help

Installation and Master Guides: http://service.sap.com/instguides

Scenario & Process Component List: http://service.sap.com/scl

SAP Upgrade Technology: http://tinyurl.com/upgrade-tech

SAP Upgrade Info Center: http://service.sap.com/upgrade

Java Support Package Manager Documentation:
http://service.sap.com/jspm

Multiple Components in One Database (MCOD):
http://tinyurl.com/sdn-mcod

Multiple Components in One Database- Programming Recommendations for Developers: http://tinyurl.com/mcod-dev-rec

Software Maintenance Tools: http://tinyurl.com/sw-maint

Installation: https://www.sdn.sap.com/irj/sdn/installation

System Copy Procedures: http://tinyurl.com/sys-ls-copy

System Copy & Migration: https://www.sdn.sap.com/irj/sdn/systemcopy

Chapter 4

Process Orchestration and SOA Guidelines for Best-Built Applications

What is "process orchestration"? And why does SAP recommend using SOA (service-oriented architecture) when developing applications? The answers come from industry trends.

Today, most SAP customers run their applications to extend SAP Business Suite in the same datacenter where they run the Business Suite. Indications are, however, that this is changing. In coming years, many extension applications may run in a different data center than the one in which SAP Business Suite is running—these applications are then referred to as running remotely.

Three use cases are driving the need for this type of configuration:

- **Networks of trading partners:** Companies are linking their systems more closely to those of their partners and customers. These integrations often involve a remote system accessing SAP Business Suite using standards-based communication such as web services

- **Integration of subsidiaries:** When one company purchases another, they often use extension applications to tie the systems together. The extension application may run at the headquarters' data center or in the subsidiary's data center, but either way, the extension application is running remotely with respect to one of the systems it extends, necessitating the use of services to invoke functionality on the remote system

- **Hosted applications:** An extension application could be running in the cloud or offered as a service. In this case, the extension application would naturally be remote from the backend system

These business and technology trends mean that applications will increasingly be delivered in a location-independent way. This is the motivation for many of the recommendations in this chapter. SAP's movement toward service-oriented architecture (SOA) is in response to business and technology trends and to enable flexibility moving forward.[1]

Like many significant technology shifts, SOA has been the subject of debate. In January 2009, Anne Thomas Manes of the Burton Group famously declared "SOA is Dead" (http://apsblog.burtongroup.com/2009/01/soa-is-dead-long-live-services.html), but then clarified that while the acronym "SOA" has "become a bad word," architectures based on service-orientation are still the critical prerequisites for the rapid integration of business processes, BPM, SaaS, and cloud computing. Manes explained:

"Successful SOA (i.e., application re-architecture) requires disruption to the status quo. SOA is not simply a matter of deploying new technology and building service interfaces to existing applications; it requires redesign of the application portfolio."

This is the approach SAP recommends: not merely service-enabling software components, but also architecting applications for flexibility.

Process Orchestration

For applications that extend SAP Business Suite, the best way to architect for flexibility is to think in terms of end-to-end business processes that might someday need to be changed in unexpected ways on short notice. Applications may need to be extended, combined with other applications, or split into parts to be used in a new sequence or by new users.

"Process orchestration" is the ability to fluidly reorganize software components to support business process innovation. Such changes to business processes and the way applications support them sometimes require software components to be running remotely, as described above.

Driving development based on business processes provides a high-level, technology-agnostic, business-driven perspective. Technology must serve business and is not worth adopting for its own sake.

Starting with business processes leads logically to model-driven development. This development strategy is an important direction to consider.

SAP follows this approach to give customers increased business agility with stable, high-quality components. An ISV application that follows this approach will enable an SAP customer to integrate the ISV application into the customer's unique, differentiating business processes that are based on SAP software. An application developed by a customer development team that is architected in

---

[1]   For a more detailed introduction to SOA, see "The Enterprise SOA Handbook," an 85-page document available for download from SDN (see http://tinyurl.com/sdn-soa-handbook)

this way will allow maximum flexibility when business processes within the company need to be adapted based on changing requirements.

SOA-BPM-1. SAP recommends that developers consider architecting an application as a set of components that can be orchestrated using business process modeling techniques.

A Brief Glossary of Terms

Business Object:[2] An entity that represents a specific view on well-defined business content, for example, a purchase order, sales order, or customer.

Business Process Management (BPM): As a management discipline, a systematic approach that helps companies standardize and optimize operational processes to reduce costs, improve quality, and increase agility. As a technology, a framework of tools to design, model, implement, run, monitor, operate, and improve business processes flexibly throughout their lifecycle (http://www.sdn.sap.com/irj/sdn/nw-bpm).

Composite Application: An application consisting of one or more business processes—where each process step is either a user interaction or a service call to a potentially remote backend system.

Enterprise Services: Web services using a common enterprise data model based on process components, business objects, and global data types, and following consistent communication patterns. SAP exposes software functionality as enterprise services.

Enterprise Service Bus: A message broker that supports web services, to simplify and accelerate reliable communication.

Enterprise Services Repository (ESR): A design-time environment where application developers model enterprise services, business objects, and business processes according to SAP's SOA meta model. These meta-level models and definitions are used to generate platform-specific representations.

Global Data Types: A business-oriented data model. SAP uses GDTs to provide a consistent data model across product lines. They are based on the UN/CEFACT Core Component Technical Specification and are published in the Enterprise Services Repository. Examples include Delivery Terms and Product ID.

Process Orchestration: The ability to fluidly re-organize software components to support business process innovation, through modeling

---

[2] There's business objects and then there's BusinessObjects. A "business object" is completely different from "SAP BusinessObjects," the SAP analytics products. The similarity in naming is purely coincidental.

the business process and developing or re-using components to improve the automation of that process.

Services Registry: While the ESR contains content that describes a service and is useful at design time, the Services Registry holds the reference to the executable endpoints of that service needed at runtime.

SOA: Service-oriented architecture is an adaptable, flexible, and standards-based IT architecture, where functionality is packaged as interoperable services to enable re-use.

Web Services: Software with interfaces designed to support interoperable machine-to-machine interaction over a network based on web protocols, in particular HTTP/HTTPS.

WSDL: Web Services Description Language. An XML-based language for specifying web service interfaces.

Composite Applications

SAP uses the term "composite application" to describe applications consisting of one or more business processes—where each process step is either a user interaction or a service call, and the service calls are loosely coupled to backend systems through service-oriented interfaces.

Even if today it appears that an application would never be used remotely or integrated into an unexpected business process, developers should consider investing the time to make their applications loosely coupled in order to "future-proof" the application, to prevent having to rewrite their applications at some future date when customers demand more flexibility.

Composite applications fill the role of flexible applications that can run remotely from a backend system. This section examines an enterprise-ready architecture for a composite application, starting with the key characteristics of a composite. (Bear in mind that the terms composite, composite application, and SOA-based application are treated as synonyms in this document.)

These characteristics can be summarized as follows (please refer to Figure 4-1 for details):

- Composite applications follow a layered approach, consisting of a business process layer, a UI layer, and a business object and service layer

- The business process layer concentrates on highly innovative collaborative business processes that bring companies a competitive advantage. Composite applications are not intended to reimplement existing standard functionality already available in packaged applications such as SAP ERP. Look for processes that distinguish your customer from their competition

- The UI layer should be task-oriented. The UI of a composite is tailored to the needs of the current role. Where the data is retrieved from is irrelevant for UI design

- The business object and services layer provides all the necessary services that the UI and process layers require. This can be new business logic, data persistency, or simply connecting to external services

- Composite applications are loosely coupled with their backend systems. That means that composite applications only define their business needs using a clearly defined interface description (called a service contract) with a short explanation about the business functionality they require to work correctly. How this interface is implemented is not important for the composite. Composite applications benefit from this approach as service implementations can be replaced as needed. This feature brings additional flexibility, especially where business needs frequently change

- Composite applications have their own lifecycles. There are no dependencies between composites and called backend systems, so their release cycles can be independent of releases of the integrated applications

- Composite applications work only on data that their business processes require. The composite architect should always be guided by the specific business process that the composite addresses. Concentrate only on the business entities the composite requires and for each business entity, use only the necessary fields. Reduce the number of attributes for a business entity to the bare minimum

- Composite applications are not invasive, so no adaptations to backend systems are required to benefit from a composite (see "Adapting SAP Software" in Chapter 3 for other approaches that do require changing backend systems in some way; composites offer less complexity)

Composite applications rely on a canonical data type system: they do not reuse proprietary data types available in the connected backend systems[3] because this would make the composite dependent on the reused data types, which we want to avoid.

Here are some additional questions that you can pose to decide whether it makes sense to write a composite application to fill a gap in functionality. If you answer these questions in the affirmative, it is likely that a composite is warranted:

- Is it a new process that complements existing processes?

- Does it rely on existing functionality? Does the functionality reside in several systems?

---

[3] There is one exception from this rule: if you are using GDTs as the canonical data type system (which is both valid and recommended), you are using data types that are also used by enterprise services in SAP's Business Suite (and thus are indeed used in backend systems). But that's OK.

- Will the application be reused (if developed for one customer) or sold as a packaged solution (if developed by a partner)?
- Is flexibility a fundamental requirement?
- Is it important to adapt the application to changing landscapes?

To Learn More

Examples of composite applications (and business process models on which those composites are based):
http://tinyurl.com/composite-examples

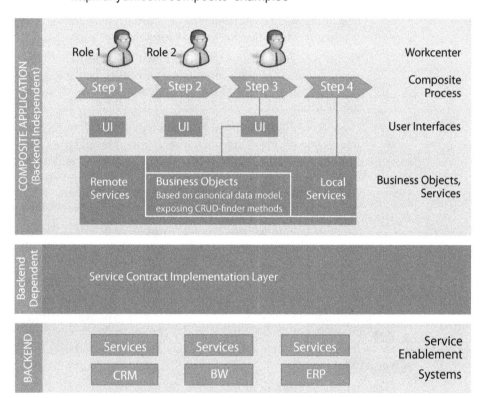

Figure 4-1. Architecture of a Composite Application

Figure 4-1 summarizes the architecture just described: you can identify the backend-independent composite application at the top, the layer containing the backend systems at the bottom and, in between, the backend-dependent service contract implementation layer. This architecture clearly separates responsibilities: the composite application takes care of the new business processes, the backend systems provide required services the composite is relying on, and the service contract implementation layer fulfills the mediation between the two in a loosely coupled manner.

The composite application comprises new business functionality. It is built using only a so-called **canonical data type** system. This means that you apply a universal cross-system data model that is used to define business data aspects of an interface or of the business entities your application works on. It's important not to expose the raw data model of the backend system.

SAP provides the Global Data Types (GDT) as a canonical data model that you could use. It is also a valid approach to define your own data type system. What is important is having such a type system in place. However, if you are working in an SAP environment, using GDTs is highly recommended because they are reused in SAP's enterprise services as well as in SAP NetWeaver Process Integration (PI). Using GDTs will significantly reduce the need for data type mappings within the service contract implementation layer. The guideline states:

SOA-GDT-1. SAP recommends modeling business objects based on global data types.

Global Data Types

SAP global data types are based on UN/CEFACT's Core Component Technical Specification for global data types. Details of this standard can be found at http://www.unece.org/cefact/ebxml/CCTS_V2-01_Final.pdf.

Global data types can be simple, having only one field, such as EmployeeID or ProductID, or aggregated, such as DeliveryTerms, Item, or Address, having multiple fields or constructed of multiple entities.

A no-cost license for the global data types is available to SAP partners that certify their applications under the ESR Content certification. SAP customers are licensed to use global data types under their customer licenses.

A catalog of global data types is available for download on SDN at http://tinyurl.com/sdngdtcatalog.

Composites should have no need for type transformations at all because they should be based on a harmonized data type system. Using a harmonized data type system significantly eases the development of composites. Don't allow your composite to get polluted with backend-specific data types. It's a clear indicator that you are leaving the path of independence.

Besides implementing new business functionality, a composite also defines external service needs in the form of a **service contract**. The interface comprises the signature of the service call from the composite's point of view: it should be lean and restricted to the fields the composite actually requires (taking a top-down approach). The description of the interface is expressed using the WSDL standard. It is a good idea to add some comments in prose to the interface that describe briefly the required business functionality so that the implementer of the interface knows what must be delivered to the composite. In defining the interface itself, we use exactly the same canonical data type system used in the composite earlier.

The service contract can now be fulfilled by the service contract implementation layer. Because it resides between the composite application and the backend systems, its focus is totally of a technical nature. It must negotiate between the composite's requirements and the available functionality of the backend systems. Keep the main advantage of this separation of concerns in mind: you can implement the interface (and with it the needed business functionality) in many different ways depending on the IT landscape you are programming against without requiring changes to the composite. This is the key point to understand regarding the flexibility and agility of SOA-based applications.

Loose Coupling Through Web Services

This edition of the guidelines for Best-Built Applications exclusively focuses on full-blown loosely coupled composite applications written in Java or .NET, calling web services implemented in ABAP, Java, .NET, or potentially other languages.

> **SOA-WS-1. SAP recommends implementing remote consumption of business functionality using loosely coupled, asynchronous, stateless communication using web services. If you develop your own web services, SAP recommends that you:**
>
> * **Use WS standards WSDL 1.1, WS-Policy 1.2, XSD 1.0, SOAP 1.1, and WSRM 1.1**
>
> * **Keep XSD structures simple**
>
> * **Publish services to the Services Registry**

But are web services enough? Not alone. The design of composite applications requires additional thought about their architecture. These applications are loosely coupled and typically use asynchronous communication. The services they invoke are stateless.

The following sections unpack some of these concepts in detail, including the meaning of loose coupling, the rationale for using asynchronous communication (especially for write operations), and what it means for a service to be stateless. It then describes the architecture of a composite application, followed by a methodology for designing such an application.

What Is Loose Coupling?

Traditional applications are one large piece or tightly coupled.[4] Composite applications are loosely coupled. But what does loose coupling mean? How can it be measured? Frequently, it is reduced to whether an application communicates synchronously or asynchronously with its peers. Although this is certainly one aspect, it doesn't cover all relevant dimensions of loose coupling. The goal of loose coupling is to reduce dependencies between systems. Therefore, the answer to how tightly an application is coupled to other systems can be found by asking a simple question: What are the consequences for system A (the calling system) if you make changes in system B (the called system)? Most probably, this question already reveals many dependencies

---

[4]   The following explanation of loose coupling is adapted from a blog by Volker Stiehl (http://tinyurl.com/loose-coupling-blog).

between your application and others that go farther than a classification of the communication style between them.

Here are additional dimensions for evaluating whether applications are loosely coupled:

- **Location of the called system (its physical address):** Does your application use direct URLs for accessing systems or is the application decoupled via an abstraction layer that is responsible for maintaining connections between systems? The Services Registry and the service group paradigm used in SAP NetWeaver CE are good examples of what such an abstraction might look like. Using an enterprise service bus (ESB) is another example. The point is that the application should not hard code the physical address of the called system in order to truly be considered loosely coupled

- **Number of receivers:** Does the application specify which systems are the receivers of a service call? A loosely coupled composite will not specify particular systems but will leave the delivery of its messages to a service contract implementation layer. A tightly coupled application will explicitly call the receiving systems in order; a loosely coupled application simply makes calls to the service interface and allows the service contract implementation layer to take care of the details of delivering messages to the right systems

- **Availability of systems:** Does your application require that all the systems that you are connecting to be up and running all the time? Obviously, this is a very difficult requirement especially if you want to connect to external systems that are not under your control. If the answer is that all systems must be running all the time, the application is tightly coupled in this regard

- **Data format:** Does the application reuse the data formats provided by the backend systems or are you using a canonical data type system that is independent of the type systems used in the called applications? If you are reusing the data types of the backend systems, you probably have to struggle with data type conversions in your application, and this is not a very loosely coupled approach

- **Response time:** Does the application require called systems to respond within a certain timeframe or is it acceptable for the application to receive an answer minutes, hours, or even days later?

There can be even more dependencies, but the message here is that loose coupling is not one-dimensional.

Benefits of loose coupling include flexibility and agility. A loosely coupled approach offers unparalleled flexibility for adaptations to changing landscapes. Since there are no assumptions about the landscape your application is running against, you can easily adapt the composite application as needed. This is especially important for ISVs and system integrators who develop applications once and install and configure them at diverse customer sites. The application itself stays untouched.

Another aspect to consider is the probability of landscape changes during the lifetime of the application. Due to mergers and acquisitions and system consolidations, the landscape underneath the application is constantly changing. Without loose coupling, you'll be forced to adapt your application again and again.

In essence, loose coupling means reducing the number of assumptions to a bare minimum. The goal of loose coupling is to minimize dependencies between systems. However, note that loose coupling comes at a price—every form of loose coupling has disadvantages (especially with regard to complexity) that must be considered.

Table 4-1 compares tight coupling and loose coupling at a very high level along a number of different dimensions. Decisions have to be made for each dimension and in most cases not all characteristics have to be applied at the same time. This table draws on information from the following books: *Enterprise SOA: Service-Oriented Architecture Best Practice* by Krafzig, Banke, and Slama (Prentice-Hall PTR 2004) and *SOA in Practice* by Josuttis (O'Reilly Media 2007).

Table 4-1. A High-Level Comparison of Tight and Loose Coupling

	Tight Coupling	Loose Coupling
Physical Connection	Point-to-point	Via mediation[a]
Communication Style	Synchronous	Asynchronous
Data Model	Complex common types	Simple common types
Type System[b]	Strong	Weak
Service Discovery and Binding	Static	Dynamic
Dependence on Platform-Specific Functionality	Strong/many	Weak/few
Interaction Pattern	Via complex object trees	Via data-centric, self-contained messages
Transactional Behavior	Controlled by a central transaction manager (e.g., two-phase commit)	Compensation[c]
Control of Process Logic	Central control	Distributed control
Deployment	At the same time[d]	Different point in time if desired
Versioning[e]	Explicit/forced upgrades	Implicit upgrades

[a] Mediation implies that some mechanism must handle communication between the composite application and the backend system, filling the role of the service contract implementation layer. This layer can be handled by an enterprise service bus (ESB), SAP NetWeaver BPM, Java code, service composition, SAP Composite Application Framework (SAP CAF), or some other means.

[b] Data types can range from weak to strong. Very weak data typing means using just a few generic data types such as string, decimal, and boolean. Strong data typing entails using highly specialized data types that are probably used only within one singular system with strong restrictions on what can be stored within them. In this case, weak is better (weak here means flexible, while strong can mean rigid or easily broken). While it may not be necessary to restrict yourself to generic data types, it is best to stay on the weak end of the spectrum. Strong data

types are fine if nothing ever changes, but weak data types make applications easier to change moving forward, providing increased agility for future modifications.

[c] Compensation means that for every modifying service, a dedicated compensational service must explicitly be developed for rollback purposes. If the modifying service is part of a service chain that has to be executed as one transaction and an error occurs, the compensational service helps to undo the first modifying operation and sets the system back to its initial state.

[d] For tightly coupled applications, the parts must always be deployed at the same time. Loosely coupled applications do not have this requirement (though of course the parts could be deployed at the same time). Consider an interface change for a web service that performs a write. When a tightly coupled service is called, if the interface has changed, it simply will not work. A loosely coupled service operation will write the data to the service contract implementation layer and continue. Once the new write operation is in place, it can handle all buffered calls.

[e] Consider versioning of services. If a service provider changes the interface of a service, it is probable that not all consumers can update their applications at the same time. In case of tight coupling, all consumers must explicitly update their applications as well. With loose coupling, the provider offers separate versions at the same time so that consumers don't have to update their applications. Alternatively, the provider supports the new functionality behind the old interface and fills new parameters with default values (an implicit upgrade that does not affect the consumer).

Why Use Asynchronous Communication?

SAP recommends that composite applications use asynchronous communication, especially for write operations, in order to potentially be remote, that is, not running in the same data center as the SAP Business Suite.

Why is this so? In a loosely coupled environment, we never know how many systems are involved, whether the systems are available, or how long it takes to complete certain change operations in the backend systems. In addition, all kinds of errors can occur, which must be handled appropriately. It is (almost) impossible to handle business-critical change operations in such an environment synchronously. Developers must not only consider the best case, in which everything works perfectly, but also must explicitly consider all kinds of error situations (technical and business errors) and how to respond to them. This goes well beyond simple request-response web service calls and it has severe implications for the composite application's architecture. Especially if the services you want to call are only synchronous ones, you have to decouple the calls between the composite application and the service contract implementation layer using asynchronous means. This can be achieved by introducing an enterprise service bus, but that is not the only way to handle it. It is also possible to achieve this solely using SAP NetWeaver Composition Environment or other development tools.

Note that asynchronous services are especially recommended for write operations. Read operations can also be handled asynchronously, for even better loose coupling. If your application uses synchronous reads and as a result there are performance problems, one solution is to copy some data (especially master data) to the composite application for caching.

What Are Stateless Web Services?

As the guideline states, SAP recommends that in loosely coupled SOA-based environments, the services providing the required business functionality should be stateless. Stateless refers to the internal state of the service instance. After the service call, the internal temporary variables and objects are deleted. It does not relate to whether the service saves state in external systems. One example is stateless session beans in the Enterprise JavaBeans world. Stateful services by contrast typically lead to tightly coupled implementations that do not scale well.

Using an Enterprise Service Bus

An Enterprise Service Bus (ESB) is software that supports flexible and reliable messaging. ESBs provide a variety of features. SAP NetWeaver Process Integration (SAP NetWeaver PI) is one such ESB. Table 4-2 provides an overview of the features of SAP NetWeaver PI.

Table 4-2. Features of SAP NetWeaver Process Integration

Core messaging and eventing	Support for synchronous, asynchronous, one-way and two-way interaction patterns
	Support for publish/subscribe and many-to-many interaction patterns
	"EOIO" (exactly once in order) delivery of messages
Standards support	Web service standards for message exchange patterns (SOA) and event-driven architecture including security, policy-based configurations, and management
	Metadata-related standards (WSDL, XSD, UDDI v3)
	Service component architect (SCA) and service data objects (SDO)
	Integration-centric orchestration (BPEL)
Service enablement and connectivity	Ability to wrap non-WS enabled (legacy) applications and expose them as managed and reusable services
Mediation capabilities	All routing patterns including dynamic routing
	Data mapping and transformation (semantic bridging)
	Graphical micro-flow-based development of flexible mediations
Performance and scalability	Ability to handle high volume messaging scenarios
	Low latency (milliseconds, not seconds or minutes)
	Ability to handle large message sizes
Protocol switching	Interoperability between consumer and providers with different bindings, typically JMS vs. SOAP/HTTP as well as proprietary protocols. Enabling this protocol switch in a meta-driven configuration-based way
Extensibility	Ability to add additional transports/bindings cartridges
	Ability to add additional mediation capability for message enrichment
Integration into metadata management	Integration with ES Repository and Services Registry
	Enable design-time and run-time governance
Monitoring/management	Local (embedded) management
Security	Support for message-level and transport-level policy-based security

A Best Practices Methodology for Designing a Loosely Coupled Composite Application

The aim of this section is to provide a methodology that can help developers to collect all the relevant information about a composite application: the process flow, the UI, the data on which the application works, and the services it will call. After all this information is collected, it can be handed over to a developer for implementation.

In the interest of space, this section does not provide a detailed, running example. To see this methodology fleshed out with an example, review "Guidelines for Specifying Composite Applications" by Volker Stiehl (http://tinyurl.com/composite-guidelines).

Start with the Business Need

To see where a composite is needed, start with the business process. Are there gaps in the way that the process is handled that could be automated? What need is driving the application? This analysis is the foundation of designing the application, but it has nothing to do with technology but with the problem to be solved, the gap to be filled.

Describe the business problem that this composite will solve and the idea behind the solution. How will the composite improve the process? Describe the business benefits of your solution.

Estimate usage. It's important at this stage to get an idea of the usage level for the proposed application. For example, how many users are there likely to be? How frequently will they use the application? How many business objects are affected (which is a measure of the complexity of the application)?

Processes

Depending on the complexity of the application, multiple processes may be involved. List each process and describe it briefly. For each process, specify it in more detail using the following steps.

Writing a process description. The process description contains general process information, including:

- **When and how the process starts:** Is the process executed regularly or does it depend on a specific event? Is the process started manually or automatically?

- **Preconditions for the process:** What must happen before this process can start?

- **Timing:** Is timing important? Must the process be completed within a specific timeframe?

Listing the roles for the process. List each role that will be involved in the process.

Visualizing the process flow. The next step is to visualize the process flow. BPMN offers an especially helpful way to sketch out processes.

SOA-BPM-3. SAP recommends using Business Process Modeling Notation (BPMN) to create process models.

Why BPMN?

From the time the first flowchart was drawn, people in many different fields have used process models. However, BPMN has achieved something that most other notations have not accomplished to date: the ability to have the models understood and accepted both by businesspeople, who know the process, and technical people, who understand how the process should be implemented in a technical sense. In the past, developers used tools like UML while businesspeople used tools like event chain processing (particularly in project management). BPMN is a notation that can be understood both by business and technical people alike. Model-driven development aims to start with process models and ultimately make them executable.

For more information on BPMN, go to http://tinyurl.com/sdnbpmn.

Providing information on each step in the process. Enter information about each process step, numbering each step. For each step, list:

- A description of the business action for each step
- The data the step works on
- The action performed on the data (one of Create/Read/Update/Delete, or "CRUD")
- How the business logic flows in detail
- Whether services are called and, if so, which services
- If the step is interactive, the input the user must enter
- Optional or mandatory
- Timing relative to the previous step, if applicable (as in 12 hours or less after step 1; 3 days after the process starts)
- The name of the role that executes the step

Exception handling. What kind of exceptions might occur and how should the process flow handle them?

If an exception is recognized during an automated step, what is displayed to the user?

How should the process recover from the exception? Can processing continue (by going to a subprocess designed for that purpose or going to another step) or must it be resolved first? Should the process terminate or generate an alert?

Business Objects/Data

The next step is to identify business objects needed for this process, focusing on those fields that are relevant for the composite application.

For each business object, include important attributes, which may appear as fields in the UI, as well as its relationship to other business objects and what may happen to this business object during the process.

Consider the relationship between business objects, whether it's a composition or an association type of relationship.

- What should happen if the business object with which your business object has a relationship is deleted? Should your related business object also be deleted? If so, that's a composition relationship. One example is a purchase order with line items stored as separate objects. If the purchase order is deleted, the line items should also be deleted

- On the other hand, if you delete a sales order, you would not delete the customer. That type of a relationship is called an association

Determine cardinality:

- 0..1 A sales order might have a confirmation

- 1..1 A sales order must have a customer

- 0..n A customer may have many orders or no order at all

- 1..n If there's a sales order, there has to be at least one item on it

Mapping to business objects in the backend system. If the business object exists in the SAP backend system, include information that maps the business object being used in the composite application to the business object in the SAP backend system. For example, include:

- The field name in the composite

- System information of the backend system: manufacturer (SAP), system type (ERP), and version number (Business Suite 7.0)

- The name of the business object in the backend system if you know it

- The name of the field in the backend system if you know it or the parameter in the related service calls. For example, the enterprise service PurchaseOrderByIDResponse_sync returns the field PurchaseOrder.Item.Quantity (Of course, this is only applicable if such a field exists in the backend system)

To finish describing the needs related to business objects, consider the following questions:

- How many business objects of this type do you expect? This helps in determining the expected load on the application

- How will the business object be used within the composite? Will the object be generated or accessed only for reading, writing, or deletion?

- Will the business object survive the business process or is it a temporary object?

- If the business object is found in a backend system, can it be changed from an alternate UI in the backend while being used in the composite? If so, think about conflicts during write access and how the composite's process can be notified if its state becomes invalid because of a change in the backend system. However, this should be implemented only if the backend is able to send notifications of these changes out of the box, for example, via eventing

UIs

The next step in the methodology entails creating a user interface mockup, a drawing of the user interface. This mockup can be created using any tool that you are comfortable with, whether SAP NetWeaver Visual Composer, which is ideal for mocking up UIs, or PowerPoint.

The mockup should take into account linkages to business objects, whether fields can be modified, whether they are mandatory or optional, the type of UI element that should be used, and the validation checks needed.

Services

Services represent the core of the composite application. As shown in Figure 4-1 earlier in this chapter, services can be divided into local services and remote services. Typically, you build local services and you discover remote services.

Local Services

Composite applications usually contain some business logic, with a lightweight composite having less business logic. Local services are a way to put business logic into the composite application.

For each service, consider aspects such as conflicts if the service changes data and how that should be handled. Input parameters, output parameters, and exceptions should be outlined along with business logic.

Some local services can have parameters externalized so that business users can change them. One way to capture this type of logic is in the form of business rules.

If a composite uses a business rules engine to represent some of its business logic, it is necessary to define the rules.

> **SOA-BRM-1. SAP recommends that business logic be expressed as business rules where appropriate. ABAP applications should use Business Rules Framework plus (BRFplus) to define rules. Other applications developed with SAP design tools should use SAP NetWeaver Business Rules Management to define rules.**

A service might be defined as a business rule if it is highly volatile and will very often be changed by business people, consisting of business logic that can be expressed as if-then-else expressions or decision tables. Examples of business rules include validation rules, rate calculation rules, decision rules, recommendation rules, personalization rules, internationalization and localization rules, exceptions and special rules, and optimization and configuration rules.

Business rules require a description of input/output parameters. Once the data on which the rule works has been defined, the logic of the rule must be explained. Decision tables can be created in a simple tool like Excel and flow rules can be created using the graphical flow modeler shipped with SAP NetWeaver Business Rules Management, descriptive prose, another kind of graphical representation (for example, a structogram), or pseudo code.

To Learn More

> SAP NetWeaver Business rules management:
> http://www.sdn.sap.com/irj/sdn/nw-rules-management

Remote Services

You build local services, but you discover remote services. The ES Workplace, described later in this chapter, enables discovery of all the enterprise services supported by SAP Business Suite. Services are of course available from non-SAP sources as well.

Implementing Process Orchestration

As mentioned earlier, you want to design your application in terms of business processes, giving you the ability to fluidly reorganize software components in support of business process innovation.

Process orchestration is therefore an architectural concept; the tooling that you use to implement that architecture is SAP NetWeaver BPM.

Why is SAP NetWeaver BPM explicitly recommended? SAP NetWeaver BPM is SAP's strategic direction, and it is tightly integrated into the SAP NetWeaver CE stack. It uses the latest technology and standards (BPMN with direct execution) and it is optimized for composite development especially in SAP environments.

SOA-BPM-2. SAP recommends using SAP NetWeaver BPM for business process modeling. SAP also recommends using the SAP Business Workflow tool for workflows within a pure, ABAP single-instance application. SAP does not recommend using:

- *SAP Business Connector, which has been replaced with functionality in SAP NetWeaver*
- *Workflow Modeler, except for applications that enhance SAP CRM*
- *SAP NetWeaver Business Warehouse process chains (process chains are recommended for loading but not for workflow)*
- *SAP NetWeaver MDM workflow*
- *Java ad-hoc workflows*

Another technique that is not recommended is the use of Guided Procedures (see UI-FLOW-1 in Chapter 5).

If SAP NetWeaver BPM is not an available option, any BPM tool that supports BPMN and integrates with SAP can be used, although this is not encouraged.

To Learn More

Business process modeling:
http://www.sdn.sap.com/irj/sdn/nw-processmodeling

SOA

Web services offer flexible, standards-based methods for communication from a remote, composite application to one or more backend systems.

Enterprise Services

SAP calls its web services "enterprise services." This is more than mere terminology, however. Enterprise services follow a particular methodology, implement consistent design patterns, and use a canonical data model.

Composite applications should use web services, and for integration with SAP backend systems should use SAP's enterprise services:

SOA-WS-2. SAP recommends using enterprise services to integrate with SAP applications if at all possible.

Over 3,000 enterprise services are now (2011) supported by SAP Business Suite and SAP continues to add services. A rich collection of functionality has been service enabled, so developers should look to see if they can reuse an enterprise service rather than developing their own service. Developers may find that they need to add services, however.

To get the same benefits of consistency that enterprise services provide, ISV developers may want to create their own services that comply with SAP's enterprise service methodology. For more information on this topic, see "Partner-delivered Enterprise Services" later in this chapter.

Web Services

Short of reusing SAP's enterprise services or creating similar services of your own, web services are the next best option. In particular, use of non-service-oriented SAP interfaces is not encouraged.

RFCs and BAPIs

If you choose to use older interfaces such as RFCs or BAPIs, SAP recommends wrapping them as web services:

> *SOA-WS-3. If access is needed to SAP application functionality that has not yet been service-enabled, SAP recommends wrapping remote function calls (RFCs) or BAPI® programming interfaces as web services. Direct access to RFCs or BAPIs is possible, but it is not encouraged.*

In some special cases, using RFCs or BAPIs directly may offer better performance, as long as the consumer and provider of the interface are in the same location. However, you should balance this benefit against the flexibility gained by using a service-oriented approach.

Service Discovery and Testing

How can you find out what enterprise services are available from SAP so that you can reuse them and optimize your development efforts? Once you develop your composite, is there an SAP backend system you can use to test your services?

The Enterprise Services Workplace

One way to find the complete set of the enterprise services SAP has released is in the Enterprise Services Workplace, available at http://esworkplace.sap.com. The search feature in the ES Workplace allows you to search for services that are related to a particular business object (the search itself is generalized, but this is one approach to using the search feature). After you find a service, you can drill down into the WSDL for that service. The ES Workplace can also be used to test enterprise services and also provides simple sample applications that you can use as guides in developing your own applications that reuse enterprise services. Getting access to all the functionality of the ES Workplace requires a free user account, registration for which is available at http://www.sdn.sap.com/irj/sdn/soareg.

Options for Testing Services

While the ES Workplace provides an environment for service discovery, it does not allow developers to make changes to the backend system. For example, if the implementation of a service requires a certain version, update, change, extension, or customization, access to the backend system is required to make that change. These types of changes are not possible with the ES Workplace. In such cases, you need access to a backend system that can be modified.

The SAP Discovery System is an appliance-based deployment of SAP Business Suite 7 that can be used for service discovery and testing with its own local ESR. The SAP Discovery System is a full SOA implementation that can be modified and whose purchase includes the SOA Experience Workshop, a two-day hands-on workshop that enables participants to learn the principles of enterprise SOA in the context of examples that are applicable to the participant's business needs.

Access to hosted backend systems can also be purchased from the SAP ICC. The SAP Remote Access and Connectivity (SAP RAC) Service offers a hosted environment against which composite applications can be tested. SAP RAC

Service is available in several forms, some of which are shared environments while others are dedicated or exclusive.

To Learn More

Discovery System: http://www.sdn.sap.com/irj/sdn/discoverysystem

SAP Remote Access and Connectivity Service:
http://www.sdn.sap.com/irj/sdn/saprac

Licensing and Services

The publication "Licensing SAP Products: A Guide for Buyers," which can be downloaded from http://tinyurl.com/licensing-guide, addresses licensing issues related to service consumption.

Here is a brief excerpt from this document, which is publicly available from sap.com:

- Users of any non-SAP software indirectly accessing SAP software or any handheld-device users must also be licensed as named users

- A licensee needs to hold the relevant package licenses for the SAP software being accessed by the non-SAP software or by the handheld devices

- Beyond the package licenses and named user licenses, SAP does not require additional licenses for the use of technical interfaces like enterprise services or the BAPI® programming interface

Web Services Characteristics

If you develop your own web services for use in an enterprise application, what characteristics should they have? Here is a guideline that outlines these characteristics (based on SAP's approach to developing enterprise services).

SOA-WS-4. SAP recommends that services:

- *Be self-contained. A consumer of a service should send all the data necessary to the service provider to continue the business process asynchronously. The provider should not have to "call back" the consumer for additional information*

- *Be robust in the case of accidental double calling. Implement services so that they ignore any duplicate calls (that is, they are idempotent)*

- *Use compensating services to reestablish consistency. Have pairs of write operations: a modifying service and a second service for undoing the business outcome of the modifying service, to be called when needed*

- *Practice forward error recovery. The receiving system must not send an error to the calling system if that error could be handled closer to the receiving system*

- *Combine service calls where possible. Combine and orchestrate multiple calls into one coarse-grained service rather than make many fine-grained calls*

Each of these points requires a bit of additional explanation, provided in the following sections.

Make Messages Self-Contained

A consumer should send the service provider all the data necessary to continue the business process asynchronously, so that the service provider never has to "call back" the service consumer for additional information.

Write Idempotent Services

Service calls should be executed exactly once. This can be accomplished by adding a parameter that allows a service consumer to add a request ID, that can be used by the provider to identify whether the request has already been received or whether it is a new request. This allows service providers to ensure that services that change data make such changes exactly once.

Here is a common real world example. Some ecommerce forms ask users not to hit the Submit button more than once or they will create multiple orders. Applications should not be designed in such a way that users must take responsibility for idempotency.

Use Compensating Services

Compensation helps ensure that the state of all involved business process instances is consistent. Executing a business process may entail several service calls that probably depend on each other (from a business perspective). If any of those calls runs into trouble during execution, the application needs to roll back changes to make the overall system state consistent again.

One approach is to have pairs of write operations: a modifying service and a second service for undoing the business outcome of the modifying service, to be called when needed. Another approach is to use the same service, called with different data.

Practice Forward Error Recovery

Errors in an application should be handled as closely as possible to where the error occurs. In other words, the consumer must not be sent an error message that the provider generates if that error could be handled closer to the provider.

However, forward error recovery may cause problems for the recipient of a message if done improperly. Typically, a message is accepted by a messaging infrastructure in the receiver system. The messaging infrastructure then passes the message content to the business application. If the application cannot process the message, it becomes stuck in the messaging infrastructure. Usually, this messaging infrastructure has only generic tools to handle these errors, and these tools are typically not suited for business users—even if the root cause of the error may be a business problem. This causes delays and high effort to fix the errors.

Here are examples for two typical situations along with possible solutions:

- A production system receives orders through messages. The production system allows the quantity to be updated as long as production has not yet started. After that, the quantity can no longer be changed

  - **Problem:** The sender of the message does not know when production starts. If an updated order message is received after production has started, the update will be rejected and the message will be stuck

  - **Solution:** Use separate fields or even separate business objects for content that can be updated by messages. For example, have both an ordered quantity and a production quantity. The ordered quantity can be updated even after production starts—it is then the task of a business user to deal with the problem on a business level

- Checking whether it is possible to post a transaction to a financial account can be complex (for example, depending on the date of the transaction or account type). This information is typically only available in the financial system

  - **Problem:** If the financial application rejects transactions, the messages are stuck. Often, the problem cannot be solved in the financial system because changes (such as a posting date) in the sender system are required. Such late changes often require cancellation of the original document

  - **Possible solution:** The sender can call a synchronous check method in the financial system to simulate the posting. If there are errors, the user can do the necessary changes immediately. This synchronous call should be optional so the transaction can be completed if the synchronous call cannot be performed

Error recovery can be complex. Here are some rules of thumb to follow:

- Message inbound processing should only reject messages if there are technical errors (such as a letter in a numeric field). Design your application such that inbound processing is not halted because of business errors

- If business errors occur in the receiving system but can only be fixed in the sending system, use synchronous calls to check methods in the receiving system that simulate the transaction

Additionally, consider the circumstances around these two call types and the differences with regard to business and technical errors:

- **Synchronous Read:** The user is waiting. An error message has to be displayed. Business errors probably can be resolved by the user, but technical errors should kick off a process for administrators to handle behind the scenes

- **Asynchronous Write:** Errors of any kind should be handled close to the place where the error occurs, but they will be handled by different people. Business errors should be handled by experts that specialize in the business at hand, while technical errors must be handled by administrators

Combine Calls Where Possible

Although use cases vary, in general, it is preferable to orchestrate services so that they are combined into higher value "coarse-grained" interfaces rather than making many fine-grained calls. Looping and nested callbacks between systems are detrimental to performance.

SOA Governance

SOA development has many moving parts and is a more granular approach than is used in traditional monolithic applications. That means work can be done independently, which is a strong benefit but in turn implies that it is possible to duplicate efforts or implement different parts in an inconsistent way.

SOA governance is the design-time and deployment-time methodology for putting rules and processes in place for managing aspects of SOA development such as the number of services, their versioning, and their reuse.

SOA-MGMT-1. SAP recommends implementing a SOA governance process to drive clear decisions about the use of service-oriented architecture in software products and to align its use with business goals and strategy.

Service Metering

To measure usage patterns, SAP NetWeaver meters all web service and enterprise service calls.

SOA-MGMT-2. SAP recommends that developers who connect their applications to SAP solutions from non-SAP platforms should add application-specific and customer-specific information to the SOAP header of all web service calls to SAP solutions to improve the measurement of usage patterns.

To Learn More

SAP note 1358528 (specifically the PDF document in the note):
http://service.sap.com/sap/support/notes/1358528

Achieving Application Integration

The following sections describe how developers can integrate their solutions with SAP applications in a way that ensures consistent semantic and communication paradigms. The resulting business solutions ensure simple inter-enterprise communications (also referred to as business-to-business or

B2B). Application integration allows semantic agreement between the service consumer and service provider (for example, address and name mean the same thing to both parties).

Technical Interoperability

Technical interoperability can be achieved by the following:

- Unified transport protocols (for example, TCP/IP)
- Security standards (for example, Web services security)
- Formats for structured communication (for example, XML, SOAP, and others)
- Multi-component landscapes require compatible interfaces with well-defined change management procedures (see Chapter 3 for details on change management)
- Integration with non-SAP products requires compatibility with international standards. For example, SAP complies with WS-I Basic Profile (http://www.ws-i.org/Profiles/BasicProfile-1.1.html) for interoperability guidelines for core web services specifications (such as SOAP, WSDL, and UDDI) or SAML (Security Assertion Markup Language, http://docs.oasis-open.org/security/saml/v2.0/saml-2.0-os.zip) for exchanging authentication and authorization data between security domains. See Chapter 9 for more information about SAML

Standards

SAP follows many SOA-related industry standards, including those outlined in Table 4-3.

Table 4-3. SOA-Related Standards That SAP Supports

Standards Area	Standards
Metadata Infrastructure	CWM, EMF, ISO 11179, MOF/JMI/XMI, ONS, UDDI, WS-MetadataExchange, XML NDR, XML Schema
Messaging	ICE, MTOM, SOAP and SOAP bindings, WS-Addressing, WS-Notification, WS-ReliableMessaging
Profiles	WS-I Basic Profile, WS-I Basic Security Profile, WS-I Sample Application
Management	CIM, CMIS, WS-Management, WS-MetadataExchange
Security	SAML, SPML, WS-SecureConversation, WS-Security, WS-Trust, XACML, XML Encryption, XML Signature
Policy	JSR265, WS-Policy
Ontology Definition Languages	OWL, RDF
Process Definition Languages	BPEL4People, BPMN, UML, VoiceXML, WS-BPEL
Service Definition Languages	EPCIS, UML, WSDL
Message Definition Languages	UML, UN/CEFACT CCTS

Software Migrated to Run in the SAP Environment

Whether it's an application consuming services provided by an SAP backend, or software providing services for SAP applications to consume, great SOA software often comes from Java developers who developed their code on another Java platform and then migrated it to run on SAP NetWeaver.

The methodology for moving a Java EE application to SAP NetWeaver is straightforward. Migrating a working Java application from one platform to another could take a few hours, a few days, or a few weeks. The best approach is to consider every migration of an application, however small, as a project. In this way, you will include all the needed steps to ensure that the application is working properly on the new platform.

Implementing such a migration entails following a process. This section outlines an approach to this process based on the experience of SAP developers.[5]

Conduct a Migration Analysis: Before starting the migration project, a migration analysis should be conducted by someone who knows the application well and someone who knows the target platform well (in this case, SAP NetWeaver). This migration analysis should incorporate an estimate of the effort involved in the migration.

Migrate to the Latest Version of Java: If the application doesn't currently run on JDK 5 or Java EE 5, migrate it to run on the same release the target platform supports. This will smooth the migration process.

Use Sun's Java Application Verification Kit. Check your application against the spec using Sun's Java Application Verification Kit, available at http://java.sun.com/j2ee/avk. This will tell you where your application does or does not conform to the spec. Making your application conform to the Java specifications will make the migration process smoother.

Migrate the Application: If you've prepared the application using the preceding steps, the migration is often the least difficult phase of all. The most important thing is not to consider yourself done until you take the steps described next.

Conduct Functional Testing: Using JUnit or your preferred testing tool or plan, the application should be tested throughout (for JUnit, see http://junit.org). Some of the known differences between Tomcat, for example, and SAP NetWeaver include Tomcat's tolerance for application elements that are not capitalized the way they are supposed to be. SAP NetWeaver exactly follows the spec in these areas. As a result, the application as a whole may appear to work, but buttons that are invoked using a statement that is not capitalized correctly according to the spec may not work (even though they did work on Tomcat). Functional testing needs to be thorough to ensure that the migration was in fact a success.

---

[5]   Two articles on SDN provide more detail on migrating Java EE applications to SAP NetWeaver. "Migrating/Porting Java Enterprise Applications to SAP NetWeaver" can be downloaded from http://tinyurl.com/migrating-java-ee; an article that provides an example migration using the PetStore2.0 application can be found at http://tinyurl.com/migrating-petstore.

Performance Testing and Enterprise Readiness: After the application is successfully running on SAP NetWeaver, you may wish to use facilities of the SAP NetWeaver platform to tune performance and to prepare the application for enterprise deployment. For example, Tomcat has a single JVM; SAP NetWeaver can spread requests across multiple JVMs for better performance and robustness. Applications have to be modified to take advantage of such features on the SAP NetWeaver platform.

Software Connected with SAP: Developers Using Microsoft .NET

SAP and Microsoft collaborate on SOA interoperability through supporting web services standards. SAP and Microsoft test their interoperability at the service level before releasing their code.

WCF

The Windows Communication Foundation is the part of the .NET framework where the web service implementation resides. Support for standards like WS-Security, WS-Reliable Messaging, and XML exist in the Windows Communication Foundation.

SOA-NET-2. SAP recommends that .NET developers use .NET framework version 3.0 or higher.

Enterprise Services Explorer for .NET

Most .NET developers use Microsoft Visual Studio. SAP's Enterprise Service Explorer is a plug-in for Visual Studio that developers can download from SDN at http://tinyurl.com/esefordotnet.

Here is a guideline related to SAP tools for .NET:

SOA-NET-1. SAP recommends that .NET developers use the SAP Enterprise Services Explorer tool for Microsoft .NET. SAP does not recommend using the SAP Connector for Microsoft .NET.

SAP recommends the Enterprise Services Explorer (ESE) instead of the SAP Connector for Microsoft .NET because the ESE supports the latest versions of Microsoft Visual Studio (2005 and 2008) while the SAP Connector for .NET is no longer being maintained and is supported only with Visual Studio 2003. Furthermore, the SAP Connector for Microsoft .NET supports only BAPIs/RFCs, whereas the ESE is SOA-based.

The ESE integrates access to enterprise services either in the ES Workplace or in the local Services Registry to make it easy to incorporate enterprise services in .NET code.

Consuming Services via .NET

Many use cases involve consuming services via .NET. This allows integration of SAP information into .NET-based applications through service calls to the SAP backend systems.

Providing Services for SAP Systems to Consume

The SAP Enterprise Services Explorer can be used to provision services that will be consumed by SAP applications. One example is a credit check based on .NET. An SAP business process, such as sales order creation, might involve a credit check. The SAP system could call a .NET-based credit check service in order to check the credit of the buyer and consume this service.

Another example of a .NET-based service provision is a product lifecycle management process that stores documents in a SharePoint-based repository. The business process might call a .NET-based service to interact with the document repository at various points.

PDK for .NET

The PDK for .NET is a tool for integrating .NET code into the SAP NetWeaver Portal. The PDK for .NET has a specialized use: as a UI tool and not as a development tool. Recently, SAP released version 3.0 of the PDK for .NET.

To Learn More

Microsoft .NET and SAP by Juergen Daiberl, Steve Fox, Scott Adams, and Thomas Reimer (Microsoft Press 2009):
http://tinyurl.com/dot-net-sap-book

SDN's .NET page: http://www.sdn.sap.com/irj/sdn/dotnet

Microsoft's SAP page: http://www.microsoft.com/isv/sap

Software Connected with SAP: Developers Using IBM WebSphere

SAP and IBM work closely together through the IBM and SAP Alliance. One of the efforts that the two companies have undertaken is achieving bidirectional synchronization between IBM WebSphere's Web Services Registry and Repository (WSRR) and SAP NetWeaver's Services Registry. This bidirectional synchronization enables organizations with deployments of both WebSphere and NetWeaver to see the available services from either registry. Details on how to set up this bidirectional synchronization are available in an SDN article by IBM's Martin Herzog (http://tinyurl.com/registry-interop).

For most Java applications running on WebSphere, however, services can be called in a straightforward point-to-point fashion. The interoperability described here shows the close alignment between SAP and IBM. Both companies are strong supporters of open standards.

SOA-IBM-1. SAP recommends that developers working with IBM WebSphere review the efforts of IBM and SAP to achieve interoperability between their Java EE application servers.

To Learn More

WebSphere page on SDN: http://tinyurl.com/sdn-websphere

The IBM and SAP Alliance page: http://tinyurl.com/ibmsapalliance

Partner-delivered Enterprise Services (PdES)

Partners that want to create their own services according to the SAP SOA methodology and offer them to SAP customers can develop such services as a result of the Partner-delivered Enterprise Services (PdES) initiative. (As the name implies, this initiative is relevant primarily for partner developers, not for developers at SAP customers.)

SOA-WS-5. SAP recommends that ISVs service-enable the functionality of their applications according to SAP's SOA methodology and certify these applications under the ESR Content certification.

Creating such services involves following the same methodology and steps that SAP uses to create enterprise services.

Why would you want to do this? There are three main reasons:

- **Semantic alignment:** By reusing SAP's business objects and their definitions, when SAP says "sales order" and partners say "sales order," both are speaking the same language, and it's easier to communicate with mutual customers

- **Interface patterns and naming rules:** Enterprise services offer standard patterns for interfaces. If there's a Find service operation, you'll always find it under the Query interface. Similarly, a Read and a Create will be under the Manage interface. Naming is also done in a standard way. If you follow the same rules as SAP, interoperability is easier

- **Standards-based data typing:** SAP bases its data typing on the UNCEFACT/CCTS standard for Core Data Types. In addition, SAP has predefined data types that have higher-level business semantics, referred to as Global Data Types. Using a common data model simplifies integration at the message element level and eliminates many types of problems in translation between data models

One step in developing a "methodology-compliant" service is signing SAP's Enterprise Services Provisioning License, a no-cost license for SAP SOA-related intellectual property. The SAP education course SOA300 ("Design Time Governance in SOA"), part of the enterprise service development curriculum, shows ISVs how to build SAP methodology-compliant interfaces that can then be certified by the SAP Integration and Certification Center (SAP ICC) under the ESR Content certification (certification interface NW-ESR-CNT). Note that partners retain full control of selling their service-enabled components.

Governance and Enterprise Services

One key difference between developing a web service and developing an enterprise service concerns governance. By following SAP's SOA methodology and working with SOA governance, the net result is service harmonization.[6]

SAP's SOA methodology can be viewed as helping create an effective service. Governance ensures efficiency. The purpose is to create services that are mutually exclusive (they don't overlap) and collectively exhaustive (they do everything that needs to be done). SAP is still working on the latter, but with more than 3,000 enterprise services available at this writing, the effort is clearly far along. Through the PdES initiative, you can participate in the effort to create a group of services that are collectively exhaustive.

Development Choices

In general, services can be implemented in any language. Key aspects for selecting a language may include:

- Shipping mode of the composite (the language in which you've implemented the composite should be used for the service as well as to reduce additional transport and installation overhead)

- Implementation complexity/effort (extending a service can be achieved more easily and with less effort on the system in which the original service resides)

- Communication overhead (if the new service combines several services from one backend system, it makes more sense to write the new service within the environment in which the reused business functionality resides)

- Performance of the language in question

- New services versus extending existing services

- Reuse of existing functionality (more easily achievable in the system in which the functionality resides)

ABAP, Java, and .NET in particular can be considered for service provisioning.

Relevant Tools

The tool for creating this type of service is the Enterprise Services Builder, which is part of the Enterprise Services Repository (ESR). The ESR itself is available with shipments of SAP NetWeaver CE and PI from release 7.1 onward.

If you implement such a service in Java, you'll want to use SAP NetWeaver Developer Studio, which is based on Eclipse. Its integration with the ESR makes it a natural tool for implementing methodology-compliant services.

If you implement in .NET using Visual Studio, you will want to install the Enterprise Services Explorer, available for download at http://tinyurl.com/sdn-ese.

---

[6] "For Busy People: Understanding ES Governance + ES Methodology = ES Harmonization" by Joachim von Goetz (https://www.sdn.sap.com/irj/scn/weblogs?blog=/pub/wlg/10836).

The PdES Wizard

The SAP Co-Innovation Lab (COIL) created an "ES Methodology wizard" prototype to make some of the steps required for creating a PdES easier. The output is a model of the service and an Excel spreadsheet listing the information you will need when defining the service.

To Learn More

Screencam of the PdES wizard: http://tinyurl.com/pdeswizardblog

PdES wizard download site: http://tinyurl.com/pdeswizard

Creating a Methodology-Compliant Service

First, you analyze the business context, determining from a business standpoint what type of service you want to create.

Next you provision the service. This happens in four steps:

* Modeling
* Defining
* Implementing (whether in Java, .NET, or ABAP)
* Publishing, that is, making the service available for use

Modeling

Modeling involves creating a picture of all the pieces you'll need, including a process component, business object, service interface, and enterprise service. The PdES wizard handles this interactively, generating a model such as the one shown in Figure 4-2.

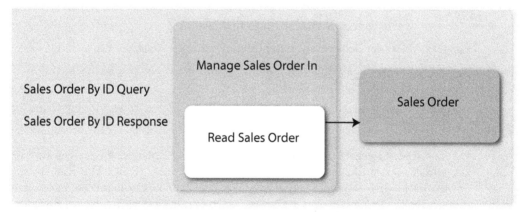

Figure 4-2. A Model Created with the ES Methodology Wizard

Although the wizard facilitates some of the steps involved in creating a PdES, it is no replacement for an SAP education course such as SOA300, which provides needed background.

Defining

Defining the service involves taking the entities you modeled and providing definitions for them using the Enterprise Services Builder. The steps involved include:

- Creating service interface and operation definitions
- Assigning the previously created model entities to the respective definitions
- Creating message types and fault message types
- Creating message data types
- Detailing the message structure down to the element level
- Data typing

SDN offers a blog with a screencam (http://tinyurl.com/pdesblogpt4) that walks you through each step in this process. The Excel spreadsheet created by the PdES wizard provides many of the values that are used during the course of this process.

Implementing

Next comes implementing the service, using the WSDL generated in the definition step. The implementation can be developed in Java, .NET, or ABAP.

Because the implementation details are specific to the programming environments, here are links to the relevant blogs on SDN:

- Java (http://tinyurl.com/pdesblogpt6)
- .NET (http://tinyurl.com/pdesblogpt7)
- ABAP (http://tinyurl.com/pdesblogpt8)

The final step, publishing the service, lies in the hands of the ISV.

Creating a methodology-compliant service enables ISVs to provide their customers with services that offer the advantages of SAP's enterprise services and that harmonize with the customer's SAP landscape.

To Learn More

Partners already offering SAP SOA methodology-compliant services: https://www.sdn.sap.com/irj/sdn/pdes

SOA300 - Design Time Governance in Enterprise SOA: http://tinyurl.com/ngt5o2

SAP Global Data Types Catalog – Complete: http://tinyurl.com/mvpupu

SAP Enterprise Service Development Curriculum: http://tinyurl.com/nwgmp5

Web Services Description Language Tool (Wsdl.exe): http://tinyurl.com/lmrb4e

SAP Help: Web Services: http://tinyurl.com/mkxydb

Developing Enterprise Services for SAP (from SAP Business Press):
http://tinyurl.com/la6lx9

Services Registry Documentation: http://tinyurl.com/service-registry-help

Classifications in the Services Registry:
http://tinyurl.com/registry-classification

Chapter 5

User Interface and User Experience Guidelines for Best-Built Applications

Developers have many choices when designing their applications. The most fundamental from the standpoint of an application's usability is the user interface. An intuitive and consistent user interface can smooth the user experience and make applications easier to consume, improving productivity. This chapter offers guidelines for developers creating user interfaces for applications that integrate with SAP Business Suite.

The chapter starts with an overview of user interface (UI) principles and best practices. It then describes SAP's approach to UI harmonization, which calls for a consolidated and harmonized look and feel for application UIs displayed in both a "canvas" (the main screen area) and a surrounding "shell" area, which exposes the UI client's menu and navigation.

The next section describes the front-end client software that customers might have in place, including the SAP NetWeaver Portal and the SAP NetWeaver Business Client. Following this, the chapter turns to a discussion of specific UI technologies, including guidance regarding SAP UI technologies. It discusses Web Dynpro ABAP, including tools such as the Floorplan Manager, the Page Builder, and the Personalized Object Worklist (POWL). It also describes Web Dynpro Java, optimal uses for Visual Composer, various Rich Internet Application technologies such as Adobe Flash and Microsoft Silverlight, mobile UI guidelines, and last but not least, output and forms.

Principles of UI Development

No matter what technology platform you use, certain principles hold true. This section outlines four important principles, including:

- Separating business logic from UI coding

- Implementing user-centered design to ensure that the UI meets users' needs
- Harmonizing the user interface for consistency and ease of use
- Making the interface accessible to as many users as possible

Separation of Concerns: Business Logic and UI Coding

One of the principles of Timeless Software described in Chapter 1 is separation of concerns, and this concept is critical for UI development. Business logic coding and UI coding should be separated to ensure maintainability of applications over time. Development of business logic is therefore discussed in other chapters of this book. Changes to the UI, in terms of look and feel, should not be tied to business logic.

UI-PROG-1. SAP recommends that business logic be separated from UI coding.

In other words, a change to the user interface should not affect the business logic behind the scenes.

User-Centered Design

User-centered design (UCD) is a flexible, collaborative process for software development projects that enables teams to more effectively meet the needs of users and their customers.

Donald Norman coined this term in the 1980s in his research at the University of California San Diego and he uses the term in his book, *The Psychology of Everyday Things*, published in 1986. Since that time, a number of methodologies that specifically put the user in the middle of the design process have emerged. Agile modeling principles such as active stakeholder participation advocate getting a prototype into the hands of users early to get input on a concrete design.

Simply put, user-centered design looks at the tasks being performed from the perspective of the user and attempts to make user interfaces both intuitive and consistent.

Agile modeling builds on the principles of user-centered design. Broad participation in creating user interfaces leads to more effective user interfaces. Putting early prototypes into the hands of users is more effective than describing a user interface at length.

To achieve this, it is important to have stakeholders who can collaborate on user interface design and user interaction issues. From developers to interaction designers (if available) to project managers to those closest to the users (often support staff) to the users themselves, designing software in this way can improve usability and consistency.

These collaborative activities take place in five distinct phases: Plan, Research, Design, Adapt, and Measure, a process that enables iterative improvement (see Figure 5-1).

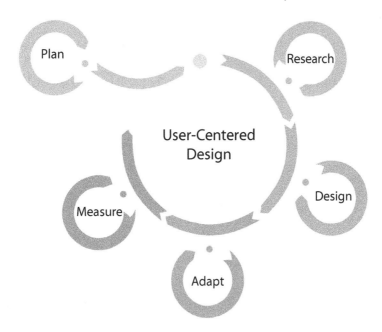

Figure 5-1. User-Centered Design

- **Plan:** Determine all activities needed and the necessary resources
- **Research:** Before designing, understand the users' goals and tasks and the market needs
- **Design:** Define the system from the user perspective
- **Adapt:** Adapt based on need for changes discovered during development
- **Measure:** Measure usability, which is comprised of effectiveness, efficiency, and satisfaction

UI-UCD-1. SAP recommends adopting the philosophy and methodology that SAP has adopted for developing user interfaces: user-centered design.

During the Design phase, developers choose which UI technology to use for their applications. Read on for information about how to choose a UI technology that fits your use case.

To Learn More

"User-Centered Design" by Ulrike Weissenberger & Carola Thompson: http://www.sapdesignguild.org/resources/ucd_paper.asp

UI Harmonization

A major role of governance is to ensure consistency across user interface screens.

Without a clear governance process that reviews UI designs for consistency, it is hard to achieve UI harmonization. The consistency required has numerous dimensions, as shown in Figure 5-2.

5 Levels of UI Harmonization: Aligning Look and Feel

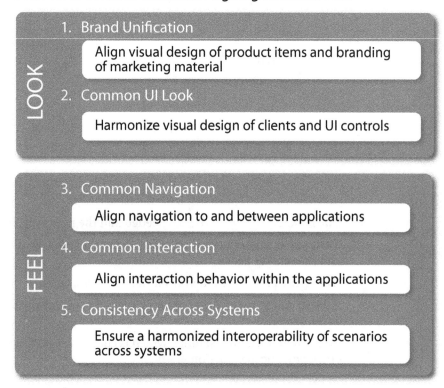

Figure 5-2. Dimensions of UI Harmonization

SAP recognizes the importance of harmonization to the user experience. To that end, several of the tools mentioned in this chapter help developers to achieve consistency by following a template style approach. No matter what tool a developer uses, however, developing a consistent approach is beneficial for end-users.

UI-GOV-1. SAP recommends implementing a user interface governance process to ensure harmonization, to drive clear user interface decisions that are aligned with business goals and strategy, and to effectively implement those goals.

Creating a consistent process for approving UI designs is one step toward UI governance.

To Learn More

> Simplified User Experience in SAP Business Suite:
> http://wiki.sdn.sap.com/wiki/x/HIFVAw

Accessibility

Accessibility is a general term used to describe the degree to which software is accessible by as many people as possible. Increasingly, accessibility is a legal requirement, especially for software sales to the public sector.

SAP believes that companies should make their applications accessible to as many users as possible:

UI-STD-1. SAP recommends making applications accessible by ensuring that all user interface elements and relevant information in an application are available to and usable by users with disabilities.

The best place to learn more about accessibility is the W3C's Web Accessibility Initiative site. This site covers accessibility laws, the latest standards developments, and how to develop a business case for implementing accessibility. Although this site is called "web accessibility," it covers a variety of areas, including user agent accessibility, web content accessibility guidelines, and mobile accessibility guidelines.

Internally, SAP has an Accessibility standard that SAP applications must meet and that partners must address during the application certification process with the SAP Integration and Certification Center (SAP ICC). Accessibility is covered extensively in the Service Marketplace.

The SAP Design Guild's Accessibility page has a rich set of accessibility resources as well, including a paper on the topic by by Josef Köble, Tanja Schätz, and Dewi Gani.

To Learn More

> W3C's Accessibility: http://www.w3.org/WAI

> SAP ICC: http://www.sap.com/ecosystem/partners/icc/index.epx

> Accessibility on Service Marketplace: http://service.sap.com/accessibility

> SAP Design Guild on Accessibility:
> http://www.sapdesignguild.org/resources/acc.asp

> Accessibility paper by Josef Köble, Tanja Schätz, and Dewi Gani:
> http://www.sapdesignguild.org/resources/acc_paper.asp

The Shell and the Canvas

People are creatures of habit, and intuitive UIs make things easy for users by putting navigational elements in the same place on every screen. Once a user is oriented to a given UI, if the other screens follow the same pattern, there is no need to search and wonder what to do.

In accord with UI harmonization (making things both consistent and easy for users), SAP chose to split the screen, or main window of an application, into a design framework known as the shell and the canvas. The shell is shaped like an upside down "L" around the canvas. The shell can contain standard menu items across the top and down the left side. The canvas is the body of the screen, which displays information, such as transactions or processes in progress. The canvas can be used to display almost any other type of UI within it.

Figure 5-3 illustrates the shell and the canvas.

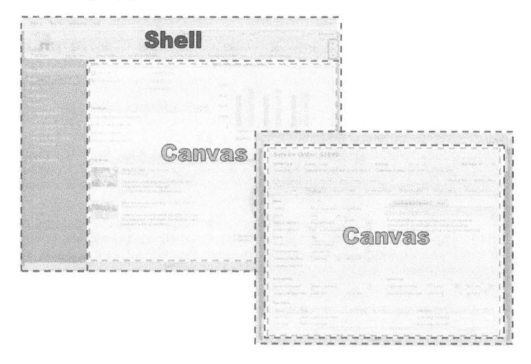

Figure 5-3. The Shell and the Canvas

The canvas is often further divided into subareas, depending on the application's requirements and the user interface framework being used. For example, SAP UIs sometimes include the use of a side panel to the right of the canvas where mashable elements may be included (see the section on Page Builder later in this chapter).

Front-End Client Software

Note: The decision about which front-end client to deploy rests with the customer and has dependencies on the customer landscape. SAP customers may choose to deploy only one or multiple types of front-end clients at various points in their system landscapes.

In addition to the traditional SAP GUI client for accessing classic Dynpro applications, such as those in the SAP Business Suite, SAP provides front-end clients to its application servers, the SAP NetWeaver Portal and the SAP NetWeaver Business Client (SAP NWBC). Both the Portal and NWBC provide the consistency of the shell (the upside down "L" is part of the client itself) and the canvas, in which a partner-developed or customer-specific application can run.

Figure 5-4 shows comparative information about the three options for front-end client software.

Figure 5-4. Front-End Client Software

SAP GUI	SAP NetWeaver Business Client	SAP NetWeaver Portal Client
☑ Windows ☑ MacOS/Linux ☑ Browser	☑ Windows ☑ Browser	○ Windows ☑ Browser
Key Attributes	**Key Attributes**	**Key Attributes**
• Classic Transaction Launcher	• Includes SAPGUI (embedded)	• Includes SAPGUI (embedded)
• Menu-Based Access	• Role-Based Access	• Role-Based Access
• Desktop Integration	• Application Launcher	• Application Launcher
	• Client-Side Integration	• Client- & Server-Side Integration
	• Browser Functionality Integrated	• Collaboration Enablement
	• Desktop Integration	• Content Mgmt. Enablement
Typical Use Cases	**Typical Use Cases**	**Typical Use Cases**
• ABAP Environment	• Mainly ABAP Environment	• ABAP and Java Environment
• Focus on Dynpro Transactions	• Focus on Multiple UI Technologies	• Focus on Multiple UI Technologies
	• Access to One Main System	• Additional Focus on Portal-Like Scenarios
	• Partial Access to Other Systems	• Access to a Large Set of Systems

User interfaces developed using the various technologies described later in this chapter can be used with either the SAP NWBC or the SAP NetWeaver Portal. Such user interfaces can also be used in standalone or web-based applications.

Developers should understand the differences between these front-end clients because, for maximum flexibility for their end customers, they may want to architect their applications to run in both the SAP NetWeaver Portal and the SAP NWBC.

The following sections provide a brief overview of the characteristics developers should know about the three options for front-end client software.

SAP GUI

SAP GUI is the classic user interface for the SAP Business Suite. Applications that run in SAP GUI are developed using ABAP Dynpro. This user interface technology provides a consistent look and feel and runs on a variety of platforms (Windows, Mac OS, Linux, and browsers).

SAP does not recommend creating new applications using this UI, however, because more flexible options are now available to developers. Development for SAP GUI uses Dynpro and not Web Dynpro. However, if you are extending an existing SAP GUI application, or adding a new small application onto a series of SAP GUI applications, then keeping the user interface consistent is a more important consideration.

> **UI-TECH-9. SAP does not recommend developing new applications in SAP GUI.**

The SAP GUI page on SDN covers information about supported versions of SAP GUI on various platforms.

To Learn More

SAP GUI on SDN: http://www.sdn.sap.com/irj/sdn/sap-gui

SAP NetWeaver Business Client

SAP NetWeaver Business Client (SAP NWBC) is a UI client that allows multiple UI technologies to be integrated in one user interface. NWBC combines the ability to display classical SAP GUI/ABAP Dynpro UIs and web UIs, whether SAP or non-SAP. SAP NWBC supports all the latest features of Web Dynpro ABAP, including the Floorplan Manager, Page Builder, and Personalized Object Worklists, all of which are described later in this chapter.

SAP NWBC is a standalone Windows client. In terms of backend system landscapes, SAP NWBC is ideally suited for simpler system landscapes involving fewer systems, with access to one main system and partial access to other systems. On the other hand, the SAP NetWeaver Portal excels at integrating numerous heterogeneous backend systems.

SAP NWBC offers role-based access to backend systems. This means that users see only the options, context, and data that their roles, defined in the backend systems, permit them to see and interact with.

SAP NWBC supports multiple windows and incorporates a window manager.

To Learn More

SAP NWBC on SDN: http://www.sdn.sap.com/irj/sdn/nw-businessclient

SAP NetWeaver Portal

The SAP NetWeaver Portal is a central UI client, designed to enable running multiple SAP applications across various systems and business roles. From the perspective of end-users, the NetWeaver Portal is the entry point to many if not all of the different applications needed for their daily work. For developers, having an application available in the portal is important in order to ensure that users can find the application easily. The SAP NetWeaver Portal offers out of the box integration with applications written in ABAP, Java, or other technologies (for example, .ASP or PHP) together with advanced system discovery tools and role management capabilities that make it possible to bring together applications from various backend systems, both SAP and non-SAP.

User interfaces developed in Web Dynpro ABAP, Web Dynpro Java, or the WebClient UI Framework can be deployed in the SAP NetWeaver Portal.

As a client, the SAP NetWeaver Portal offers the following advantages:

- **Content management:** The SAP NetWeaver Portal offers document management and content management capabilities using Web Page Composer. Web Page Composer provides managed content in the context of business applications. Document management capabilities are also key portal features

- **Collaboration integration:** The portal offers collaboration features such as wikis and discussion forums

- **Support for Java:** While the SAP NWBC offers mainly ABAP support, the SAP NetWeaver Portal supports both ABAP and Java stacks

- **Platform independent and browser-based:** Since the portal runs in the user's browser, it is accessible from anywhere, on any platform, using any browser supported in the Product Availability Matrix

- **External facing applications:** Portal-based applications can be provisioned to people who are not employees of SAP's customers, such as (the customer's) customers or partners

- **Personalization and branding:** SAP administrators can set up the portal so that it offers personalization and preferences for individual users as well as corporate branding

An important use case for customers is to make some of their applications externally available without exposing all of them. With an external facing SAP NetWeaver Portal, this is possible. Such an external-facing portal is exposed outside the company firewall, typically via the Internet, for use by customers, suppliers, distributors, and so forth. However, designing an external facing portal requires paying special attention to performance, scalability, reliability and security. An eClass provides more information and covers best practices. Accelerated application delivery (AccAD) is one tool that can help with ensuring LAN-like performance for external facing portals. One particularly helpful blog on this topic is "Network Infrastructure for SAP Application-based Landscapes" by Joerg Nalik. (Links for these resources are listed below.)

To Learn More

Product Availability Matrix (Service Marketplace user required):
http://service.sap.com/pam

SAP NetWeaver Portal on SDN:
http://www.sdn.sap.com/irj/sdn/nw-portal

eClass on implementing external-facing portals:
http://tinyurl.com/external-portal-eclass

AccAD on SDN: http://www.sdn.sap.com/irj/sdn/nw-accad

"Network Infrastructure for SAP Application-based Landscapes" blog:
http://www.sdn.sap.com/irj/scn/weblogs?blog=/pub/wlg/7447

Roles in UI Clients

Developers who want to provide maximum flexibility in running their applications in the canvas of either client must ensure that roles are handled as the target client expects. Reading roles from backend systems ensures proper authorization and allows navigation and content to be personalized based on the user's role. It allows the front-end clients to offer role-based access to applications so that users see only the options, applications, and information that are relevant to their roles.

The SAP NWBC reads roles from a standard ABAP backend (via PCFG, the transaction for reading roles). The SAP NetWeaver Portal reads roles from the Portal Content Directory (PCD). (Note furthermore that roles from PCFG can be uploaded into the PCD.)

Identity management systems can help with managing roles and identities across system landscapes. See Chapter 9 for more information on identity management.

To Learn More

SAP Help on PCFG: http://tinyurl.com/pcfg-roles

Reading roles from the PCD: http://tinyurl.com/66kekzl

Object-Based Navigation in SAP UI Clients

In many types of navigation, the program references a particular URL. Object-Based Navigation moves this to a semantic level, where instead of calling a particular URL, you can call an operation on a business object, such as a sales order. From that sales order, the user could navigate to an item record. However, Object-Based Navigation checks the user's role to ensure only the correct access is allowed. For example, only certain users may be able to change information about an item, but others may be allowed to view the information.

Object-Based Navigation is available both in the SAP NetWeaver Portal and in the SAP NetWeaver Business Client.

To Learn More

Object-Based Navigation and SAP NetWeaver Portal:
http://tinyurl.com/object-based-nav

Object-Based Navigation and SAP NetWeaver Business Client:
http://tinyurl.com/object-based-nav-nwbc (see section 5.11)

UI Technology and Tool Recommendations for Developers Using SAP Tools

Developers can use various UI technologies to provide content for the canvas. While the choice of front-end client rests with the customer, the choice of the tool used to develop the application in the canvas rests with the developers.

Note: The following sections provide technology and tool recommendations for developers using SAP tools. You may note that there are very few recommendations that relate to developers of applications that simply integrate with the SAP Business Suite via enterprise or web services, for example. Such developers make independent decisions about how to create their UIs, but should take into account the information outlined in "Principles of UI Development" earlier in this chapter.

Developers using SAP tools need guidance when it comes to developing new applications. What technologies does SAP recommend? Which are less relevant for new application development?

The following sections go through some of these recommendations to provide background information. The rest of the chapter describes recommended technologies in various areas.

Recommended UI Technologies

Developers using SAP tools can select one of three recommended SAP UI technologies for developing new user interfaces: Web Dynpro ABAP, Web Dynpro Java, and the WebClient UI Framework (which is used in SAP CRM).

> *UI-TECH-1. SAP recommends that developers using SAP tools select one of the following user interface technologies:*
>
> - *Web Dynpro ABAP with the Floorplan Manager*
> - *Web Dynpro Java for development on the SAP NetWeaver Java stack*
> - *WebClient UI Framework for development of applications that complement SAP CRM*

For more detailed information on these UI technologies, see the relevant sections later in this chapter.

Note that this recommendation applies to the canvas area as a whole. It is possible to embed Rich Internet Applications in the canvas using these recommended tools. See "UI Technologies for Rich Internet Applications" later in this chapter for details.

UI Technologies That Are Not Encouraged

Having said which tools are recommended for developers using SAP tools, this section specifies the UI technologies that are not encouraged for new development.

UI-TECH-6. SAP does not encourage use of the following user interface technologies:

- ***Business Server Pages (BSP)***
- ***HTMLB***
- ***Portal Framework***
- ***XHTML or plain HTML***
- ***ITS flow logic***
- ***ABAP Dynpro***

Table 5-1 provides a list of alternatives to UI technologies that are not encouraged.

Table 5-1. Modern Alternatives to Deprecated UI Technologies

UI Technology Not Encouraged	Alternatives
Business Server Pages (BSP) and HTMLB	Web Dynpro ABAP
	WebClient UI Framework (for CRM-related applications)
Portal Framework	Web Dynpro ABAP
	Web Dynpro Java
XHTML or plain HTML	Web Dynpro ABAP
	Web Dynpro Java
Internet Transaction Server (ITS) flow logic	Web Dynpro ABAP
	Web Dynpro Java
ABAP Dynpro	Web Dynpro ABAP

The content in this table warrants a bit more explanation in some cases:

- Use of BSPs directly is not encouraged. However, the WebClient UI Framework is built on BSPs and its use is encouraged for applications related to SAP CRM
- Use of ABAP Dynpro is not encouraged because it is not a Web UI. When adding screens to existing applications that were built using ABAP Dynpro, however, use of ABAP Dynpro is a valid option

While ABAP Dynpro should not be used for developing new applications, UI harmonization, discussed earlier in this chapter, means that if a UI is written in one technology, adding a screen in a second UI technology could be jarring to the user. If a developer is creating an extension to an application (which will be used on the same display as that application), using the same UI technology as the original application improves the user experience. This is one of the few valid reasons to use a UI technology that is not encouraged, such as ABAP Dynpro.

Deciding Which SAP UI Technology to Use

As a developer, you may have some questions at this point.

- Which UI technology should I use?
- If I am using a certain UI technology, what capabilities can I take advantage of?
- Are those capabilities in older releases as well?

The next few sections will help answer these questions. We start out with a comparison of Web Dynpro ABAP and Web Dynpro Java.

We then go into each of the recommended technologies in more detail, highlighting important information about Web Dynpro ABAP, Web Dynpro Java, and the WebClient UI Framework. Please note that each of these frameworks enables embedding of Rich Internet Applications, which are covered in a separate section later in this chapter. This chapter also covers UI recommendations related to migrating Java applications to SAP NetWeaver and recommendations related to output and forms.

Web Dynpro ABAP and Web Dynpro Java Capabilities

Web Dynpro ABAP and Web Dynpro Java have important elements in common. They use the same programming paradigm, models, UI control sets, and so on. Although they each have important strengths, they are not identical (see Table 5-2).

Table 5-2. Web Dynpro ABAP and Web Dynpro Java Capabilities

	Web Dynpro ABAP	Web Dynpro Java
Runtime Environment	SAP NetWeaver 7.00 and higher[a]	SAP NetWeaver CE 7.20 and higher
Designtime Environment	ABAP Workbench (SE80) (As of SAP NetWeaver 7.00)	Eclipse-based SAP NetWeaver Developer Studio
Developer Skill Set	ABAP programming, ABAP Objects, ABAP development tools	Java programming, Java development tools
Backend Data Access	Access to data in remote SAP systems via Enterprise Services (recommended). Access to data sources in the local ABAP system via native ABAP coding (not encouraged for applications that might be distributed). In addition, RFCs are supported (All as of SAP NetWeaver 7.00)	Access to various data sources in ABAP backend systems exposed as Enterprise Services (recommended). In addition, BAPIs, Remote Function modules via Adaptive RFC 2 model, Web Services, EJBs and JDBC stored procedures are supported
Lifecycle Management	Integrated into ABAP Lifecycle Management (correction workbench, transportation and change management system, security environment, translation, MIME repository, enhancements)	Integrated into the NetWeaver Development Infrastructure (NWDI) and NetWeaver's change and transport system CTS+

[a] As of the July 2011 revision of this chapter, SAP NetWeaver CE 7.30 and SAP NetWeaver 7.0 EhP2 are the newest general available releases.

Adaptation	Enhancement Framework support for modification-free enhancements. Support for built-in adaptation on configuration and customizing level carried out by developer and administrator. Support for end-user personalization of application UI. Support for component-defined application and component configuration. Support for customer-defined enhancement fields in ABAP dictionary structures (All as of SAP NetWeaver 7.00)	Support for implicit personalization[b] flavors (customize application UIs as administrator for single users or groups of users, personalize application UIs as end-user). Support for customer-defined enhancement fields in ABAP dictionary structures end-to-end without code modification using the Adaptive RFC model
UI Infrastructure and Services	Integration into Floorplan Manager for Web Dynpro ABAP. Usage of SAP List Viewer ABAP, POWL, (Personalized Object Worklist), Page Builder, and Select Options. ABAP Dictionary types directly available. Reuse ABAP Dictionary Search Help	Usage of SAP List Viewer Java
UI Openness (same for both)	SAP Interactive Forms by Adobe, Business Graphics, JNet, JGantt (as of SAP NetWeaver 7.0) Integration of Adobe Flash Islands (as of SAP NetWeaver EhP1) Integration of Silverlight Islands (as of SAP NetWeaver EhP2) Microsoft Project support	Integration of Adobe Flash and Microsoft Silverlight Islands, Microsoft Office, Microsoft Project, SAP Interactive Forms by Adobe, Business Graphics (based on Internet Graphic Server or IGS), Network (JNet) and JGantt. Other integrations such as Geographic Information Systems (GIS) are possible. Microsoft Project support
Mobile Devices	Not supported	Supported
Front-end Integration	Integration into SAP NetWeaver Portal and SAP NetWeaver Business Client (As of SAP NetWeaver 7.00) Integration into SAP NetWeaver BPM (As of SAP NetWeaver AS 7.0 EhP2)	Integration into SAP NetWeaver Portal and SAP NetWeaver Business Client Integration into SAP NetWeaver BPM (As of SAP NetWeaver CE 7.30)
UI Element Library Distinctions	ACFExecute, ACFUpDownload, Panel, PanelStack, FormLayout, ThresholdSlider, MultiPane (As of SAP NetWeaver 7.0 EhP2)	AnalyticsChart, Calendar UI elements, ColumnLayout, Splitter, Spinner, RFIDReader, WebWidget (As of SAP NetWeaver CE 7.20)

[b] Implicit Web Dynpro Java personalization is only supported for applications running as an NW 7.0 Web Dynpro iView in SAP NetWeaver Portal

SAP UI Technologies and Business Process Management

Business Process Management (BPM) is a discipline related to easily and rapidly adapting business processes to the changing needs of a business. Increasingly, development tools are offering options to integrate the creation of business process models with (lower-level) coding.

The following UI tools provide out of the box integration with SAP NetWeaver BPM:

* Web Dynpro Java
* Visual Composer
* Web Dynpro ABAP (as of SAP NetWeaver 7.3)

With Web Dynpro Java and Visual Composer, UIs can be automatically generated from the process context data in a BPM model.

In addition, the Task Management API in SAP NetWeaver BPM (as of SAP NetWeaver 7.3) can be used to integrate with other UI technologies, such as those used for developing mobile clients.

To Learn More

SAP NetWeaver Business Process Management and Composition:
http://www.sdn.sap.com/irj/sdn/bpm

SAP UI Technologies and Tools for ABAP Developers

SAP technologies and tools for ABAP developers include Web Dynpro ABAP (which includes the Floorplan Manager, Page Builder, and POWL tools) and, for SAP CRM, the WebClient UI Framework.

Web Dynpro ABAP

Web Dynpro ABAP is the preferred UI development platform for ABAP developers. It offers a model-based, declarative methodology for UI development. It includes several tools that enable UI developers to design applications in a consistent way that will be intuitive for SAP customers, such as the Floorplan Manager, Personalized Object Work List (POWL), and the Page Builder. These tools enable developers to reduce the total cost of development (TCD) while creating applications that follow a consistent structure and flow. Developers should use the latest version of Web Dynpro ABAP.

To Learn More

SDN page on Web Dynpro ABAP:
http://www.sdn.sap.com/irj/sdn/nw-wdabap

The Floorplan Manager

Available as of SAP NetWeaver 7.01, the Floorplan Manager is a Web Dynpro ABAP framework that can be used to configure an application based on reusable building blocks. These components do not have to be implemented again but can be reused by leveraging the framework provided by the Floorplan

Manager. In this way, using the Floorplan Manager decreases the amount of coding and implementation effort, reducing the cost of development.

This UI Building Block (UIBB) approach to UI development also ensures consistency between screens of the UI. Central functionality like navigation, messaging, and personalization is embedded in the framework and can be defined using APIs. Even after the application is delivered, customers can adapt the UI to their needs using simple configuration options.

Developers can incorporate their own components into UIs designed using the Floorplan Manager as well as integrating Rich Internet Applications, such as Flash Islands and Silverlight Islands, into their UI screens.

Because it offers both ease of development and consistency across screens, SAP recommends using the Floorplan Manager tool:

UI-TECH-2.1. For development of new applications via Web Dynpro ABAP, SAP recommends using the Floorplan Manager to increase consistency among user interfaces.

To Learn More

SDN page on the Floorplan Manager for Web Dynpro ABAP:
http://tinyurl.com/fpm-wd-abap

Wiki page on WebDynpro ABAP Floorplan Manager:
http://tinyurl.com/fpm-wiki

Page Builder

Page Builder is a Web Dynpro ABAP-based framework for combining smaller pieces of relevant UIs into one harmonized yet highly configurable page for the end user. While what appears in an area created using the Floorplan Manager for Web Dynpro ABAP is an application, the Page Builder for Web Dynpro ABAP offers a framework for creating mashups. The UI elements in this case are called Collaborative Human Interface Parts or CHIPs. CHIPs often appear in a side panel on the right side of the interface.

In the Page Builder, a CHIP catalog lists all the CHIPs available for a page; when configuring them, a person simply drags and drops them onto the page. Pages can be configured in this way at three levels: developers, SAP administrators, and users. Developers and SAP administrators can determine what is included in the CHIP catalog and thus be made available for users to add to pages.

A predefined CHIP is included to integrate web content, that is, any content that is addressable with a URL. This includes material such as Google Maps. Page Builder can also incorporate CHIPs for interactive windows such as chat and analytic elements. Figure 5-5 shows a screenshot from a demo available on SDN that shows the Page Builder and CHIPs in action.

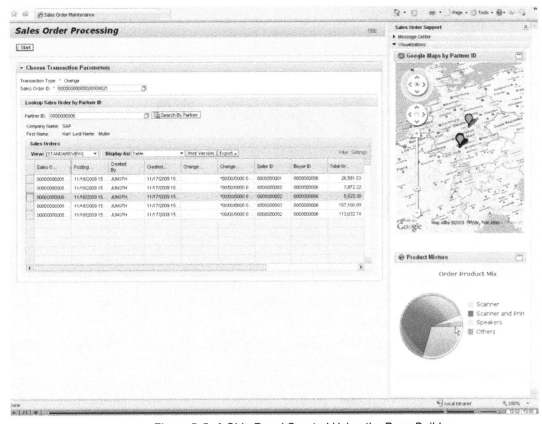

Figure 5-5. A Side Panel Created Using the Page Builder

CHIPs can communicate with applications developed via Web Dynpro ABAP via a technique called wiring. ABAP developers can create their own CHIPs using transaction SE80.

To Learn More

Page Builder demo on SDN: http://tinyurl.com/pagebuilder

SAP Help on Page Builder: http://tinyurl.com/helppb

Floorplan Manager versus Page Builder

The Floorplan Manager and Page Builder complement one another. You use the Floorplan Manager to build traditional applications that are transactional and that read and write data (for example, maintaining customer information). Page Builder is not used for full-blown transactional applications, but for overview information that is read-only. UI Building Blocks (UIBBs) in Floorplan Manager are tightly coupled; CHIPs, as is the model for mashup elements, are loosely coupled.

Additionally, Page Builder allows for a side panel to be created that draws on data from the main application.

Figure 5-6 compares the use cases for Floorplan Manager and Page Builder.

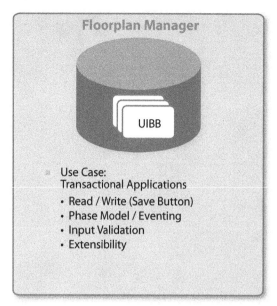
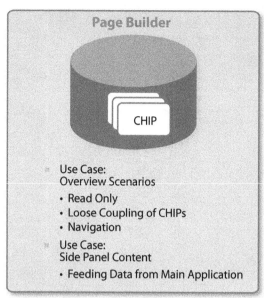

Figure 5-6. Floorplan Manager versus PageBuilder

The Personalized Object Worklist

The Personalized Object Worklist or POWL is a reusable Web Dynpro ABAP component with special functionality.

The POWL allows developers, with very little coding, to create a list of tasks for a particular user, "pushing" their work to them and allowing them to work through the list task by task.

Characteristics of the POWL include:

- Central personalized access to all relevant individual work lists

- Direct visualization of the number of business objects on the overview screen

- Work pushed to the user via automatic update

- Capability of handling a great number of work lists, business objects, and documents

- Easy personalization of the selection criteria and layout of the list by end-users

- Easy creation of new work lists by end-users

The POWL consists of a query area and a list area (see Figure 5-7). Users can access all queries via tab navigation. Application-related buttons provide object-based functionality. Queries can be created, changed, categorized, or temporarily hidden as needed. Selection criteria can be changed temporarily without changing the whole query. Filtering within the data table is supported. Further settings can be made to personalize the data table (examples include which columns are shown, the number of rows, and sort order).

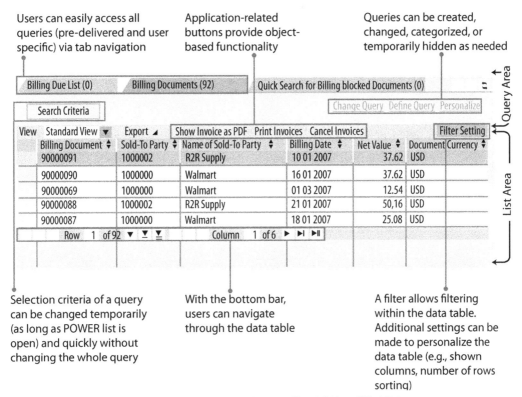

Figure 5-7. Personalized Object Worklist

Using the POWL, developers can implement queries and enable users to launch external applications.

To Learn More

POWL on SDN Wiki:
http://wiki.sdn.sap.com/wiki/display/Found/POWER+List

WebClient UI Framework

The WebClient UI Framework (WebClient UIF) is useful for developing applications that integrate tightly with SAP CRM. It is a highly configurable and customizable UI framework based on Business Server Pages. It has been part of SAP CRM since CRM 5.2 and part of SAP ERP starting with Enhancement Package 4. Architecturally, the WebClient UIF is not part of SAP NetWeaver, but is part of the Business Suite Foundation Layer.

The Component Workbench is the tool for building user interfaces in the WebClient UI Framework. Screens created with the WebClient UI Framework ultimately render as HTML screens and can be further tailored by a developer in this form.

The CRM Interaction Center Web Client is one application that uses the WebClient UI Framework.

UI-TECH-2.2. For development of new applications that should be strongly integrated with SAP CRM, SAP recommends using the WebClient UI Framework to increase consistency among user interfaces.

To Learn More

WebClient UI Framework on SDN: http://tinyurl.com/wcuif-scn

Article on SAP Design Guild:
http://www.sapdesignguild.org/community/readers/reader_crm_web_client.asp

UI Guidelines for the WebClient UI Framework:
http://www.sapdesignguild.org/resources/CRM-UI-Guidelines-Customers.pdf

SAP consulting training course: http://tinyurl.com/webui-course

SAP CRM Web Client Customizing and Development (SAP Press):
http://tinyurl.com/webui-book

SAP UI Technologies and Tools for Java Developers

Web Dynpro Java is a technology with many attractive characteristics. Its design time is based on the Eclipse IDE and is tightly integrated with SAP's Java development environment and landscape. Further, it offers scalability, speed of development, and out-of-the-box integration with SAP data sources. It is particularly well suited for development of new applications that integrate multiple data sources (as well as, of course, for extending existing Web Dynpro Java applications).

On the other hand, SAP has decided that Web Dynpro Java will no longer be enhanced. It is still a supported product and certainly will be supported through 2018. Web Dynpro Java continues to be a valid UI development tool, but alternatively, so are standards-based alternatives such as JavaServer Faces (JSF):

UI-TECH-10. For Java UIs, SAP recommends either Web Dynpro Java or standards-based development using JavaServer Faces (JSF).

Also, developers using Web Dynpro Java should be aware of dependencies on the NetWeaver platform. Web Dynpro Java applications built on SAP NetWeaver 7.1 or higher can be used on the SAP NetWeaver 7.3 stack without migration. Applications built using Web Dynpro Java on SAP NetWeaver 7.0 require migration to run on SAP NetWeaver 7.3.

Another SAP tool for Java developers is Visual Composer, which is a design time tool for rapidly creating Web Dynpro Java UIs. Visual Composer can be used effectively for mocking up and designing UIs, but is not ideal for developing complex UIs. Furthermore, as a UI design tool, it offers integration with SAP NetWeaver BPM; design the UI in Visual Composer, then continue development in SAP NetWeaver BPM.

For both Web Dynpro Java and Visual Composer, the new release of SAP NetWeaver 7.30 allows customers on the 7.0, 7.01, and 7.02 releases to enjoy all the capabilities that were formerly only available in the NetWeaver CE release, including significant improvements in terms of efficiency (performance and scalability), and usability as well as other new features (see links below).

To Learn More

Web Dynpro Java on SDN: http://www.sdn.sap.com/irj/sdn/nw-wdjava

Web Dynpro Java Demo Kit for SAP NetWeaver CE 7.11 and CE 7.20:
http://wiki.sdn.sap.com/wiki/x/OIAnCg

Visual Composer: http://www.sdn.sap.com/irj/sdn/nw-vc

Visual Composer features in 7.3 and migration issues:
http://tinyurl.com/vc-and-7dot3

Guided Procedures and Guided Activities

There's a frequent requirement to create a logical sequence of steps in a UI that guides a user through a process step-by-step. Guided Activity Floorplans, part of the Floorplan Manager, offer a way to create a UI to support a logical sequence of steps.

Guided Procedures are now a deprecated UI technology, although customers using them are still supported by SAP.

UI-FLOW-1. SAP does not recommend using Guided Procedures for new development efforts.

To Learn More

Guided Activity Floorplans on SDN:
http://tinyurl.com/guided-activity-floorplans

Help for Guided Activity Floorplans:
http://tinyurl.com/help-gaf

Java UI Technologies for Migrated Software

Java developers may choose to develop on another platform, such as Tomcat or IBM WebSphere, and migrate their applications to run on SAP NetWeaver.

UI-TECH-3. SAP recommends that Java applications that are migrated to run on SAP NetWeaver use JavaServer Faces (JSF) technology.

In contrast, you should not use Java Server Pages (JSP); this recommendation is in accordance with a general movement in the Java community away from JSP and toward JSF and Facelets.

UI Technologies for Rich Internet Applications

Different UI technologies offer different features and capabilities. To complement their functionality, Web Dynpro and the WebClient UI Framework provide the ability to plug in other technologies in their canvas area. These elements are referred to as islands. Interactive dashboards are an example of using islands on a screen.

UI-TECH-5. SAP recommends using Adobe Flash or Microsoft Silverlight in Web Dynpro Islands or WebClient UIF Islands.

Flash Islands and Silverlight Islands are available with Web Dynpro ABAP and Web Dynpro Java as well as with the WebClient UIF. Flash Islands and Silverlight Islands provide equivalent opportunities for Rich Internet Applications in combination with standard SAP applications. Based on a dedicated event model and rich graphic capabilities, developers can create a new user experience with both technologies. Content from SAP backend systems can be reused via a simple data binding mechanism.

Although developing applications entirely in Flash or Silverlight is possible, use of islands is recommended to preserve UI harmonization (see section earlier in this chapter) and so that the island has access to the services of the SAP framework and runtime.

Mixing Silverlight and Flash islands on the canvas entails loading both Flash and Silverlight and negatively impacts application performance.

To Learn More

Flash Islands: http://tinyurl.com/flash-scn

Silverlight tutorial for Web Dynpro Java:
http://tinyurl.com/silverlight-tutorial

Silverlight in SAP Help: http://tinyurl.com/silverlight-help

Mobile User Interfaces Guidelines

User interface guidelines for various mobile devices, including the iPad, iPhone, Blackberry, and Android, are available on the SAP Service Marketplace. UI design guidelines for creating dashboards are also found in the same location.

To Learn More

SAP Service Marketplace UI Design (Media Library; user required):
http://service.sap.com/uidesign

Output and Forms

Output and forms are key topics for enterprise customers, and SAP has specific recommendations in this important area:

UI-TECH-8. SAP recommends using SAP Interactive Forms by Adobe for forms that are printed or used online or offline. SAP does not recommend that developers use SAPscript.

SAP Interactive Forms by Adobe can be used in three different ways:

- The print scenario
- The interactive offline scenario
- The interactive online scenario

The print scenario is supported out of the box with SAP NetWeaver. The interactive offline and online scenarios require the purchase of an additional license.

SAP has worked hard to improve performance and scalability of forms for enterprise customers and has introduced the concept of a hub, a centralized platform that allows forms to be deployed in a more scalable fashion. Customers often have a complex system landscape, but using the hub, they can run one server in a heterogeneous system landscape that serves forms for numerous systems. A blog on SDN describes the Adobe Document Services hub functionality.

SAP offers an eLearning Series on this topic that was produced by the SAP NetWeaver RIG, covering such topics as:

- SAP Interactive Forms by Adobe for Online Processing in Java
- SAP Interactive Forms by Adobe for Offline Processing in Java
- SAP Interactive Forms by Adobe for Processing with Email
- SAP Interactive Forms by Adobe Working with the PdfObject and PdfDocument APIs
- Securing Online Interactive Forms by Adobe

To Learn More

The output management section in Chapter 3

SAP Interactive Forms by Adobe on SDN:
http://www.sdn.sap.com/irj/sdn/adobe

Adobe Document Services hub:
http://www.sdn.sap.com/irj/scn/weblogs?blog=/pub/wlg/16622

Chapter 6

Enterprise Information Management Guidelines for Best-Built Applications

Information is a valuable asset to be used for enabling end-to-end business processes and for making specific decisions at all levels. Although this sounds like a simple and self-evident fact, it is increasingly becoming a challenge for many companies faced with today's flood of information. Ever-increasing volumes of data—if not properly managed—can lead to unnecessarily high operational costs, poor business decisions, damaged customer and partner relationships, lost business opportunities, and steep penalties for failure to comply with regulations. In short, enterprise data itself is useless unless it is converted into information and then into enterprise knowledge.

ISVs can help SAP customers manage the data explosion and more effectively turn their information into enterprise knowledge in a variety of ways. In a straightforward sense, ISVs could build a connector that brings information from a specialized system into SAP NetWeaver Business Warehouse. But no matter what the ISV application does, it is important for ISVs to understand how SAP's enterprise information management (EIM) portfolio works and what SAP recommends that ISVs do for each area of enterprise information management.

This chapter first lays a groundwork of describing the pillars of EIM, including data integration and data quality, master data management, enterprise search, enterprise data warehousing, information lifecycle management, and enterprise content management.

The combined EIM solutions from SAP address the trusted data requirements of customers' operational and analytic initiatives, and support the data governance process that enables these initiatives. They help organizations create a strategic enterprise information management vision while transforming their data into competitive advantage. Several acclaimed sources underpin the importance of having an EIM strategy in place to avoid compliance issues, and benefit from the bottom-line and top-line impact of steady enterprise information. According to the IT Policy Compliance Group, 90% of all businesses still do not have sufficient policies in place to meet data governance regulations.[1] In this context, Gartner states that an "average organization loses $8.2 million annually through poor data quality."[2]

Figure 6-1. Enterprise Information Management

In summary, enterprise information management is the business activity of gathering, cleansing, integrating, managing, and governing all information assets used by an organization. It enables corporate initiatives such as business transaction processing, business intelligence, data warehousing, data quality management, data migration, data integration, master data management, and information lifecycle management. SAP helps companies with their business strategies for enterprise information management by providing software and technology within the SAP BusinessObjects portfolio, the SAP NetWeaver technology platform, and SAP Business Suite software. With SAP solutions, companies can optimize their business performance by empowering their users and business processes with trusted information that is complete, accurate, and always accessible. EIM encompasses the following key areas:

- Data Integration and Data Quality
- Master Data Management
- Enterprise Search

[1]   Matt Hines, "Report: 90 percent of companies fail compliance," Infoworld, July 16, 2007, http://www.infoworld.com/t/business/report-90-percent-companies-fail-compliance-223.

[2]   Jeff Kelly, "Poor data quality costing companies millions of dollars annually," SearchDataManagement.com, August 25, 2009, http://tinyurl.com/Kelly-data-quality.

- Enterprise Data Warehousing
- Information Lifecycle Management
- Enterprise Content Management

SAP has a site devoted to EIM at http://www.sap.com/solutions/enterprise-information-management where you can see how particular SAP products are aligned with these categories. To find partner certified solutions, visit http://www.sap.com/ecosystem/partners/icc/index.epx.

To Learn More

Enterprise Information Management overview page:
http://www.sdn.sap.com/irj/sdn/nw-informationmanagement

Database Considerations

Before delving into the pillar areas of EIM just listed, there are some foundational concepts to put in place. First and foremost, ISVs should attempt to decouple their software from the underlying database. This provides the maximum flexibility for enterprise customers.

EIM-DB-1. SAP recommends that ISV applications that use a relational database support at least two databases listed on the product availability matrix, for example, Oracle and IBM DB2 or MaxDB and Microsoft SQL Server. SAP also recommends making applications agnostic concerning the underlying database and operating system wherever possible.

To Learn More

Supported databases, see the product availability matrix:
http://service.sap.com/pam (SAP Service Marketplace user required)

Data Integration and Data Quality

Data integration is concerned with the problem of bringing in data from a wide variety of sources and normalizing it. Data quality is all about ensuring that the data is clean, does not have missing or duplicate values, and is reliable.

Because computer systems and software are always changing, as well as the system landscape in a company affected by mergers and acquisitions, the issues of data integration and data quality present ongoing challenges for most companies.

This section of the chapter covers using SAP BusinessObjects Data Services to address these important issues as well as covering some more specialized tools, including SAP Business Objects Data Federator and SAP Business Objects Text Analysis.

Using SAP Business Objects Data Services for Data Integration and Data Quality

ISVs know that problems for companies often signal an opportunity to help companies achieve their goals. SAP BusinessObjects Data Services is of particular interest to ISVs because it can handle both SAP and non-SAP systems. It can also be used to help with the quality of data persisted into an ISV's applications.

Table 6-1. Data sources with which SAP BusinessObjects Data Services integrates

Databases	Applications	Files/Transport	Mainframe (with partner)	Unstructured Data
• Oracle	• JD Edwards	• Text delimited	• ADABAS	• Any text file type
• DB2	• Oracle Apps	• Text fixed width	• ISAM	• 32 languages
• Sybase & IQ	• PeopleSoft	• EBCDIC	• VSAM	
• SQL Server	• Siebel	• XML	• Enscribe	
• Informix	• Salesforce. com	• Cobol	• IMS/DB	
• Teradata	• SAP BI	• Excel	• RMS	
• ODBC	• SAP R/3	• HTTP	• Both direct and change data	
• MySQL	– ABAP	• JMS		
• Netezza	– BAPI	• SOAP (Web Services)		
	– IDoc			

In order to make their solutions accessible to SAP BusinessObjects Data Services, ISVs should consider integrating via web services. The ISV application can call a web service to send data to SAP BusinessObjects Data Services and a second call to retrieve the data. Further, the ISV application can be the source for web services, although calling web services to communicate from an ISV application to SAP BusinessObjects Data Services is the more common case.

To Learn More

"SAP BusinessObjects Data Services Integrator's Guide:"
http://tinyurl.com/ds-integrator-guide

A concrete example might be a case where the ISV application uses SAP BusinessObjects Data Services to extract data for master data management and persist it back into the application. SAP BusinessObjects Data Services features could be used to normalize address data, eliminate duplicates, clean up the data using predefined rules, and send it back to the ISV application. Such proactive use of data quality and data integration techniques helps ensure that new data persisted in the application is clean before it is stored.

Data profiling is another feature of SAP BusinessObjects Data Services. Data profiling means handling the inconsistencies seen in data. When data comes in through a single interface, the program can validate data as it is entered. But in many other cases, data comes in a much less consistent way, with improperly formatted social security numbers, invalid values for certain fields, missing data, and the like. SAP BusinessObjects Data Services can help with data profiling, which can address all these types of problems to ensure that data is complete, consistently formatted, and valid. ISVs should be aware of these capabilities so that they can help enterprise customers integrate disparate data sources when appropriate and leverage the SAP BusinessObjects tool set.

Perhaps one of the most well known uses for SAP BusinessObjects Data Services is to integrate data from multiple sources into a data warehouse, for example. ISVs can use this tool to help customers integrate and deliver structured and unstructured data from various data sources using its extraction, transformation, and loading (ETL) capabilities.

Data quality is another key concern for enterprise customers. When adding data to their enterprise data stores, it makes sense to ensure that the data is of high quality before it is added, whether the record is added through an ISV application or directly using the SAP Business Suite. For example, when a user creates a new customer record in ERP, users should see existing customers with correct addresses to ensure that they don't enter duplicates.

SAP BusinessObjects Data Services, the Data Quality part of it, delivers data quality functions (standardize, parse, cleanse, enhance, match) to help centralize the discovery, correction, and prevention of data quality issues.

By ensuring that the data is of high quality before it is added, ISVs can help ensure that their additions to the data store are accurate and do not duplicate existing information.

EIM-DIDQ-1. SAP recommends using the Data Quality features of SAP BusinessObjects Data Services to support customers in improving the quality of existing and incoming data.

ISVs may develop software that entails moving data between application systems on a regular basis. There are a variety of methods for doing this. Remote function calls (RFCs) are a fast but SAP proprietary method for moving data, but they are not applicable to third-party systems. Enterprise Service Bus (ESB) functionality can be used. (Table 6-2 compares SAP BusinessObjects Data Services with ESBs.) Web services are good for moving small amounts of data and provide flexibility, standardization, and agility since they follow a service-oriented architecture (SOA) approach (see Chapter 4). SAP BusinessObjects Data Services can be utilized for high speed transfer of data between systems in scenarios where:

- Data must be moved multiple times per day
- Complex transformations are required
- Data has to be checked and possibly corrected before being integrated into the target system

Table 6-2. Extract, Transform, and Load versus Enterprise Service Bus

	Extract, Transform, and Load (ETL)	Enterprise Service Bus (ESB)
Core Use Case	Data replication and data synchronization in real time Examples: Asynchronous bulk load of a data warehouse, data migration	Event-driven message-based integration in synchronous and asynchronous scenarios Example: Synchronous process automation across ERP and CRM systems
Data Characteristics	Bulk data	Single messages with small, medium, and large payloads
Transformation Characteristics	Lightweight to sophisticated transformations Embedded data quality transforms (cleansing, matching)	Lightweight to sophisticated transformations
Integration Process Characteristics	Single-step stateless integration processes only Point-to-point or point-to-multipoint connectivity with clearly defined sources and targets	Multistep stateful integration processes requiring workflow/ business process management (BPM) engine to handle process status Bus architecture with publish & subscribe and sophisticated routing rules
SAP product	SAP BusinessObjects Data Services	SAP NetWeaver Process Integration

Special Integration Cases

This section covers two additional integration cases: integrating unstructured data into structured data stores and integrating data while leaving it in the source system (data federation).

As described in the Enterprise Content Management (ECM) section of this chapter, many data sources, from emails to text messages to notes on an order, contain unstructured data. Deciphering this data and deciding what to keep is an important challenge.

SAP BusinessObjects Text Analysis reads and classifies text in unstructured data sources so that it can be incorporated into BI systems. In order to determine the value of information, the value and meaning must be analyzed.

SAP BusinessObjects Text Analysis can convert unstructured data like emails, documents, all kinds of free form text in an ERP system or databases into structured information by taking the text portions, understanding the grammar of the given language and extracting defined meanings.

Note that Text Analytics is available as a Transform from within SAP BusinessObjects Data Services for all sources that SAP BusinessObjects Data Services can read from.

For some use cases, moving large amounts of data between systems or integrating data from many systems into one using ETL is not practical or efficient. In these cases, data can be left in place and analyzed remotely. This is called data federation. Data federation involves the idea of shipping queries, where you basically distribute the queries to various application systems and then get the results back and aggregate them. In this way, companies can integrate heterogeneous data sources for unified reporting.

SAP BusinessObjects Data Federator can be used for querying data from different data sources in place for BI reporting purposes when the limitations of such an approach are recognized. Generally, virtual queries involve a certain risk that the source data in scope is not 100% consistent. In addition, if large quantities of data are being integrated using data federation, there could be a noticeable load on the source systems, which could impact source system performance impact and should be considered. Data federation is best used for smaller data sets that answer specific queries—such as fetching Q2 sales for California—than for larger scale integration and reporting.

There are many adapters available for SAP BusinessObjects Data Federator, and ISVs may wish to ensure that their products can be queried through one of these adapters (two generic ones include JDBC and ODBC).

To Learn More

> SAP BusinessObjects Data Federator, download its user guide:
> http://tinyurl.com/data-federator
>
> Data Integration and Quality Management overview page:
> http://www.sdn.sap.com/irj/sdn/im
>
> Data Integration and Quality Management discussion forum:
> http://forums.sdn.sap.com/forum.jspa?forumID=305
>
> SAP Data Services Tips and Tricks wiki page:
> http://tinyurl.com/data-tips-tricks
>
> SAP Help Knowledge Center for DI/DQ:
> http://help.sap.com/content/bobj/im/index.htm

Master Data Management

Have you ever gotten a mass mailing with your name spelled wrong? Have you ever contacted a company by one channel, only to have to repeat your story (or correct your account information) all over again using another channel such as the telephone?

This lack of unified data about customers is one of the main drivers for master data management, and it is a common problem for large companies. SAP customers may find themselves with separate customer data in multiple SAP and non-SAP systems and need to unify and reconcile that data to create a " golden record," a record in which not only is all the data consistent, but it is the best data available for a particular entity (such as a customer), with all information properly formatted and the like.

This section details more about master data management and master data governance to assist ISVs in understanding the problems customers face, the solutions SAP offers, and the opportunities for complementing the products offered by SAP in this important area.

SAP can help customers manage and govern multidomain master data across heterogeneous IT landscapes. Typical usages include, for example, customer data integration, product information management, and global data synchronization. Generally, when companies plan to adopt an enterprise master data management (MDM) strategy, they can either pursue a decentralized or a centralized approach (see Figure 6-2). In the decentralized case, the original data ownership lies in the local system, which is also where data is created (step 1 on the left side of Figure 6-2). In such a context, the MDM instance serves as a central hub for subsequent consolidation of globally relevant master data information (step 2 on the left side of the figure) that can propagate the consolidated information across the system landscape to ensure overall data quality (step 3 on the left side of the figure).

By contrast, in a centralized approach, the primary goal is to drive the creation of high-quality data upfront using central authoring and governance principles. In this case, the data is created centrally on the MDM system (step 1 on the right side of the figure) and propagated to the application systems (step 2 on the right side of the figure).

On a typical path towards central authoring as an ultimate stage, companies start at a local scale with getting their data ready quality-wise, then integrate data into a central MDM hub for central consolidation and harmonization, and finally adopt central data governance mechanisms to ensure data accuracy upfront.

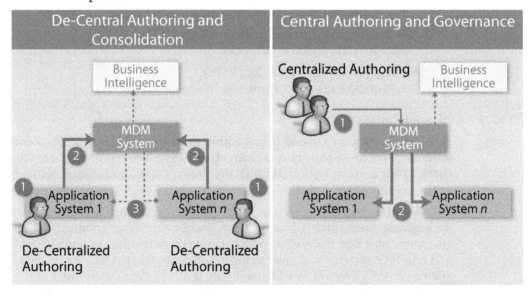

Figure 6-2. Decentralized Authoring and Consolidation versus Centralized Data Authoring and Governance

Accordingly, an MDM strategy can comprise the following incremental usage patterns:

- Ensure data readiness at local scale (that is, in a single system)
- Integrate and cleanse data at local scale
- Consolidate and harmonize data at global scale (that is, across the entire system landscape, regardless of geographic location of systems)
- Manage data centrally at global scale

The adoption of these usage patterns is not necessarily incremental. An enterprise may pursue a mixed MDM strategy according to specific data domains and organizational areas. This means, for example, that local data readiness may be appropriate for a specific data domain and area within the organization while central master data management and data governance principles at global scale may be relevant for another data domain.

Governance and Master Data Management

Governance is an important aspect of managing master data, ensuring that data is consistent across the system landscape.

To apply a master data management and governance strategy ensuring master data consistency in cross-system IT landscapes and at data creation, SAP provides a comprehensive portfolio, facilitating an incremental implementation approach:

- **SAP BusinessObjects Data Services** for ensuring data readiness at local system scale, and when it comes to integrating and cleansing data (as described earlier in this chapter), SAP BusinessObjects Data Services can be used as the underlying data quality engine for de-central authoring and consolidation and for central authoring and governance. Because SAP BusinessObjects Data Services does not persist data, this requires a master data management solution on top.

- **SAP NetWeaver Master Data Management (SAP NetWeaver MDM)** to consolidate and harmonize multi-channel master data in heterogeneous landscapes—including product, supplier, customer, or user-defined data objects—using a single platform. SAP NetWeaver MDM targets scenarios focused on globally relevant master data attributes for use in SAP and non-SAP applications

  SAP NetWeaver MDM is applicable for de-central authoring and consolidation focused on globally relevant master data attributes for use in SAP and non-SAP applications. In conjunction with SAP NetWeaver BPM it provides a flexible infrastructure for central authoring and governance with a focus on globally relevant master data attributes for use in SAP and non-SAP applications

- **SAP Master Data Governance** is focused on central authoring and governance for use in SAP applications. SAP Master Data

Governance, version for financial data is a ready-to-run governance application for specific master data domains, providing pre-built validation against SAP business logic. SAP Master Data Governance, version for financial data can be used to govern financial master data (such as chart of accounts or cost center data) at its creation in SAP ERP to deliver consistent data across general ledger software and facilitate regulatory compliance

Based on SAP NetWeaver MDM's nature as a flexible infrastructure component with versatile data integration and data modeling capabilities, it is best suited for a great variety of multi-domain use cases in heterogeneous system landscapes.

Integrating SAP BusinessObjects Data Services with SAP NetWeaver Master Data Management with their complementary capabilities helps customers to achieve utmost master data quality and a consolidated master data stock across the enterprise.

To Learn More

"SAP BusinessObjects and SAP NetWeaver MDM - Bringing Together The Best of Two Worlds:"
http://www.sdn.sap.com/irj/scn/weblogs?blog=/pub/wlg/13144

"Integrating SAP NetWeaver MDM with SAP BusinessObjects Data Services" page on the MDM wiki on SDN:
http://wiki.sdn.sap.com/wiki/x/FgCFCg offers links to many resources on this topic

Predefined MDM Business Content facilitates implementations of SAP NetWeaver Master Data Management for master data consolidation and harmonization scenarios in SAP landscapes. For more information, see the SDN page on this topic at http://www.sdn.sap.com/irj/sdn/mdm-business-content.

> **EIM-MDM-1. SAP recommends that partners gain expertise in using both SAP NetWeaver Master Data Management and SAP BusinessObjects Data Services because of their complementary nature.**

In this context, business packages that SAP has developed based on SAP NetWeaver MDM include:

* Aggregate Physician Spend
  (http://weblogs.sdn.sap.com/pub/wlg/18641): Facilitating a single view on physician master data to ensure consolidated reporting (as required by the U.S government)

* Optimized Supplier Spend
  (http://tinyurl.com/optimized-supplier-spend): Facilitating a single view on supplier master data to ensure consolidated reporting (to streamline global sourcing and purchasing)

- Continuous Data Quality Assurance
  (http://www.sdn.sap.com/irj/scn/weblogs?blog=/pub/wlg/17620):
  To measure prevailing master data quality statistically and trigger
  follow-up action for sustained data control

- Collaborative Master Data Maintenance Processes (e.g., governed
  material creation)(http://weblogs.sdn.sap.com/pub/wlg/18640): To
  control master data at the point of creation and ensure compliance
  with company standards upfront

How ISVs Can Leverage MDM

However, given the great variety of ways to use MDM, there is enough untilled
ground for ISVs to build add-on solutions on top of SAP NetWeaver MDM.
SAP currently offers two certifications in the area of MDM.

To Learn More

SAP Integration and Certification Center's page:
http://tinyurl.com/mdm-cert

Integrating with MDM

Another way to build on SAP NetWeaver MDM is using web services and other
open interfaces.

> *EIM-MDM-2. SAP recommends using SAP NetWeaver MDM openness
> (for example, MDM Enrichment Architecture, APIs, and web services)
> to add ISV integration content (for example, system connections
> to automated translation engines or third-party data enrichment
> services).*

MDM offers several types of integration points, including:

- Web services
- ABAP API
- Java API
- .NET API

The MDM ABAP API provides a programming interface for accessing SAP
MDM 7.1 using ABAP. The interface is easy to configure and convenient to use.
The MDM ABAP API is delivered for SAP NetWeaver AS ABAP as a separately
installable package. It is optimized for ABAP developers and available using
ABAP Objects and function modules. It includes the core services performed
on the records (create, retrieve, update, delete, query, etc) as well as metadata
(tables, fields, etc.) and administrative functions (such as repository) are
delivered.

To Learn More

MDM ABAP API: http://tinyurl.com/mdm-abap-guide

The MDM Java and .NET APIs enable users to write applications that interact with the MDM server to perform various operations. The APIs expose a granular and comprehensive set of functions for basic operations such as searching and editing data, as well as for advanced functionality such as repository administration.

To Learn More

These APIs: http://tinyurl.com/mdm-java-net-guide

MDM uses a specific MDM Connector to provide connectivity between the MDM Server and J2EE applications. In particular, the connector can be used within SAP NetWeaver Portal to configure connections to MDM repositories in the portal system landscape. Apart from the portal, any J2EE application can use the MDM Connector to establish a physical connection to an MDM Server, while allowing J2EE server-wide connection pooling, configuration, and monitoring.

The MDM Connector is based on the SAP Connector Framework.

To Learn More

SAP help on the topic of MDM APIs: http://tinyurl.com/mdm-apis

Composing Data Governance Applications

In the context of data governance, creation of master data follows a particular business process. By using SAP NetWeaver MDM in conjunction with SAP NetWeaver BPM, a repeatable business process can be created for creating master data.

Integrating SAP NetWeaver Business Process Management with SAP NetWeaver Master Data Management provides a flexible, service-based environment to govern data creation and maintenance processes where new master data (for example, a customer, supplier or material record and its globally relevant attributes) can be requested, checked, approved and finally created in a comprehensive process flow that coherently spans across multiple systems. This integration is available as of support package 4 for SAP NetWeaver MDM 7.1.

To Learn More

Blog on this topic:
http://www.sdn.sap.com/irj/scn/weblogs?blog=/pub/wlg/17698

"Error-free Consistent Master Data Starts at the Source:" an article reprinted on SDN from SAP Insider provides additional insight into how SAP NetWeaver MDM and BPM can work together:
http://tinyurl.com/mdm-bpm-article

EIM-MDM-3. SAP recommends an architecture with a process layer, a UI layer, and a services layer for centrally governed data creation processes (i.e., globally relevant master data information) in heterogeneous landscapes with:

- *SAP NetWeaver MDM, SAP BusinessObjects Data Services, and SAP Business Suite application services*
- *WebDynpro-based user interfaces*
- *BPM as a process orchestration layer*

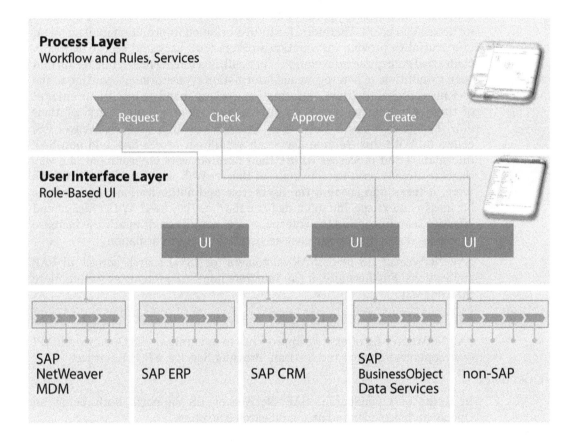

Figure 6-3. Process, UI, and services layers for a data creation process

To Learn More

Master Data Management overview page:
http://www.sdn.sap.com/irj/sdn/nw-mdm

Master Data Management discussion forum:
http://forums.sdn.sap.com/forum.jspa?forumID=55

Enterprise Search

In the not-so-distant past, all data resided in a single monolithic system and experts were able to search and filter that data through standard and ABAP SQL queries. Today data is both structured and unstructured and scattered over many source systems. At the same time, despite this complexity and the proliferation of data itself, users of all types demand the same Google-like search response that they get from their browsers.

In part, the volume of structured and unstructured content is rapidly growing because of the ubiquity of tools for creating it (from word processors to online blog writing tools to email clients). In addition, vast volumes of business-critical data reside in business applications and these systems are often not designed for occasional users. Therefore, for future-oriented information management, it is crucial to provide information workers with easy and secure access to contextual enterprise information – typically via intelligent search agents that span a multitude of heterogeneous information repositories. According to the McKinsey Global Institute, "information workers spend an inordinate amount of time searching for the right information, approximately 40% of their day." This is where SAP NetWeaver Enterprise Search (SAP NetWeaver ES) comes in. With this solution users can seamlessly access SAP and non-SAP information and processes within their familiar work environment in a way they are already used to from state-of-the-art Web search standards. What's more, it takes into account the users' role and authorizations, and enables business-context-specific zooming in on the data they need. With efficient and effective searches across the enterprise, companies can dramatically increase people productivity through easy access to the right information.

SAP NetWeaver ES helps SAP customers (or ISVs) search across all SAP applications. Furthermore, it can integrate non-SAP systems as well in more than one way.

Approaches to Integration with SAP NetWeaver Enterprise Search

SAP NetWeaver ES offers two approaches to integration: the OpenSearch API (www.opensearch.org) and the Data Provider Service, a SOAP service.

OpenSearch

In terms of OpenSearch, SAP NetWeaver ES supports both being an OpenSearch provider and an OpenSearch consumer.

This means that if an information source supports the OpenSearch APIs, SAP NetWeaver ES can query it and consume its search results. In this case, the search index would live on the information source's system rather than being integrated into the index of SAP NetWeaver ES.

As an OpenSearch provider, results from SAP NetWeaver ES could be consumed by a service such as Microsoft Desktop Search.

Other systems that both provide and consume using the OpenSearch APIs include Microsoft SharePoint. So SharePoint search results could include results from SAP NetWeaver ES, and SAP NetWeaver ES results could include results from a Microsoft SharePoint search.

Data Provider Service

The SAP NetWeaver ES provides another option as well. Using the Data Provider Service (DPS), a SOAP service can be created that essentially tells SAP NetWeaver ES to go out and index a backend system of some type. Creating this service entails modeling the data objects in the target system so that SAP NetWeaver ES knows what to index and the structure of those data objects. This modeling capability is built into SAP NetWeaver ES.

In this way, the DPS provides ISVs and others with great flexibility in designing connectors for third-party systems and for integrating the search of those systems into SAP NetWeaver ES.

To Learn More

Connectors: http://tinyurl.com/search-object-connectors

"SAP NetWeaver Enterprise Search Data Provider Services (DPS) - Developer Documentation" by Holger Gockel: http://tinyurl.com/dps-developer-doc (WSDL files are also available from this link)

OpenSearch versus DPS

How can ISVs decide between OpenSearch and DPS?

ISVs that want to consume SAP search results for use in another application or that provide the results of their search functionality to SAP NetWeaver Enterprise Search should use OpenSearch.

ISVs that want to make their content indexable and searchable by SAP NetWeaver Enterprise Search should use DPS.

EIM-ES-1. SAP recommends using SAP NetWeaver Enterprise Search to collect structured and unstructured data that is dispersed across heterogeneous landscapes into a single work environment.

To Learn More

SAP NetWeaver Enterprise Search page: http://www.sdn.sap.com/irj/sdn/nw-search

SAP NetWeaver Enterprise Search discussion forum: http://forums.sdn.sap.com/forum.jspa?forumID=202

Enterprise Data Warehousing

The practical reality for most organizations is that their data infrastructure is made up of a collection of heterogeneous systems. For example, an organization might have one system that handles customer relationships, a system that handles employees, systems that handle sales data and production data, and yet another system for finance and budgeting data. In practice, these systems are often poorly or not at all integrated. Simple questions such as "How much time did salesperson A spend on customer C? How much did we sell to customer C? Was customer C happy with our service? Did customer C pay his bills?" can be very hard to answer, even though the information is available "somewhere" in different data systems.

Another problem is that ERP systems are designed to support relevant operations in detail. For example, a finance system might keep track of every single widget purchased, when it was ordered, when it was delivered, and when it was paid for. The system might offer accounting principles (like double entry bookkeeping) that further complicate the data model. Such information is great for the person in charge of buying widgets or the accountant trying to sort out an irregularity, but the CEO is definitely not interested in such detailed information. The CEO wants answers to questions such as "What's the cost? What's the revenue? and Did our latest initiative reduce costs?"

Data warehousing is a complex process that starts with the acquisition of data of varying quality from a wide variety of sources. It continues with the consolidation, harmonization, and consistent, detailed persistence of data. Finally, the data is aggregated as reliable information in analyze-optimized formats and structures that are provided at a favorable price for analytical applications.

SAP NetWeaver Business Warehouse (SAP NetWeaver BW) is model-driven and enables these complex processes to be modeled and designed in a platform-independent manner in a data warehouse application. Data structures, transformations, and data flows are described using modeling objects on a meta level. The SAP NetWeaver BW metadata repository administrates this meta level and makes it accessible.

SAP NetWeaver BW provides an integrated data warehouse platform that provides features such as:

- Business oriented modeling via modeling patterns and business content that enables fast implementation

- Reliable data acquisition with openness and data quality by SAP NetWeaver BW's native ETL capabilities and SAP BusinessObjects Data Services (Data Integrator and Data Quality)

- Streamlined operations for cost efficient data management using scheduling, monitoring, and data consistency. In SAP NetWeaver BW, you use process chains to control and manage internal processes. These process chains can also be inserted in SAP NetWeaver BW scheduling tools, such as Redwood Chronicle for data flow management that crosses BW boundaries. In a sophisticated case, you can fully automate and centrally monitor ETL processes that may span a Manufacturing Execution System (MES), an ERP system, and a BW system

- SAP NetWeaver BW Accelerator runs on specifically configured hardware from SAP partners and can help improve the performance of queries, shorten batch times, and reduce administration tasks through in-memory acceleration techniques

For SAP NetWeaver BW customers, EIM solutions help maximize their investment by providing additional functionality for ensuring their BI system gains trusted information.

EIM-BW-1. SAP recommends that source system data be replicated into the SAP NetWeaver Business Warehouse component and stored there persistently if any of the following data integration requirements need to be fulfilled:

- *Consolidating data from heterogeneous transactional systems in one location (if necessary, leverage SAP BusinessObjects Data Services tools to cleanse or qualify external data for analytical purposes in the Business Warehouse)*

- *Organizing and integrating high volumes of data*

- *Merging, standardizing, and cleaning historical data*

- *Providing high availability and performance data for analysis*

- *Isolating high-performance transactional systems from analytical queries*

An ISV Example

An ISV wants to bring historical weather information into SAP NetWeaver BW for analyzing ice cream and beverage sales.

To do this, information from all weather stations has to be consolidated including data elements such as temperature, humidity, and amount of rainwater per square mile, as well as dimensions such as weather station location and geographical area. The dimensions also have to be mapped against the sales regions using postal codes or something similarly granular.

The large data volume has to be considered and the data would probably reside on cheaper storage devices such as archives. Nevertheless the access speed for the weather data should meet the Service Level Agreements given to the Information Consumer side by IT.

EIM-EDW-1. SAP recommends using SAP BusinessObjects Metadata Management to analyze metadata coming from SAP NetWeaver Business Warehouse and combine it with metadata from other models (BI, Data Services, RDBMS, and third-party tools) to see impact analysis and data lineage for the end-to-end BI to data source environment.

Considering this guideline in the context of our weather data example, analysis shows that the meta models of BW Sales Analysis and the German Weather Agency are certainly different. In order to get these two worlds mapped to each other, a powerful meta model browser such as the SAP BusinessObjects Metadata Manager (SAP BOMM) is helpful.

> **EIM-EDW-2. SAP recommends that ISVs who want to ease the integration of data from their applications into SAP NetWeaver Business Warehouse use naming conventions that ease the process and, when possible, reuse SAP business objects.**

For our example, this would mean that all modeling objects and source coding the ISV brings into SAP NetWeaver Business Warehouse with their product must be implemented in a separate namespace following the rules of a software add-on (see ALM-PRD-7 in Chapter 3).

To Learn More

Enterprise Data Warehousing overview page:
http://www.sdn.sap.com/irj/sdn/edw

Enterprise Data Warehousing discussion forums:
http://forums.sdn.sap.com/category.jspa?categoryID=4

Information Lifecycle Management

SAP can help customers implement an information lifecycle management (ILM) strategy that balances the cost of storing information while ensuring accessibility to support business processes and audit requirements. With its data volume management and retention management capabilities, ILM helps control the overall growth of the corporate information environment and meet legal retention requirements. SAP NetWeaver Information Lifecycle Management enables you to decommission redundant SAP systems while preserving full auditing and reporting capabilities for stored data. Retention-relevant data from such systems can be transferred to a central retention warehouse to satisfy auditing and reporting needs. ILM also allows you to define retention rules, enabling you to retain different business records for different periods of time according to policy or legal requirements.

Partner products that help with document retention include the following. SAP Document Access by Open Text provides a single point of access to SAP and non-SAP data and documents via virtual content folders. SAP Archiving by Open Text helps with archiving data from SAP systems.

> **EIM-ILM-1. SAP recommends that ISVs enable information lifecycle management best practices for their products to ensure that ISV and SAP applications conform to a complete and uniform ILM solution.**

ISVs using SAP development tools or that have migrated their software to the SAP environment should enable customers to relocate retention-relevant data from an application database to an archive using the standard SAP data archiving function in accordance with relevant governance.

> ***EIM-ILM-2. SAP recommends that every ISV application component support the major ILM cornerstones:***
>
> - ***Data volume management—supports system load reduction and compliance with relevant internal and external governance***
>
> - ***Retention management—provides tools and methods for retention of information based on relevant governance***
>
> - ***Retention warehousing—provides a standardized solution for legacy system decommissioning***

To Learn More

Information Lifecycle Management overview page on SDN:
http://www.sdn.sap.com/irj/sdn/ilm

Enterprise Content Management

According to the Association for Information and Image Management, "Enterprise Content Management (ECM) is the strategies, methods and tools used to capture, manage, store, preserve, and deliver content and documents related to organizational processes."[3] ECM tools enable management of unstructured information.

In an enterprise environment, the majority of content that users deal with in their daily work is unstructured information. To leverage this business-relevant information, it's essential to support content-rich business processes by tightly integrating ECM services into business applications.

Because unstructured information is very often an underutilized information source, ISVs can find many opportunities to offer software that complements the offerings of the SAP Business Suite in this important area.

SAP offers an integration layer in SAP NetWeaver for integrating ECM products via web services, described next.

The ECM Integration Layer in SAP NetWeaver

SAP NetWeaver Composition Environment allows customers and partners to build content rich composite applications by leveraging the ECM integration layer of SAP NetWeaver. The ECM integration layer is a platform component that deals with how to integrate and consume ECM-related services within an application that you build on top of the SAP NetWeaver CE.

The ECM integration layer facilitates the consumption of ECM services provided by SAP created and by partners, as shown in Figure 6-4.

---

[3] "What Is ECM?"
http://www.aiim.org/What-is-ECM-Enterprise-Content-Management.aspx.

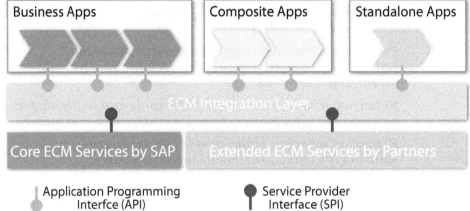

Figure 6-4. ECM integration layer

ISVs that use SAP tools can use the ECM integration layer within SAP NetWeaver CE to provide document management services via the service provider interface (SPI) or to consume document management services via the application programming interface (API) if they build their own application on top of SAP NetWeaver Composition Environment.

Since SAP NetWeaver CE also includes SAP NetWeaver Business Process Management and SAP NetWeaver Business Rules Management, ISVs can also build a process within BPM and leverage these capabilities.

An emerging open standard, OASIS Content Management Interoperability Services (CMIS) is widely supported by vendors including SAP, Microsoft, IBM, EMC, Open Text, and Alfresco. It is a standard for integrating third-party repositories and services.

CMIS defines a domain model for interacting with an ECM repository via a service-oriented Web interface (it supports both SOAP and REST bindings).

To Learn More

CMIS including the specification: http://tinyurl.com/oasis-cmis

Examples of ECM Products

Both SAP and its partners offer ECM products.

SAP Extended ECM by Open Text helps customers manage unstructured content across its entire life cycle, from capturing, filing, accessing, or relating it to business applications, collaborating on it, and archiving it and disposing of it. ISVs may want to be aware of this product, which can be accessed via the ECM integration layer in SAP NetWeaver referenced earlier in this section. While SAP NetWeaver Portal provides basic knowledge management capabilities, SAP Extended ECM by Open Text offers more advanced capabilities like input management, records management, content-centric workflows and archiving.

SAP Digital Asset Management by Open Text helps SAP customers take advantage of new distribution channels by enabling a complete end-to-end process for digital asset delivery and monetization. This product is integrated with SAP CRM.

SAP PLM Document Management System allows customers to manage documents in a secured place and link them with other SAP business objects such as Material Master, Customer Info Record and so on. Enterprise services are available to interact with SAP PLM DMS for partners that wish to interface with SAP PLM. Use cases for these enterprise services are highlighted in the Technical Document Management Connectivity ES bundle (see http://wiki.sdn.sap.com/wiki/x/DQ0).

To Learn More

Enterprise Content Management overview page on SDN:
http://www.sdn.sap.com/irj/sdn/nw-ecm

Getting Experience with EIM Tools: The SAP Discovery System

ISVs who are interested in learning more about such EIM tools as SAP NetWeaver MDM, SAP BusinessObjects Data Services and Data Federator as well as SAP NetWeaver BW may wish to work with the SAP Discovery System, as shown in Figure 6-5.

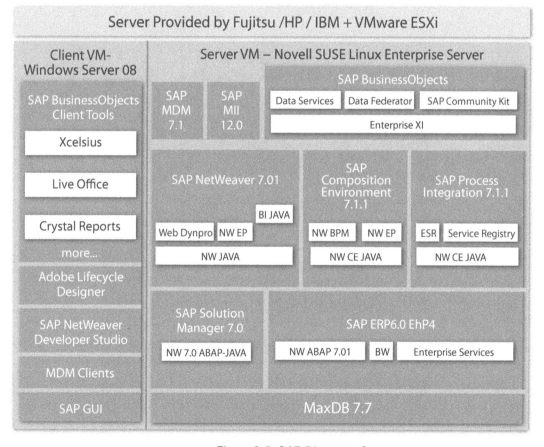

Figure 6-5. SAP Discovery System

The SAP Discovery System enables ISVs to work with included SAP software and analyze its relationship to their own application portfolio.

To Learn More

Discovery System: http://www.sdn.sap.com/irj/sdn/discoverysystem

Chapter 7

Business Intelligence Tools Guidelines for Best-Built Applications

Enterprises collect considerable data through their use of ERP systems for all their business activities and through the use of SAP partner solutions that integrate with the SAP Business Suite.

While transactional data offers information about customers and related business interactions, the data has additional value as a source of information for businesses. Insights gathered from analysis make better, more informed decisions possible. Business Intelligence (BI) generally refers to the techniques, tools, and software applications that are used to perform this analysis and support the decision-making process.

To be useful, business data needs to be actively managed in order to make it a reliable source for extracting further business intelligence information. Such information must also be made accessible to those who need it. Chapter 6 on Enterprise Information Management (EIM) addresses this important topic.

Once reliable data is provided, data is further analyzed and presented (for example, as reports or dashboards) to business users. That is the focus of this chapter.

SAP recognizes that ISVs must make a significant choice: either to build a "generic" application that can work equally well with any enterprise application (with or without SAP backend systems) or to build an "SAP-specific" application that integrates especially tightly with SAP backend systems and the NetWeaver platform. A generic application may help an ISV serve a larger market while an SAP-specific application can provide additional features that are not possible using a generic approach. SAP provides BI tools to support both the generic and the SAP-specific approach.

SAP recognizes that customers face a similar choice. They have both SAP and non-SAP applications. SAP BusinessObjects BI solutions can be used to leverage both SAP and non-SAP data sources. Customers decide how to provide business intelligence information to users, and therefore face development choices about embedding SAP tools in their environment and in applications they develop. Since SAP BusinessObjects BI tools support both SAP and non-SAP applications (indeed, there are many SAP BusinessObjects customers who do not even run the SAP Business Suite), developers at large customer installations have an array of choices about how to provide BI tools to business users. Furthermore, since they often have licenses for the tools described in this chapter because of their status as SAP customers, they may not realize all the options for BI tools that are available to them.

This chapter introduces SAP BusinessObjects BI tools specifically as they relate to integrating and embedding BI capabilities into customer- or partner-developed applications. The information contained in this chapter applies generically to all backend systems including (but not limited to) the SAP Business Suite.

The SAP BI frontend strategy is to focus development on the SAP BusinessObjects BI tools.

BT-BO-1. SAP recommends using SAP BusinessObjects BI tools for analytics.

The following SAP Business Explorer business user tools, BEx Report Designer, BEx Analyzer, and BEx Web Analyzer, are now in maintenance and new applications should be based on SAP BusinessObjects BI tools. SAP BEx tools are not covered in this book.

BT-SAP-1. For new development SAP does not encourage use of the following SAP Business Explorer business user tools: BEx Report Designer, BEx Analyzer, and BEx Web Analyzer.

As described in the Preface, the phrase "does not encourage" in a guideline indicates that if you use these tools currently, you should consider switching in the long term and not use them for new projects.

SAP BEx Web Application Designer (SAP BEx WAD) remains the tool of choice for customers and partners to design web-based analytical and planning applications connected to SAP NetWeaver Business Warehouse, and SAP BEx Query Designer remains the tool of choice for IT departments to model BEx Queries on top of BW data providers.

One of the key issues in building a generic application is that the various data formats in the many potential data sources might not be efficient for direct use. With the SAP BusinessObjects business intelligence (BI) solutions, an intermediate adaptation through the semantic layer enables a common access point to all sources of enterprise data. In this way, the semantic layer acts as a sort of middleware, providing translation and adaptation for backend data sources into language and vocabulary that a group of business users understands.

Figure 7-1 offers a high-level view of how SAP BusinessObjects BI tools access data sources.

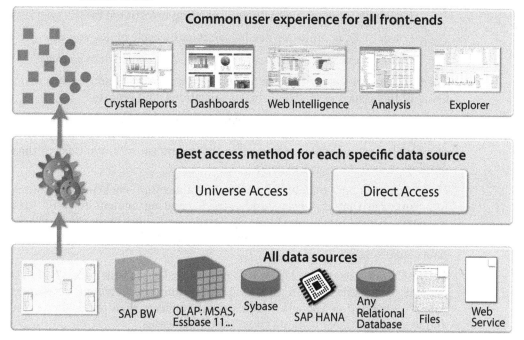

Figure 7-1. How BI Tools Access Data

Data sources are shown at the bottom of the diagram. These data sources are further described in Chapter 6, which covers enterprise information management.

The middle tier shows how those data sources are accessed. The SAP BusinessObjects BI platform includes a semantic layer. The semantic layer unifies the data access methods and maps data structures from complex data sources into new metadata structures designed to be understandable by business users who work with SAP BusinessObjects BI tools. These mappings are called universes.

Universe access provides the ability to:

- Model non self-descriptive sources
- Customize and enrich any source
- Add security
- Federate data from multiple sources
- Provide human-readable output (business representation of the source)

Direct access simplifies access to BEx queries. Before SAP BusinessObjects BI 4.0, data from BEx queries was flattened. Direct access generates a universe automatically and that universe (though it cannot be modified) offers a true one-to-one reproduction of all the data in a BEx query, preserving the hierarchy and offering a better visualization of that data. Direct access provides:

- Automatic modeling of self-descriptive sources
- The ability to preserve customers' existing investment in BEx queries
- Lower TCO: no universe needed, simpler lifecycle management
- Quick access to BEx queries or other self-descriptive data sources

The top layer of Figure 7-1 shows that content is analyzed and reports created using BI tools, such as dashboards, visualizations, and reports.

Developers with different types of expertise use the layers shown in Figure 7-1. Developers who specialize in various data sources work directly with or even change metadata structures in those data sources. We refer to these developers as *data source experts*.

Universe developers map terminology and values from backend data sources into language that end users understand, creating content referred to as universes. It is quite common for an SAP customer to have numerous universes for different business audiences that need slightly different terminology or data constructs.

The third community, developers who provide end users with prebuilt analytic content are referred to in this chapter as *analytics content developers*. Analytics content developers enable users to analyze their applications' data and to gain additional insights about their businesses.

Any of these layers may be used by partners or customer developers. This chapter primarily addresses universe developers and analytics content developers. These developers may embed these capabilities into their applications or provide prebuilt analytics.

Instead of developing their own proprietary BI tools, ISVs and customer developers can save time and development resources by integrating SAP BI tools into their applications. Developers can choose to bundle reports or other BI content with their applications, or they can embed BI tools into their applications.

In terms of bundling BI content:

BT-CI-1. To help end users gain immediate insight into their businesses, SAP recommends creating SAP BusinessObjects BI content (such as reports and visualizations) that is specific to their enterprise applications and data.

SAP BusinessObjects BI Tools at a Glance

Just as you'd find a range of tools in a toolbox, so the SAP BusinessObjects BI tools offer a variety of tools to meet the needs of different business users.

ISVs and customers often want to add or embed reporting to their applications.

SAP Crystal Reports, a familiar tool to many developers, allows users to extract data from data sources, create predefined formatted reports, and distribute that information to a large audience.

SAP BusinessObjects Dashboards (formerly Xcelsius) enables data visualization. It provides highly visual and interactive Flash dashboards suited for casual BI users from executive and managers to operational staff. Visualizations created using this tool are often embedded into applications.

SAP BusinessObjects Explorer provides a search engine-like user interface to enable users to find data that is relevant to their business needs. The simple user experience makes it possible for anyone to directly interact with the data online or on any mobile device and extract necessary information without help from experts or IT staff.

Some users want to go further in their analysis of data, particularly power users. For this, **SAP BusinessObjects Web Intelligence** provides ad hoc query and reporting that let users create queries and formatted reports from heterogeneous data sources either online or offline. When in-depth data analysis is required, **SAP BusinessObjects Analysis** provides online analytic processing (OLAP) analysis of large multidimensional data sets. When connecting to SAP BW, SAP BusinessObjects Analysis provides in general more functionality and better performance than SAP BusinessObjects Web Intelligence.

All of these tools (as well as some others we do not detail in this chapter) are unified by the **SAP BusinessObjects Business Intelligence platform**. The platform has its own SDK, and ISVs and customer developers who embed the platform in their applications can offer additional capabilities such as user management, group and role management, single sign-on, scheduling, report viewing, and data analysis. More about this SDK and the SDKs for embedding particular BI tools are covered later in this chapter.

With this introduction in mind, this chapter now turns to an overview of the role of the BI platform and its semantic layer, followed by a bit more detail on each tool and where you can learn more about it as well as recommendations relevant for particular tools and information about embedding BI capabilities and content into your applications.

BI Tools and the BI Platform

The SAP BusinessObjects philosophy has always been to give each user the right BI tool for the way he or she works. Power users who want to analyze data need a different experience than an executive who wants to track and monitor key metrics. In other words, business users have distinct needs and different IT skill sets. The suite of SAP BusinessObjects BI tools provides business users with access to information across different categories: reporting, dashboards, analysis, and exploration on a single, scalable BI platform.

Figure 7-2. SAP Business Objects BI Tools

BI tools and the BI platform can be embedded in applications by customers or partners. Some of the BI tools can be deployed standalone, without the SAP BusinessObjects BI platform.

The SAP BusinessObjects BI platform is the underlying infrastructure for managing users and BI content. The platform enables the BI features to scale up to serve users in the largest enterprises. From a technology standpoint, BI tools are modular additions to the BI platform. Developers and administrators can choose to deploy the BI platform along with a particular BI tool or with several tools. See Table 7-1 later in this chapter for details about which SAP BusinessObjects BI tools require deployment of the platform.

BT-BO-2. SAP recommends that developers incorporate SAP BusinessObjects software into their applications to provide data visualization and analysis.

The BI platform is included in the following products:

- SAP Crystal Server
- SAP BusinessObjects Edge
- SAP BusinessObjects BI

In practice, many development teams choose to embed BI platform services in their applications. This offers a number of advantages:

- **Scalability.** By embedding the platform into your application, you will be able to scale no matter how many users are being supported by your application on customer sites

- **User management.** This helps ensure that the right information is provided to the right users with the right authorizations

- **Scheduling and distribution of reports**

- **Ease of understanding for business users,** since a semantic layer can be used to transform complex data structures into terms that business users can understand

- **A solid foundation.** Particularly for SAP Crystal Reports, the SDKs are different for simply embedding a report in an application without a server-based solution and with a server-based solution. By incorporating the platform from the outset, developers can avoid the expense of writing code now and rewriting it later when they want more capabilities

Embedding the BI platform does not mean that developers must purchase the full range of BI tools. If only Crystal Reports or SAP BusinessObjects Dashboards is needed, developers can deploy just the tools that they currently need for their application and add additional tools later if more BI features are added in future releases.

Some tasks related to embedding the platform are particularly relevant for ISVs with an OEM relationship with SAP.

To Learn More

SAP BusinessObjects OEM program for ISVs:
    http://www.sap.com/partners/partnerwithsap/oem

The Value of the Semantic Layer

The semantic layer, which is part of the BI platform, abstracts the complexities of the underlying data structures to make them more understandable and usable by end users. The semantic layer acts as a security barrier, allowing access to only data that has been released for reporting purposes.

Anyone who has worked with data long enough knows that unifying data from a user perspective is a challenge. Large companies often have multiple data warehouses, databases, and enterprise applications in place in various divisions. Thanks to the common semantic layer, accessing data from disparate parts of the enterprise, then combining these sources in a single report is possible using universes.

A universe is an organized collection of metadata objects, which are mapped onto data structures in data source systems. They enable business users to analyze and report on corporate data in nontechnical language. These objects include their own dimension, measures, hierarchy, and attribute definitions as well as predefined calculations and functions applied to source data and queries against data sources. A universe at runtime includes connections to the data sources so that queries can be run on the data source components themselves.

The role of universes is to provide the business user with understandable business objects, such as Revenue, Country, and Year. The user is free to analyze data and create reports using relevant business language regardless of the underlying data sources and structures.

As such, the semantic layer is useful to developers who help customers with the data diversity dilemma and to ISV partners who may create universes to package particular niches of data and then resell them or bundle universes as part of their applications. A universe can bring order to many data sources and enable data exploration, reporting, and visualization.

BT-META-1. SAP recommends using the SAP BusinessObjects semantic layer as an intermediate layer between reports, analytics, queries, analysis, and dashboards and the underlying database.

Using the semantic layer, you create universes, which allow application developers to simplify access to data schemas for their users. The tool for creating universes is the information design tool, a metadata design environment that enables a designer to extract, define, and manipulate metadata from relational and OLAP sources.

Universes created using the information design tool can be used by the following SAP BusinessObjects data analysis and reporting applications starting with SAP BusinessObjects BI 4:

- SAP BusinessObjects Web Intelligence
- SAP Crystal Reports for Enterprise
- SAP BusinessObjects Explorer
- SAP BusinessObjects Dashboards

The information design tool allows you to:

- Create connections to data sources, including multidimensional and relational data sources
- Publish universes
- Create security profiles to define user access to universe data and metadata
- Perform universe maintenance

BT-UNIV-2. For new development, SAP recommends using the information design tool for universes.

For SAP BusinessObjects customers who already have considerable investment in SAP BusinessObjects solutions and in universes created with the universe design tool, universe designers can continue to use these previous versions within the 4.0 release and slowly migrate to the information design tool.

BT-UNIV-3. SAP does not encourage using the universe design tool for creating universes.

SAP Crystal Reports Business Views are maintained in the product solely for SAP Crystal Reports legacy purposes and have not been enhanced or developed in recent releases. It is not possible to convert Business Views created with Business View Manager XI 3 to a format that is compatible with SAP Business Intelligence BI 4 reporting tools. Universes are the primary way to access data for SAP BusinessObjects Business Intelligence BI solutions.

BT-META-2. SAP does not recommend using SAP BusinessObjects Business Views as the semantic layer.

Table 7-1 summarizes dependencies between BI tools, universes, and the BI platform.

Table 7-1. BI Tools and Relationship to the BI Platform and Universes

Tool	Primary use of tool	Requires BI platform?	Use of Universe as a metadata layer	How this tool can access data from SAP Business Suite
SAP Crystal Reports for Enterprise	Creating formatted reports	Yes	Required for most data sources, not needed for BW access	Either through SAP NetWeaver BW or directly
SAP Crystal Reports 2011	Creating formatted reports	No	No	Either through SAP NetWeaver BW or directly
SAP BusinessObjects Dashboards	Creating dashboards	No	Recommended	Dedicated connector to BEx queries
SAP BusinessObjects Explorer	Search and exploration of data	Yes	Recommended	Through SAP NetWeaver BW
SAP BusinessObjects Web Intelligence (applet, HTML)	Ad-hoc query and reporting	Yes	Required for most data sources, not needed for BW access	Dedicated connector to BEx queries
SAP BusinessObjects Web Intelligence Rich client	Ad-hoc query and reporting	No	Required for most data sources, not needed for BW access	Dedicated connector to BEx queries
SAP BusinessObjects Analysis, Edition for OLAP	Interactive access to multidimensional data via the Web	Yes	No	Accesses SAP HANA, SAP Netweaver BW and other OLAP sources
SAP BusinessObjects Analysis, Edition for Microsoft Office	Interactive access to multidimensional data via Microsoft Excel and PowerPoint	No	No	Accesses SAP HANA, SAP Netweaver BW and other OLAP sources

To Learn More

SAP BusinessObjects Information Design Tool User Guide:
http://tinyurl.com/infodesigntool

SAP BusinessObjects Universe Design Tool Guide:
http://tinyurl.com/universedesigntool

The BI Toolbox

This section provides more detail on each of the BI tools.

Crystal Reports

Crystal Reports offers enterprise reporting for situations where reports need to be well formatted for printing or to be distributed to a large audience. Also, developers can embed Crystal Reports into their applications (see the section on integration with SDKs later in this chapter).

Of specific consideration for the current releases of Crystal Reports is that two versions exist side-by-side. SAP Crystal Reports 2011 is a natural progression from SAP Crystal Reports 2008 with minimal incremental features. SAP Crystal Reports for Enterprise, which is where the development team has invested the majority of its effort, is a newly designed report design tool targeted at ease of use, SAP data consumption, and native support for the semantic layer in SAP BusinessObjects BI 4.0.

Crystal Reports is capable of reporting on underlying data structures with or without the use of the semantic layer offered by Universes. Typically, Universes are not used in an application if the reports are consuming data from:

- Proprietary application data
- .NET data sets or .NET data tables
- JavaBeans
- Plain Old Java Objects (POJO)
- Web services
- XML

Crystal Reports can also directly consume the data generated by stored procedures which are executed in databases.

SAP Crystal Reports for Enterprise is only capable of reporting on data coming from the SAP BusinessObjects Semantic Layer, SAP BW, SAP BEx Queries, and SAP BusinessObjects Analysis views. The initial release of SAP Crystal Reports for Enterprise does not support direct-to-data connectivity. In addition, it is dependent on the BI Platform and does not provide a standalone solution.

Creation of Crystal Reports follows a traditional workflow in which business users (or customers) request reports, and analysts or report developers create them.

The way that you implement Crystal Reports depends on what you are trying to do and how many users you anticipate. It also partly depends on your long-term BI capability and usage vision. See the section on Crystal Reports SDKs later in this chapter for further elaboration on choices in this area.

SAP BusinessObjects Dashboards

SAP BusinessObjects Dashboards is a drag-and-drop visualization tool to create interactive analytics for powerful, personalized dashboards providing flexibility through free form layout, layering of visual controls and fine grained control over mouse events.

It delivers casual BI users visual access to operational and analytical information assets, including the ability to plan scenarios with what-if analysis. Dashboards can be accessed from web applications such as portals, BI launch pad, and custom web applications. Dashboards can also be accessed from desktop application such as Adobe PDF and MS Office. Like Crystal Reports, creation of dashboards follows a traditional workflow in which users request a BI dashboard solution and developers create it. Developers often create dashboards that add visual elements to their applications.

SAP BusinessObjects Dashboards can consume data from transactional relational databases or OLAP sources. Typically, it connects to these data sources through the SAP BusinessObjects BI platform, retrieving the data via universes and BEx queries (starting with SAP BusinessObjects BI 4 Service Pack 1). Dashboards can also consume data from Web Intelligence report documents or Crystal Reports tables.

To connect to SAP Business Suite application data, SAP BusinessObjects Dashboards has a dedicated connector to BEx queries. In this scenario the SAP NetWeaver BI Java server is required.

SAP BusinessObjects Dashboards can also consume data coming from web services and XML feeds.

Query as a Web Service is an older connectivity mechanism that is superseded by the Universe Query Panel available within the Dashboard designer tool (starting with SAP BusinessObjects BI 4).

BI-DASHBOARDS-1. SAP does not recommend using Query as a Web Service as a data connectivity method for dashboards.

SAP BusinessObjects Explorer

SAP BusinessObjects Explorer is suitable for all levels of users. Users can explore information via the Web with no training and no knowledge of the underlying data model. This tool is ideal to give anyone the ability to directly answer questions, especially for those that are not already included in standard corporate reports.

SAP BusinessObjects Explorer requires the use of the BI platform.

Insight derived from SAP BusinessObjects Explorer is easily sharable with others. Explorer can be embedded quickly into web applications. It can be used online or on a mobile device or tablet. Explorer users can access their information from anywhere and continue their exploration in an ad hoc manner.

To Learn More

SAP BusinessObjects Explorer page on SDN:
http://www.sdn.sap.com/irj/boc/explorer

SAP BusinessObjects Web Intelligence

Web Intelligence is an ad hoc query and reporting tool for both business users and power users. While Explorer offers data search and exploration capabilities to all users, including casual users, Web Intelligence enables business users and power users to drill down and navigate their data.

BT-QUERY-1. SAP recommends using Web Intelligence as an ad hoc query and reporting tool.

Web Intelligence supersedes the older Desktop Intelligence:

BT-QUERY-2. SAP does not recommend using Desktop Intelligence as a query and analysis tool.

Desktop Intelligence is a legacy report-writing tool included in the product to support legacy applications. It is at the end of its support life.

Web Intelligence has more features and capabilities than the Desktop Intelligence product. It also has a rich client for offline work. Web Intelligence requires the use of the BI platform, but a standalone version of Web Intelligence called SAP Crystal Interactive Analysis does not require the use of the platform. In this case, data being explored is entirely on the desktop system.

To Learn More

SAP BusinessObjects Web Intelligence on SDN:
http://www.sdn.sap.com/irj/boc/webi

SDN page on standalone Web Intelligence:
http://www.sdn.sap.com/irj/boc/iade

SAP BusinessObjects Analysis

SAP BusinessObjects Analysis is a suite of tools for power users and analysts that provides highly interactive access to multi-dimensional data stored in SAP BW or HANA. It allows for powerful yet easy-to-use analysis of large, complex datasets.

BT-ANALYSIS-1. SAP recommends using SAP BusinessObjects Analysis to interact with multi-dimensional data.

BusinessObjects Analysis is available in two editions: Analysis, edition for Microsoft Office, which provides deep integration with Microsoft Excel and PowerPoint, allowing users who normally work in those tools to access and analyze data in that familiar environment and Analysis, edition for OLAP, which is a web-based tool that provides these analysis functions in the browser.

To Learn More

SAP BusinessObjects Analysis, edition for MS Office:
http://www.sdn.sap.com/irj/boc/analysis

SAP BusinessObjects Analysis, edition for OLAP:
http://www.sdn.sap.com/irj/boc/analysis-olap

BI on Mobile Devices

With SAP BusinessObjects Mobile solutions, you can bring BI content to users who don't normally interact with BI applications or tools.

Two applications are available: SAP BusinessObjects Mobile and SAP BusinessObjects Explorer Mobile.

SAP BusinessObjects Mobile

SAP BusinessObjects Mobile allows you to access business intelligence (BI) reports directly on mobile devices. Users can intuitively access, navigate, and analyze reports without the need for additional training.

Reports can be deployed quickly onto mobile devices because IT can leverage existing BI content and infrastructure. The architecture leverages SAP BusinessObjects BI platform functionality, such as user authentication and management and content management.

When a user requests a report using a mobile device, the SAP BusinessObjects Mobile server, a component that is deployable on the BI platform, passes the request to the Web Intelligence server, which returns the report, just like a normal Web Intelligence request. The application on the device has been designed to render the document according to the device's screen size. The benefit is that a report doesn't have to be designed specifically for a particular device or screen size. The rendered document is automatically stored on the device for offline analysis. All communication, content, and metadata (including usernames and passwords) are encrypted.

SAP BusinessObjects Explorer for Mobile

Through simple keyword search, navigation, and visualization, SAP BusinessObjects Explorer for mobile allows business users to answer business questions from a mobile device and puts business information at their fingertips.

SAP BusinessObjects Explorer for mobile automatically displays the data visually on the mobile device so that business users can get insight at a glance and share their findings using their mobile device.

To Learn More

SAP BusinessObjects Mobile: http://tinyurl.com/bomobile

Using BI Tools and Platform SDKs

Software development kits (SDKs) enable third-party developers who obtain licenses from SAP to embed the BI platform into their applications. This section describes the SDKs for the BI platform and BI tools in brief.

To Learn More

SAP BusinessObjects BI 4.X Developer SDK Library:
http://www.sdn.sap.com/irj/boc/sdklibrary

BI Platform SDKs

The BI platform SDK is the same for SAP BusinessObjects BI, SAP BusinessObjects Edge, and SAP Crystal Server.

Universe SDK

SAP BusinessObjects BI 4.0 includes the legacy Universe Designer with its COM-based SDK. An SDK for the information design tool is not currently available.

Crystal Reports SDKs

Two categories of SDKs that support the Crystal Report file type: component-based SDKs and server-based SDKs.

The runtime of a component-based SDK is composed only of runtime files. These runtime files are easy to integrate into a third-party application; they are small lightweight libraries that run in the same process with a third-party application. However, this also means that the application needs to load these files into memory and the reports are then processed and rendered within the application's memory space. This is also called in-process reporting.

On the other hand, the runtime of a server-based SDK is composed of both runtime files and a report server. The server portion is normally a Windows service or the equivalent in a Unix/Linux environment. The SDK sits between the report server and the application front end. It forwards the requests from the application to the report server and the report server does most of the work. It processes and renders the reports and then delivers the finished rendered report back to the SDK to be sent to the end user.

Server-based solutions are used when other capabilities such as report scheduling and ad hoc data access are required. Server-based solutions are also better when the application will be used by more than a handful of users or for mission critical applications. SAP Crystal Reports for Enterprise only offers a server-based runtime; component deployment is not applicable for this product.

BT-BO-3. SAP recommends using functionality from any of the following products when developing using the component deployment model:

- *Crystal Reports 2011*
- *Crystal Reports 2008*

- *Crystal Reports XI Developer*
- *Microsoft Visual Studio*
- *Crystal Reports for Visual Studio .NET*
- *Crystal Reports for Eclipse*
- *Rational Application Developer*

On the other hand, one component that is outmoded is the Crystal Reports report designer component:

BT-BO-3a. SAP does not recommend using the Crystal Reports report designer component (RDC), which is an older COM-based solution.

The following guidelines provide additional information to help partners and customers choose the right type of deployment for their needs:

BT-BO-4. SAP recommends using the component deployment model for the following situations:

- *Small, self-contained component desktop applications*
- *Small Web applications that will be accessed by a department or work group in a company*
- *Reports that are run on demand*
- *A reporting engine embedded in the application process*

SAP recommends using the server deployment model rather than the component deployment model in more demanding situations like the following:

- *For mission-critical Web applications that need report processing failover*
- *For reports that need to run at specific times or are based on specific events or the successful completion of a third-party business process*
- *For reports that share objects like formulas, SQL commands, text objects, and images in an object-oriented repository*
- *For managing shared reports*
- *For providing access to enterprise data via web services*
- *For situations with a complex semantic data layer*
- *Where robust security options for user, group, object, and folder levels are required*
- *For batch report processing*

SAP BusinessObjects Dashboards SDKs

SAP BusinessObjects Dashboards has an SDK that enables developers to create their own add-ons and extend out-of the box visualization library and data connectors. Add-ons for Dashboards 4.0 and earlier releases are developed using Adobe Flex 2.

To Learn More

SAP BusinessObjects Dashboard Design SDK:
http://www.sdn.sap.com/irj/boc/xcelsius-sdk

Web Intelligence SDKs

There are lower level Java APIs that expose a subset of the functionality available in Web Intelligence DHTML (web client) frontend.

To Learn More

Web Intelligence Report Engine Java SDK:
http://help.sap.com/javadocs/bip/40/re/en/
resdk_java_apiRef_40_en.zip
Web Intelligence Custom Data Source Framework SDK:
http://help.sap.com/businessobject/product_guides/boexir4/en/
xi4_cdp_dev_en.pdf
Object Model Diagram:
http://help.sap.com/businessobject/product_guides/boexir4/en/
xi4_rebean_omd.pdf

Open Document API

The Open Document API is used for referencing BI documents using a URL.

Packaging BI Tools with Applications

This section of the chapter deals with packaging BI tools in third-party applications. It covers topics such as:

- Authentication and authorization
- Managing users
- Packaging applications
- Installation

Authentication and Authorization

SAP BusinessObjects BI supports mapping SAP roles to roles in the SAP BusinessObjects BI platform. After you map SAP roles, users are able to log on to BI platform applications with their SAP credentials. This eliminates the need to recreate individual user and group accounts within the BI platform.

SAP BusinessObjects BI also supports LDAP, Windows Active Directory, Trusted Authentication and its own Enterprise Security. Third-party applications may have their own proprietary authentication schemes as well.

BI-SEC-1. To enable federated identity management, SAP recommends using Trusted Authentication. This technique allows developers to leverage their own security model to provide single sign-on from their application to SAP BusinessObjects BI.

To Learn More

Business Intelligence Platform Administrator's Guide:
http://tinyurl.com/bi-admin-guide

Managing Users

The BI platform allows you to perform user management. It is possible to achieve single sign-on by adding users, adding users to groups, and deleting users in the BI platform at the same time that you add users to your application. Single sign-on is when a user signs into an application and is seamlessly signed in to any BI tools to which they should have access.

BI-USER-1. When embedding the BI platform, SAP recommends that developers follow up any user management tasks in their applications with a corresponding user maintenance action in the BI platform.

For example, if a user is added to the application, that user should be added to the BI platform. Similarly, if a user is deleted from an application, that user should also be deleted from the BI platform.

To Learn More

Sample code for adding users: http://tinyurl.com/addusers

Packaging Applications: Deploying Content

SAP BusinessObjects provides the following tools for importing objects across two SAP BusinessObjects Business Intelligence platform deployments that are at the same version number.

- Lifecycle management console
- LCMBIAR Command-Line Tool

The Lifecycle management console for SAP BusinessObjects Business Intelligence platform is a web-based tool that enables you to move BI resources from one system to another system, without affecting the dependencies of these resources. It also enables you to manage different versions of BI resources, manage dependencies of BI resources, and roll back a promoted resource to restore the destination system to its previous state.

You can promote a BI resource from one system to another system only if the same version of the SAP BusinessObjects Business Intelligence platform application is installed on both the source and destination systems.

BI-PKG-2. When deploying a BI solution, SAP recommends using the lifecycle management console for importing and exporting objects.

BI content and configuration information can be backed up and packaged in an LCM Business Intelligence Archive file or LCMBIAR file. LCMBIAR files are similar to WAR files with content and a deployment descriptor and make it easier for customers and partners to package and deliver BI content with their application. They are packages of content such as dashboards, reports, queries, and universes that can be distributed with an application. All of the BI platform rights, permissions, and bindings of the content are kept intact when the content is packed in a LCMBIAR file. They can be deployed through a UI-based tool or silently deployed via a command line or Java-based API for seamless integration.

BI-PKG-1. When delivering a BI solution, SAP recommends packaging the content as LCMBIAR files.

Older versions of SAP BusinessObjects BI include a tool called the Import Wizard that can be used for moving objects across different BI systems and for the creation of archive files for distribution. The Import Wizard tool is superseded by the lifecycle management console, therefore:

BI-PKG-3. SAP does not recommend using the Import Wizard tool for importing and exporting objects.

To Learn More

Lifecycle management tool can be found in the Administration Guide:
http://tinyurl.com/lcmconsole

Installation

SAP BusinessObjects BI has an interactive setup that asks for several configuration parameters when the software is installed.

When developers embed SAP BusinessObjects BI in their applications, it is possible to create a silent installation that is embedded into other installations being performed. Developers can create a response file, which records all needed configuration options, and then can include it in their installers so that the installation is silent from the end user's perspective.

BT-INST-1. When silent installation is required, SAP recommends the use of response files to silently install SAP BusinessObjects BI.

To Learn More

SAP BusinessObjects Partner Extranet (Service Marketplace user required): http://tinyurl.com/bo-partner

Business Analytics Webinar Series: http://tinyurl.com/bowebinars

SAP BusinessObjects Support: http://service.sap.com/bosap-support

SAP Crystal Solutions Support:
https://www.sdn.sap.com/irj/boc/support

Business Analytics Community: https://www.sdn.sap.com/irj/boc

SAP BusinessObjects Downloads:
https://service.sap.com/bosap-downloads

SAP Crystal Solutions Downloads:
https://www.sdn.sap.com/irj/boc/downloads

Product Guides & End User Documentation:
http://help.sap.com/businessobject/product_guides/

Installation and Upgrade Guides (Service Marketplace user account required): https://service.sap.com/bosap-instguides

Release Notes (Service Marketplace user account required):
https://service.sap.com/bosap-releasenotes

BusinessObjects Articles (Technical Whitepapers):
https://www.sdn.sap.com/irj/boc/articles

Tutorials: http://www.sdn.sap.com/irj/scn/bi-suite-tutorials

Chapter 8

Application Development Guidelines for Best-Built Applications

For ISVs, guidelines related to application development are among the most important. How you will develop your software, what software architecture and programming language you will use, how you will deploy it, how you will test it, how to ensure it is enterprise-ready—all of these topics are highly relevant to ISVs developing applications that complement the SAP Business Suite.

Introduction

Before you even write a single line of code, it makes sense to think about how the software will integrate with back-end systems, such as the SAP Business Suite. Of course, you will decide this based on your business context—including your existing skill set, where your market is today, and where you see it headed. Naturally, form has to fit function: the technical design needs to be optimal for the intended purpose of your product.

Like all the chapters in this book, you won't find how-to information in this chapter. How to code in ABAP or in Java is not covered here. Instead, we highlight the major decisions that ISVs should consider regarding the development of their products, including integration points with the SAP Business Suite.

This chapter covers general guidelines, ABAP-specific guidelines, Java-specific guidelines (both for development on NetWeaver and migration to NetWeaver), and then third-party platform development guidelines.

A word about programming environments before we begin. At SAP, you may hear more about ABAP than Java in some areas. This is natural since SAP invented and develops ABAP and is the main source for information and tools relating to ABAP. SAP also stands behind Java and Java development, but of course is not the main or only source of information about Java. SAP supports development in multiple languages, including ABAP, Java, and others as well.

This chapter stands in close relationship to all the other chapters of this book and frequently references them. In some ways, this chapter provides a bridge between all the other chapters in the book from a high level. Here are just a few examples of guidelines that bridge from the content in other chapters to this chapter:

- SAP's Application Lifecycle Management (ALM) highlights decisions to be made to ensure the quality and supportability of your product as well as how customers should deploy and operate it. It includes aspects like aligning what operating system, database and SAP platforms your product runs on with SAP's product availability matrix or PAM (see ALM-PRD-5), how to handle software change management (ALM-REL-3), and contextualizing ITIL as an overarching industry standard from which SAP's ALM draws (ALM-PRD-1)

- Process orchestration and service-oriented architecture guidelines cover how the business logic of your programming can best integrate with the components of the SAP Business Suite. One of the key guidelines states that ISVs should use enterprise services (SOA-WS-2) when integrating with SAP applications. Additionally, the business logic layer encompasses the business process layer and the messaging layer, both of which are described in Chapter 4

- User interface (UI) and user experience (UX) guidelines cover aspects such as UI harmonization (UI-GOV-1), which can help SAP users feel at home with your application

- Enterprise information management (EIM) encompasses how a company's data is handled as a whole and so should inform application development. For example, ISVs should write applications in a way that ensures business data quality (EIM-DIDQ-1)

- Data visualization and reporting is often part of application development as well. Choosing an SDK that scales with the application can eliminate the need for later rework (BT-BO-2)

- Security is of paramount importance for everyone, but is especially relevant for enterprise-ready applications. For example, the guidelines recommend using Security Assertion Markup Language (SAML) as a way to exchange authentication and application credentials across security domains (SEC-STD-3)

Scanning through this list provides good food for thought when considering how your product should integrate with the SAP Business Suite. Figure 8-1 illustrates this view.

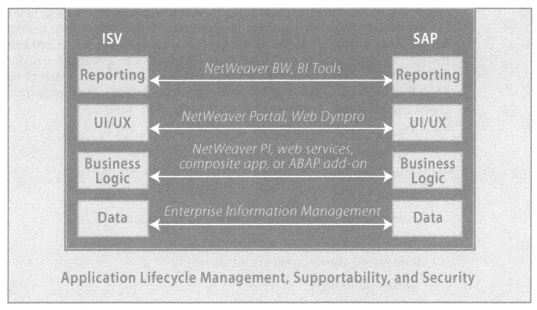

Figure 8-1: Integration Points

There is no one-size-fits-all method for integrating with the SAP Business Suite. There are a number of options to choose from and in fact multiple integration points could be used simultaneously. For instance, if you write an Add-On in ABAP that runs embedded in a Business Suite component, it would be quite natural to use all the NetWeaver capabilities together (all the light blue boxes in Figure 8-1). Another option would be to develop a .NET-based product and use just web-service based integration in the business logic layer. Integrating with the SAP Business Suite is not only about linking features and functions on the reporting, UI/UX, business logic, and data levels but it is also about integrating with SAP's Application Lifecycle Management procedures and incorporating supportability and security. In short, considering all the integration points in Figure 8-1 can help make your product "enterprise-ready," that is, ready for mission-critical business use.

The remainder of this chapter is divided into general guidelines (which apply to all ISVs regardless of the development environment that they use), ABAP guidelines, Java guidelines, and .NET guidelines.

General Guidance

In the following sections, the general guidance provided applies to any software that integrates with the SAP Business Suite, regardless of its platform.

Making Software Enterprise Ready

For any software development effort, the most expensive mistakes are made in the initial planning and design phase of a software lifecycle. If development is launched too quickly without sufficient planning, later rework can be extremely expensive. Rapid prototyping of an initial product idea can help to refine the business functions of a future product. However, although prototyping helps in understanding the use case and the features needed, before final coding begins, more guidance should be considered to design and code a product that will be "enterprise ready." Enterprise ready refers to a range of criteria. On a strategic level, consider the concept of Timeless Software as described by SAP CTO Vishal Sikka (http://vishalsikka.blogspot.com/). Eight principles characterize Timeless Software (http://tinyurl.com/sdn-timeless):

- Decoupling of "content" and "container"
- Separation of concerns between technology layers
- Componentization
- Design locality
- Adaptable provisioning, independent of consumption
- Separating intent from optimization
- Optimizing across layers of abstraction
- Design-thinking

The basic idea behind Timeless Software is that SAP's customers use a single release of their mission critical business applications often for a very long time with few if any changes to their core application deployments. This is why SAP supports its products for 7+2 years (see Chapter 3 for details). It also raises the question of how to create innovative software for customers despite the longevity of their core applications. SAP's promise to customers is to deliver "innovation without disruption," and SAP recommends that its partners commit to a similar approach.

Innovation without disruption is accomplished in part by following the eight principles of Timeless Software. One example of the use of such principles is the "separation of concerns between technology layers," which is shown in Figure 8-1. We will make further use of these principles in the rest of this chapter.

On a practical level, making software enterprise ready entails:

- Having an application lifecycle management (ALM) practice for all products to enable supportability
- Providing scalability and strong performance for large systems (with many terabytes of data and having a high-volume transactional and reporting load)
- High availability of the overall solution. A business solution needs to offer a deployment that avoids any single point of failure through redundancies so that customers can, if needed, achieve high availability of their productive landscapes for mission critical applications
- Accessibility. Software must be able to serve the needs of a diverse workforce

- Documentation (including installation, administration, tuning, reference, and security guides)
- Globalization. The software should support multicurrency, multiple languages, local handling of dates and numbers, and so on
- Security features and best practices

Componentization

The SAP Business Suite (some components of which are shown in Figure 8-2) is designed according to the Timeless Software principle of componentization, which allows SAP to deliver larger blocks of new application innovations over time without the need to replace previously deployed components.

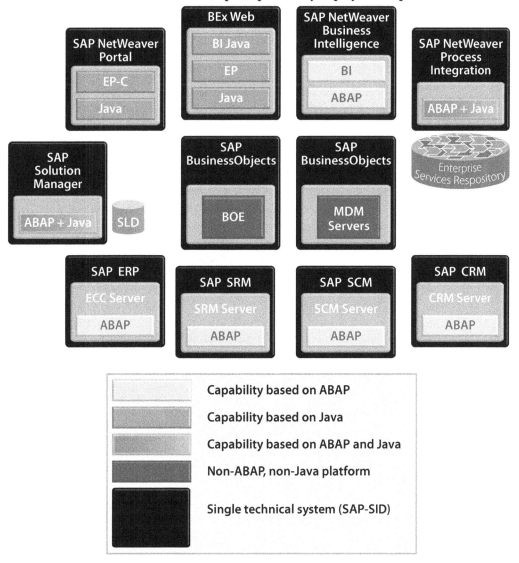

Figure 8-2. Some SAP Business Suite Components and Their Major Stack Requirements

> **DEV-COMP-1. SAP recommends componentization of business application solutions.**

Single Stack

One thing you might notice about the Business Suite is that most components run on a single stack, whether ABAP or Java.

> **DEV-AS-1. SAP recommends developing components built on a single stack, whether ABAP, Java, or a third-party platform.**

In other words, an ISV should select one platform for one application component, not mix and match different platforms. The platform in question could be SAP NetWeaver ABAP, SAP NetWeaver Java, or any third-party platform.

The platform the ISV chooses may or may not be the same platform as the runtime platform for the SAP component with which their application integrates. If the ISV application and the SAP component run on the same platform, it might be an option for customers to deploy the ISV solution on the same system. This obviates the need to maintain a separate system for the ISV solution and therefore reduces the customer's total cost of ownership (TCO).

On the other hand, there are valid reasons for an ISV to choose an alternative platform. An ISV might have experience with only one particular platform, or might want more independence from SAP releases (which can be achieved particularly if they use interfaces that SAP keeps stable over time), or might be addressing a special use case that requires a particular platform (decision to use open source, acquired products, or other reasons). Any of these might reduce total cost of development (TCD) for the ISV. So there are good reasons for an ISV solution to use the same platform as the SAP Business Suite as well as good reasons to use a different platform (but usually no good reasons to use multiple platforms for one component, which is the rationale behind DEV-AS-1 above). Good knowledge of the individual purpose of an ISV solution is needed to evaluate all trade-offs and to make a platform decision.

Integration through APIs and Composite Applications

While it's best to create an application that runs on a single stack, that doesn't exclude the idea of composite applications or the use of APIs in general. For example, an ISV might extend an app in ABAP and then write a Java composite that sits in front of it, since composite applications can be ideal for creating customer-specific solutions.

A double stack is an application that calls from one program stack to the other within a single application. Scalability is an issue with such applications.

Since composite applications are generally independent from the SAP solution platform, they offer a good way to provide innovation without disruption. Since SAP core application installations are long lived, so are the APIs to that core. In order to make SAP applications easily extensible, existing APIs are kept stable for multiple releases of SAP applications. Therefore, developing composite applications is a very good way to add innovative new functions to existing SAP installations:

DEV-COMPOSITE-1. SAP recommends creating composite applications to support new business processes or scenarios without the need to modify or enhance SAP Business Suite components.

Using SAP's composite application platform (SAP NetWeaver CE) enables the newest technology innovations to be used to front-end a range of current and older SAP Business Suite releases.

When integrating via service calls, cross-platform application communication should be lean; look at making one coarse-grained compound call that groups smaller calls into one interaction rather than making many separate fine-grained calls (see Chapter 4).

The Enhancement and Switch Framework

Using the Enhancement and Switch Framework, the SAP Business Suite follows the Timeless Software principle of innovation without disruption. Customers can pick and choose which new functionality they'd like to activate in SAP systems on the level of business functions. As ALM-PRD-3 in Chapter 3 suggests, ISVs should familiarize themselves with the Enhancement and Switch Framework and advise their customers about which SAP functionality needs to be enabled to integrate their solution. By defining the relevant dependencies between the ISV solution and SAP software on a business function level, ISVs can make sure that their solutions can be activated only if the SAP business functions the ISV solution depends on are also activated.

Enabling only those features that are needed by a particular customer when the customer wants them is what the Timeless Software principle of "separation of intent from optimization" is about. It helps our customers reduce the number of features that they need to deal with and thus reduces TCO.

If what you want to do involves adapting, that is, changing or enhancing SAP ABAP code, SAP objects in the DDIC (the SAP Data Dictionary), or other objects, it should be done using the Enhancement Framework and the classic append technology for DDIC objects, but this requires great expertise in the SAP application and its implementation.

To Learn More

"How to Get the Most From the Enhancement and Switch Framework as a Customer or Partner" by Thomas Weiss: http://tinyurl.com/blog-esf

Extensibility

DEV-COMP-2. SAP recommends that business solutions allow customizations and extensions of their functionality.

Many customers have unique requirements for their business processes and following this guideline helps them. In order to make applications extensible and maintainable over time, ISVs should keep interfaces to their solutions stable so that releases are forward- and backward-compatible.

Extensibility has multiple dimensions. The data model or business object model may require additional fields or require support for locally needed features. Another dimension of extensibility is the ability to adapt a process to meet the needs of a business. For more information on building extensible applications, see *Building Extensible Composite Applications with SAP* by Matthias Steiner (SAP Press, 2009).

Deployment

A key decision to make in the design phase is what the final deployment of an ISV product will look like in relationship to the customer's SAP landscape.

In relationship to an SAP landscape, deployment of a complementary solution can be categorized as being either "very close," "close," or "distant." Running very close or close simplifies some aspects of integrating with SAP Business Suite, both from a performance perspective and from a security perspective. This demonstrates the Timeless Software principle of design locality.

Applications that are very close to the SAP Business Suite run in the same application server instance with SAP. This includes ABAP Add-Ons, described in Chapter 3, and Java applications running on the same instance of SAP NetWeaver as the Suite.

Running close to the SAP Business Suite means having a local integration, in which the ISV application runs in the same local network[1] and security zone as the SAP Business Suite.

Running close or very close to the Business Suite allows the use of SAP-proprietary interfaces such as BAPIs and other remote enabled function modules (by means of RFC, Java Connector or .Net Connector). These proprietary interfaces have been supported for a long time, have been kept stable and backward compatible, and have been tuned for high performance. However, these interfaces often can't be used over longer distances in distributed landscapes and can't penetrate firewalls easily like enterprise services can (see Chapter 4 for details about enterprise services). Therefore, a decision to always deploy in a close or very close configuration reduces the flexibility and agility of the complementary solution.

Alternatively, a complementary solution can be designed to support a "distant" deployment so that the extension can connect via wide area networks, such as company intranets or the Internet, to a customer's core SAP applications and can span different security zones, enabling business processes that might be executed across multiple distributed locations. For this to work, potentially distant extensions need to use standard protocols and data formats for communication, such as web services. Examples of distributed process steps

---

1   The term local network refers to running in the same data center, whether that data center is in the cloud or on-premise.

include credit checks or any type of business-to-business (B2B) scenario. The use of standards-based connectivity methods enables customers to easily integrate application extensions in their existing network and security infrastructure.

Complementary solutions that can support distant deployments can also be deployed in close or very close configurations. The standard protocols that work in distributed systems work equally well in local systems. Some developers worry about performance impacts, but optimization at the cost of flexibility and agility is often a mistake. Remember the Timeless Software principle that recommends "separating intent from optimization."

Data Layer Considerations

Integrating at the data level does *not* mean accessing data or metadata in databases of SAP Business Suite components directly.

There are a couple of reasons for this. First, data integrity is critical, and requires proper locking for concurrent access control. As a result, SAP data stores must be modified only through the application layer.

Second, the additional metadata information added by SAP's application server layer (called the SAP Data Dictionary or DDIC) is not visible when accessing databases directly. Without this metadata, it is not easy to interpret what data means and what constraints it has (such as allowed value ranges).

DEV-DATA-1. SAP strongly recommends that data in SAP applications be accessed only via interfaces supplied by SAP.

Data integration comes in many flavors, and above all should support customers in managing their business data as they need to. Examples include:

* Aligning the metadata definition of business objects in order to avoid the need for extra data types and data structure conversions and transformations. (ISVs should consider adopting SAP's data model (see Chapter 4, SOA-GDT-1)

* In addition to the data exchange described under business logic layer integration earlier in this chapter, there are various import and export methods for integrating data at the data level. For example, when larger volumes of data have to be exchanged using an extract, transform, load (ETL) process, it's common to use batch processing for handling that data

* Data tools described in Chapter 6 can be used for data cleansing

* Moving data to SAP NetWeaver BW enables flexible and fast reporting

* Integrating at the data level could also entail using SAP NetWeaver Master Data Management in order to synchronize master data between SAP and the partner application

When changing data either in an ISV solution's own data store or in an SAP Business Suite component, it is important to guarantee transactional integrity by having clear commit or rollback handling. For SOA-based integration, this means there needs to be robust error handling as discussed in Chapter 4.

DEV-DB-1. SAP recommends that the persistency layer should be free of application logic.

This guideline is specifically about not using third-party database-specific constructs such as stored procedures and triggers. Doing this ties the complementary application to a particular database product, but different SAP customers have chosen different databases, and all SAP customers like to have choices. From a performance perspective, for most workloads, the application server tier offers better scalability and more efficient concurrency control than a single database instance. Executing application code on the application server is preferable to executing database-specific operations in the database that could be coded more neutrally at the application layer.

The application layer includes an abstraction of the database (for example, SAP OpenSQL), which allows the use of different database products from different database vendors without any change to application coding (this provides another example of the Timeless Software principle of componentization).

Native database access methods that use third-party database vendors' proprietary SQL syntax may be efficient, but limit applications to running on a single brand of database. What might be gained by using native methods versus standard SQL is ultimately lost when code must be modified to support another database platform.

Separation of Concerns and Interface-Driven Development

Interface-driven development provides another angle on the subject of separation of concerns (mentioned earlier in connection with the separation of concerns between technology layers).

Software is usually developed not by one individual but by a team. In fact, there may be multiple groups of developers and even multiple companies involved in development (if, for example, some development is outsourced).

Separation of concerns here relates to enabling interface-driven development by many people or groups. Componentization of software products is a prerequisite for development-related separation of concerns. Another prerequisite is following a good application lifecycle management methodology, in particular in regard to software change management as described in Chapter 3.

Functional Correctness

SAP customers have complex system landscapes, and applying changes and fixes to enterprise software requires a particular methodology (see "Change Management" in Chapter 3). As a result, ISVs should follow a high standard for functional correctness and include rigorous quality assurance testing to eliminate as many problems as possible before software is released.

> **DEV-QA-1. SAP recommends creating test plans and using state-of-the-art testing tools to ensure functional correctness before releasing software.**

Open Source

SAP NetWeaver incorporates some open source software. SAP stands behind this code and provides support for it as if it were SAP's own code.

In the same way, partners are responsible for supporting their product, including any open source software embedded in it.

Another factor to consider with open source software is the potential impact of license terms on enterprise customers. Open source software is distributed under a variety of licenses. Depending on the terms of the license, you may or may not be able to sell that software to enterprise customers without legal ramifications. For example, open source software licensed under the Apache License is generally easy to incorporate into your software. Software that is licensed under the GNU General Public License (GPL) is far more challenging because of the concept of copyleft[2] versus copyright.

> **DEV-OS-1. SAP recommends that ISVs keep track of any open source software that is integrated into their products. SAP also recommends that ISVs carefully analyze the terms of the license of any open source software that is integrated into their products, considering license terms from a business perspective.**

To Learn More

SAP's use of open source:
http://www.sdn.sap.com/irj/sdn/opensource-integration

Guidelines for ABAP Development

SAP invented and continues to update and improve the Advanced Business Application Programming (ABAP) platform. ABAP is a powerful application platform that includes the ABAP programming language, the ABAP development environment, and the ABAP application server.

As a platform, ABAP offers:

- A multilayered architecture
- Scalability
- A proven runtime environment

---

2   See http://www.gnu.org/copyleft

The ABAP platform offers features that support the entire application lifecycle. It has numerous features and functions that support workflow, organizational management, and data elements such as business objects. Programming business applications in ABAP is particularly easy because you have all these features. ABAP developers benefit from the infrastructure that SAP created for itself and shares with its partners to help streamline their development as well.

As a language, ABAP is a fourth-generation programming language that supports both procedural and object-oriented development and incorporates special support for business programming:

- Built-in vendor-independent database access with Embedded OpenSQL
- Internal tables, which store and represent the business data of the database tables in the application layer and UI layer in the same table structure
- Internationalization support
- Powerful transaction management at the server level
- Effective cooperative logical locking: as much as necessary, as little as possible
- Infrastructure such as organizational management

As a development environment, ABAP offers an efficient toolset supporting the full development lifecycle.

As an application server, ABAP is an enterprise-ready runtime machine including:

- Highly scalable, high performance synchronous and asynchronous user request processing
- Batch processing
- Output (print) management
- Sophisticated technical and business activity monitoring
- Administration tools

SAP has invested significantly to update the ABAP platform over many years. Developers who learned ABAP in earlier releases should ensure that they are fluent in "modern ABAP."

> ***DEV-ABAP-1. SAP recommends using the version of ABAP released in SAP NetWeaver 7.0 and beyond.***

SAP uses ABAP for much of its own application development (see Figure 8-2). The ABAP language continues to evolve, and now incorporates such modern concepts as ABAP Objects, a fully object-oriented version of the ABAP language.

> ***DEV-ABAP-2. SAP recommends using ABAP Objects for new programming initiatives and for significant refactoring of older programs.***

Exceptions can be made when maintaining or adding small amounts of functionality to older, procedural programs, since refactoring the entire program in ABAP Objects then may not make economic sense.

To Learn More

ABAP Objects: https://cw.sdn.sap.com/cw/docs/DOC-40131

ABAP Programming Guidelines

ABAP programming guidelines are helpful to all ABAP programmers, whether at partners, at customers, or SAP's own internal developers who program in ABAP.

Although there have been many books about ABAP programming, until recently there was no statement from SAP about how to program most effectively in ABAP. In 2009, Horst Keller, along with Wolf Hagen Thümmel, published a book called *Official ABAP Programming Guidelines* (SAP Press).

The guidelines in this book consist of 120 rules in four areas:

- Readable Programs
- ABAP Specifics
- Programming Model
- Correct and Robust Programming

For each rule, you'll find:

- Background information
- The rule itself
- Detailed information
- A bad code example
- A good code example

Some of the information contained in this book was drawn from the ABAP Keyword Documentation. Effort is being made toward folding even more of the information from the book into this area.

> ***DEV-ABAP-3. SAP recommends the SAP Press book,* Official ABAP Programming Guidelines, *to learn more about effective ABAP programming.***

To Learn More

ABAP: http://www.sdn.sap.com/irj/sdn/abap

ABAP Testing Tools

The ABAP environment provides a rich suite of testing tools so that you can verify the formal and functional correctness of your programs. Sophisticated static program checks should be part of each ABAP development process (use the Extended Program Check option in the ABAP Workbench or call it directly using transaction SLIN). The ABAP Unit testing tool supports you in writing, running, and organizing unit tests in ABAP. Together with the ABAP Coverage Analyzer, ABAP Unit provides you with the tools you need to develop according to a test-driven paradigm. You can test even more intensively with the Code Inspector. This tool also lets you automate mass testing. Extended Computer Aided Test Tool (eCATT) is used to create and execute function and integration tests. Its primary aim is the automatic testing of SAP business processes.

The ABAP Workbench offers a variety of useful tools to develop ABAP based add-ons and enhancements to existing development units.

To Learn More

ABAP testing tools: http://tinyurl.com/ABAP-testing

ABAP Test Analysis wiki: http://tinyurl.com/ABAP-Test-Analysis

Detailed information on Workbench tools can be found in the SAP NetWeaver Developer Guide in Docupedia: https://cw.sdn.sap.com/cw/docs/DOC-44656

Guidelines for Java Development

Java is an industry-standard application platform that includes the Java programming language, a Java development environment (there are many available), and a Java application server. SAP supports Java, and provides a Java development environment called the SAP NetWeaver Developer Studio, as well as a Java application server that includes SAP's own Java Virtual Machine (SAP JVM).

Like ABAP, the Java language continues to evolve. Java developers should use the versions of Java and Java EE supported in the latest version of SAP NetWeaver.

> ***DEV-JAVA-1. SAP recommends that Java developers use the version of Java and Java EE supported in the latest version of SAP NetWeaver.***

To find out which version of Java is supported in any given product, see the product availability matrix (PAM) at http://service.sap.com/pam (Service Marketplace user required).

Additional guidelines for Java developers depend on whether your application is developed on SAP NetWeaver and runs on NetWeaver, or is migrated to run on NetWeaver, or runs on a different application server entirely.

Developed on SAP NetWeaver

Developers who code on SAP NetWeaver should use SAP NetWeaver Developer Studio (see Figure 8-3).

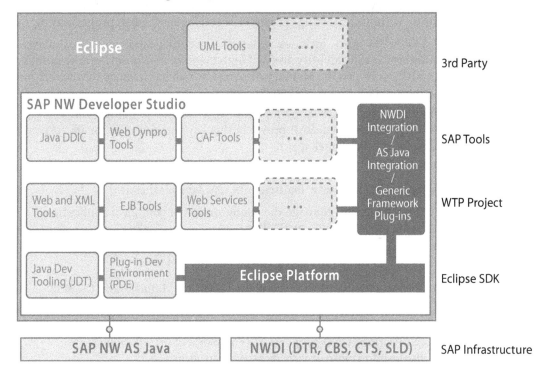

Figure 8-3. SAP NetWeaver Java Environment

SAP NetWeaver Developer Studio is based on Eclipse 3.4. It offers features especially suited to deploying code in an SAP environment. For example, to run an application on SAP NetWeaver, the EAR file should have an SAP manifest. SAP NetWeaver Developer Studio adds this manifest automatically.

Additionally, features to aid with enterprise team development are built into the components of the NetWeaver Development Infrastructure (NWDI), including:

- The Design Time Repository (DTR), a source code versioning system based on the WebDAV and Delta V open standards
- The Component Build System (CBS), a build server
- The Change Transport System (CTS), a software logistics tool[3]

DEV-JAVA-2. SAP recommends using SAP NetWeaver Developer Studio if you develop for and run on SAP NetWeaver AS Java.

---

3   If you need to do synchronous transport between ABAP and Java systems, use CTS+, which is part of the ABAP environment.

In addition to offering an SAP-aligned Java development environment, the SAP NetWeaver Developer Studio, SAP develops and maintains its own Java virtual machine, the SAP Java Virtual Machine (SAP JVM).

Unlike other JVMs, the SAP JVM allows developers to switch to debug mode on the fly without restarting the server, a convenience when programming.

The SAP JVM also includes extensive profiling and memory analysis capabilities to easily identify areas of high memory consumption and memory leaks. SAP developed the Memory Analyzer, which has been open sourced and is available at http://www.eclipse.org/mat/.

Support for the SAP JVM, as for other SAP software, follows the 7+2 year maintenance guarantee. SAP provides this support not only for its software but also for the Java stack it runs on.

Differentiating Points for SAP's Java Platform

Here are some noteworthy features of SAP's Java platform:

- Configurability. Manage the configuration of your Java application using tools provided by SAP

- Centralized software deployment. Manage software upgrades centrally using CTS and NWDI

- End-to-end monitoring using SAP Solution Manager and CA-Wily Introscope

- Built-in support to use RFC/BAPI interfaces of SAP's ABAP-based applications (JCO support), for complementary solutions to be deployed in close or very close configurations

- SAP JVM with the same behavior on 14 supported platforms

An excellent resource for learning more is *Java Programming with SAP NetWeaver*, 2nd edition, by Karl Kessler et al (SAP Press, 2008).

Guidelines for Migrating Java Apps to SAP NetWeaver

Another option for Java developers is to migrate their applications, written on another Java platform, to run on SAP NetWeaver AS Java.

A page devoted to Java EE migration and third-party integration is available on SDN (see http://tinyurl.com/Java-EE-migrate). It handles both potential dimensions of migrating to SAP NetWeaver:

- Migrating from a different application server

- Migrating to a newer Java EE release

Sample applications are available on the SDN Java migration pages.

To Learn More: Java Resources

> SAP Technology Troubleshooting Guide (covers NetWeaver Java AS issues): http://wiki.sdn.sap.com/wiki/x/wIN3Cw
>
> SDN's Java EE forum: http://tinyurl.com/Java-EE-forum
>
> Docupedia's SAP NetWeaver CE pages: http://tinyurl.com/Docuped-nwce

Guidelines for .NET Development

SAP and Microsoft have worked jointly on ensuring interoperability between the SAP Business Suite and .NET.

> *DEV-NET-1. SAP recommends that .NET developers use one of the following versions, all of which have been tested by SAP for interoperability:*
> - *.NET 2.0 with Web service enhancements 3.0*
> - *.NET 3.0*
> - *.NET 3.5*

.NET developers can integrate with the SAP Business Suite in a number of ways:

- Using RFCs and the .NET Connector
- Using SAP NetWeaver Process Integration (SAP NetWeaver PI)
- Using enterprise services
- Using Duet Enterprise

The .NET Connector enables connecting to the SAP Business Suite via RFCs. RFCs work well with tightly coupled configurations.

SAP NetWeaver PI represents a second way that .NET developers can connect with the Suite. .NET web services can be connected point-to-point or PI can be placed in a network DMZ for integration with remote .NET components.

SAP enterprise services can also be used to connect directly to .NET based applications, without PI.

To support easy integration on the user interface level, especially for Microsoft SharePoint, SAP and Microsoft have jointly developed Duet Enterprise.

To Learn More

> Duet Enterprise: http://www.duet.com

.NET developers who integrate applications with the SAP Business Suite on the business logic level can use either enterprise services and other web services, for full deployment flexibility, or SAP's RFCs, for deployments constrained to run in close or very close configurations.

SDN has an area specifically for .NET developers: http://www.sdn.sap.com/irj/sdn/dotnet. You'll find forums, articles, and blogs about .NET development.

SAP offers two tools to help with .NET development:

- The Enterprise Services Explorer for .NET helps integrate .NET applications with enterprise services
- The .NET Connector helps developers integrate their applications with RFCs

Further details about these tools can be found in Chapter 4.

To Learn More

Traditional classes: http://www.sap.com/services/education/index.epx

eLearning training classes: http://www.sdn.sap.com/irj/scn/elearn

Custom development resources: http://www.sdn.sap.com/irj/sdn/nw-development

SAP TechEd annual regional conferences: http://www.sdn.sap.com/irj/scn/sapteched

Virtual TechEd, which makes TechEd session presentations available to you at any time : http://www.sdn.sap.com/irj/scn/vste

Code Exchange is a relatively recent addition to the SDN area of the SAP Community Network. Code Exchange provides an environment where community members can share and collaboratively develop prototypes.

To Learn More

Information and to join CodeExchange: http://www.sdn.sap.com/irj/scn/code-exchange

Chapter 9

Security Guidelines for Best-Built Applications

Like medieval fortresses, IT application landscapes have multiple layers of defense against security breaches. This chapter provides an overview of how SAP partners can incorporate enterprise-ready security into their applications when planning products that integrate with the SAP Business Suite.

Security is naturally of critical concern for SAP customers. The data held in SAP and other enterprise applications is literally the lifeblood of the customer's business. Customer data, for example, must be kept private both for the sake of the customer's relationship with the company and for the sake of preventing competitors or thieves from exploiting that data. Customer data leaks have a deleterious effect on brands.

As a result, ISVs must take special care to develop their applications securely and to provide interoperability with industry standards that SAP supports.

This chapter covers topics such as:

- Secure programming guidelines
- Identity management (IdM)
- Security Assertion Markup Language (SAML) and single sign-on
- Security zones, security infrastructure, and transport security

Secure Programming Guidelines

The most critical concern for ISVs relative to security is to ensure that their applications are programmed in a secure fashion. User input should be validated to prevent a variety of attacks including SQL injection and the like.

SAP has secure programming documentation for both ABAP and Java developers (https://cw.sdn.sap.com/cw/docs/DOC-19597). The documentation covers topics such as:

- Secure programming
- Password security
- Secure Store and Forward (SSF)
- Security logging
- SAP NetWeaver Virus Scan Interface
- Secure user interface
- Cross-site scripting
- SQL injection
- Input validation
- Canonicalization (data transformation into a standard format to ensure proper signature processing)
- Directory traversal
- URL encoding and manipulation
- Cookie manipulation

Developers should read this documentation and follow the suggestions provided for secure programming. Because no document is exhaustive and security topics are constantly evolving, developers should supplement this documentation with additional information so that they can stay abreast of the latest issues related to secure programming.

Another facet of secure programming is designing an application that is auditable. Increasingly, records of changes to data (what the change was, when it happened, and who made the change) need to be available for later review by independent auditors. Your application should offer logging to provide customers with auditability of changes.

Framework-based Secure Programming Helps

Developers who code on the SAP platform, whether SAP NetWeaver Java Developer Studio or ABAP Workbench, will find that the framework itself provides some level of protection against common attacks. For example, input from a user could include malicious commands or SQL designed to crash the program and gain access to backend systems. As a result, input should be constrained, validated, or encoded to prevent such attacks. The software framework in the SAP platform helps developers with these low-level types of problems. For example, Code Inspector, part of the ABAP Workbench, offers numerous code checks, including security checks (see http://wiki.sdn.sap.com/wiki/x/VQ4 for details).

Developers who use third-party platforms, such as .NET or third-party Java frameworks, should search out the best available resources on secure programming for those environments and implement best practices.

Security Guides

ISVs should provide their customers with security information about running their applications. Security guides are product-specific, and SAP provides such guides for its products. These guides are an important reference for ISVs:

> **SEC-STD-1. SAP recommends that ISVs follow secure programming guidelines, read the SAP security guides, and adhere to relevant industry standards and SAP product standards to ensure security of customer's business-critical applications.**

Links to all the security guides can be found on the SAP Service Marketplace (Service Marketplace user required; see http://service.sap.com/security). In addition to the security guides, this area of the Service Marketplace provides links to SAP information about the following topic areas:

* Application security (includes topics such as auditing and authorizations)

* Secure collaboration (includes topics such as digital signatures, SAML, secure store and forward or SSF, and web services security)

* Secure user access (includes topics such as identity management, authentication and single sign-on, and access control)

* Infrastructure security (network-level security)

The Media Library in this same area contains many links to documentation and presentations.

Developing Security Functions

Only programmers with expertise in security should develop security functions. For example, while a security expert should be able to develop a robust custom Java login module to enable OpenID-based SSO to the SAP NetWeaver Java Application Server, a developer without the proper level of expertise might design a module that is easily hacked. For this reason, it's better to leave development of security functionality to experts and use established security libraries rather than developing your own.

Security Functions in SAP NetWeaver Application Server

The SAP NetWeaver platform has some security functions built in that you can leverage. The platform includes support for authentication, single sign-on, and user management. (User management is handled locally by the application server whereas identity management, described in the next section of this chapter, refers to the discipline of centrally managing distributed user stores with the support of an identity management system.)

Authentication, Authorization, and User Management

Authentication is very important in software security. Usernames and passwords are commonly used for authentication, but what happens when users have many usernames and passwords to remember? Identity management systems provide a solution to this problem. Users don't want to remember numerous username and password combinations (they aren't very good at it either). Furthermore, from an administrative perspective, setting up users in many different systems creates a maintenance nightmare.

As a result, a central identity management system is needed for some scenarios (see Figure 9-1 for an example landscape using SAP NetWeaver Identity Management). The process of setting up or provisioning user accounts and permissions needs to be carefully managed and monitored through approval workflows.

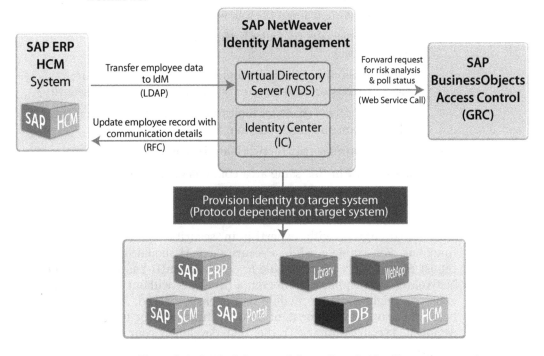

Figure 9-1. Centralizing user information via identity management

Revoking privileges and deprovisioning users is even more important and must be accomplished very quickly. IdM should also be integrated with a human resources system where hiring and discontinuing employment is processed and where authorizations are determined.

Application users typically have particular functions to fulfill, which means that they need authorizations associated with their IDs. Such authorizations are also a means to implement segregation of duties schemes for business processes where, for example, purchasing a product and paying the vendor need to be separated both for legal compliance reasons and for good business practices.

Single Sign-On

Single sign-on is a combination of two basic security concepts: authentication and authorization. Authentication means proving that users are who they say they are. Authorization relates to what you are allowed to do.

Single sign-on at an application level allows users to authenticate (prove that they are who they say they are) and then have access to a collection of applications that they are authorized to use. The opposite of single sign-on is having users sign on to each application that they access.[1]

The technology used for single sign-on is different depending on whether you are dealing with a single security domain, such as an intranet, or multiple security domains.

In a single network, such as an intranet, SSO is usually implemented using Kerberos or cookie-based technologies such as SAP logon tickets (described later in this chapter).

The problem is that although such technologies may meet initial demands, in the long term, there is often a need for a multidomain solution, that is, a solution that can cross security domains. A security domain is a network of computers that rely on one identity management system. Crossing security domains requires establishing trust between two (or more) security domains. Crossing security domains requires a different type of authentication scheme where trust can be established and credentials passed between the domains. SAP, like many other organizations, supports SAML for this purpose.

SAML

The Security Assertion Markup Language (SAML) is an industry standard from the Organization for the Advancement of Open Internet Standards (OASIS).[2] SAML is designed for exchanging security credentials and implementing SSO across security domains.

Here's an example of how it works. If an application user (called a principal) needs to authenticate to an application in another security domain (called a service provider or SP), the user could request a token from an identity management system (an identity provider or IdP). The user can then present the authentication token to the application (service provider) for authentication. The user gets an authentication token from the IdP only once per logon session and can use it for connecting and authentication to multiple different SPs without needing to do a formal user/password login for every application connection.

---

1   An excellent resource on single sign-on is *Single Sign-On mit SAP* by Martin Raepple (SAP Press, 2010), available at http://sappress.de/2409. An English translation is planned for publication in 2011.

2   OASIS propagates many standards, including the WS-* standards. For more information about SAML, see the OASIS website at http://www.oasis-open.org/specs/index.php#saml.

> ***SEC-STD-3. SAP recommends Security Assertion Markup Language (SAML) version 2.0 for central authentication and single sign-on when integrating homogeneous SAP landscapes as well as heterogeneous landscapes.***

Even if you are using non-SAP identity management, using SAML for interoperability provides a good foundation for integrating a variety of systems in a standardized way.

SAML is used in mainly two scenarios: web-browser single sign-on and single sign-on for SOAP-based[3] web services.

Web Browser Single Sign-On

In the case of single sign-on for web-based applications, SAP NetWeaver supports a number of authentication methods: basic authentication (username and password), X.509 digital certificates, SAP logon tickets (based on cookies), Kerberos, and SAML 2.0, which is the preferred approach.

SAML 2.0-based web browser SSO is supported as of SAP NetWeaver AS ABAP 7.02 SP3 and SAP NetWeaver AS Java 7.20.

To Learn More

NW IDM 7.1 SP5 Release Notes: http://tinyurl.com/nwidm [4]

Kerberos is supported only in SAP NetWeaver AS Java via the SPNEGO Login Module, described later in this section.

SAML 2.0

Of the options just outlined for web browser SSO, SAML 2.0 is the preferred choice. SAML 2.0 represents a substantial enhancement over SAML 1.1 and is in fact incompatible with SAML 1.1.[5]

SAML 2.0 provides three important benefits:

- **Single sign-on.** The ability to authenticate once and access all relevant applications.

- **Single logout.** The ability to log off all relevant applications at once (when the user signs out, the identity provider terminates all open sessions at the service providers where the user is still signed in)

- **Identity federation.** The ability to aggregate different identities (logons) in different systems

---

3   To date, REST-based web services do not use SAML's HTTP profile; at present, the best fallback solution for RESTful SSO is mutually authenticated SSL connections using client-side X.509 certificates.

4   Service Marketplace user required.

5   Earlier releases supported the SAML 1.1 standard in SAP NetWeaver AS Java 6.40 and 7.00. This support was limited to a specific profile (the Browser Artifact Profile) and a service provider role only (SAP did not ship a SAML 1.1 Identity Provider with these releases).

Authenticating via Certificates

There are two ways commonly used to authenticate using certificates in an SSO scenario. Both are based on Kerberos.

SAP NetWeaver AS Java supports Kerberos via the SPNEGO module (that stands for Simple and Protected GSS API Negotiation Mechanism). SPNEGO is an appropriate means to support SSO primarily in an intranet (that is, behind the firewall). But it can also be used as the first step of a more complex SSO scenario where a Kerberos token will be transformed and exchanged with a SAML token used by the application for SSO that crosses security domains.

To Learn More

SPNEGO: http://wiki.sdn.sap.com/wiki/x/7BwB

Microsoft Active Directory also uses Kerberos and X.509 certificates.

SAP Logon Tickets

SAP Logon Tickets are used broadly in SAP applications and components like SAP BW and SAP CRM. They are usually issued by a Portal system in an SAP NetWeaver-based landscape. An SAP Logon Ticket is—like a SAML Assertion—a statement about a successful authentication of a user. However, it is not an industry standard and can't be used for cross-domain or B2B scenarios.

SAP will continue to support but not further enhance SAP Logon Tickets. As of SAP NetWeaver 7.20, SAP fully supports and recommends SAML 2.0 (see guideline SEC-STD-3 above). For SSO within an SAP-only landscape in an intranet, the SAP Logon Ticket still remains an option if the customer does not want to run a SAML Identity Provider.

Since ISVs are often concerned about the maximum utility for their software (flexibility to be used in multiple scenarios), it makes sense to implement SAML 2.0 rather than SAP Logon Tickets.

However, SAP Logon Tickets are a valid option for SSO for those customers who have an SAP-only landscape, don't need to cross security domains, do not have high security requirements, and do not have a central identity management or directory server that could serve as a SAML identity provider.

SEC-SSO-1. SAP does not recommend using SAP Logon Tickets for single sign-on in heterogeneous landscapes, outside the corporate firewall or in an environment with high security requirements.

To Learn More

SAP Logon Tickets: http://tinyurl.com/saplogontickets

SOA Single Sign-On

SOA single sign-on is needed when one system must authenticate to another while invoking a SOAP-based web service.

Figure 9-2 shows a simple scenario. First the user authenticates to a portal, and then the portal invokes a web service, authenticating to the business system.

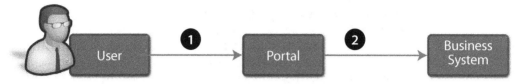

Figure 9-2. A user authenticates to the portal, and the portal authenticates to the business system in the backend.

Before SAML, there was no good security solution for this scenario. As a workaround, web service calls were done under a special account, called a "technical user," so that they looked as though they came from a single authenticated user. However, this meant that access to business systems through web services could not be traced to individual users.

All users of SAP systems, whether direct or indirect, must have a license (there are different levels of SAP user licenses, providing full or more limited access). SAP customers have agreed to—and want to—ensure that every user is licensed, but the need to allow programmatic logins for application-to-application communications via a technical user made that difficult.

With SAML, tokens can be used to authenticate each individual user that invokes a business system through web services, as specified by WS-Security. There are two confirmation methods to use a SAML token to confirm an authenticated user:

- Sender Vouches
- Holder of Key

The second approach, Holder of Key, is more consistently implemented and, in testing performed by SAP, has proved more likely to be interoperable. It allows for a specialized service called the Security Token Service (STS) to issue tokens based on trust relationships between various entities. This helps with interoperability because a Kerberos ticket can be presented to an STS in exchange for a SAML token, simplifying interoperability between different types of systems while ensuring security.

SEC-STD-4. SAP recommends that web service calls be authenticated with SAML tokens that use the SAML Holder of Key confirmation method to ensure auditability and interoperability.

To Learn More

More details: http://wiki.sdn.sap.com/wiki/x/AlGhBg

Identity Management

Identity management systems act as an identity provider in SAML scenarios. SAP NetWeaver Identity Management is increasingly the preferred method for provisioning users versus the Central User Administration (CUA) found in SAP NetWeaver.

SAP NetWeaver Identity Management has several advantages over CUA:

- For SAP-only landscapes, it provides management of users across both the SAP Portal and the Business Suite

- It provides centralized user management across heterogeneous vendor application landscapes

- It helps organizations to implement IT governance measures including self-service password resets, advanced workflows, controls, and auditing

Because SAP customers will be increasingly moving toward SAP NetWeaver Identity Management from CUA, it is important that ISVs ensure that their products work well with SAP NetWeaver Identity Management. [6]

SEC-STD-2. SAP recommends that ISVs delegate authentication and role management to SAP NetWeaver Identity Management. Solutions built on SAP and non-SAP platforms can continue to use platform-specific authorization concepts, but SAP recommends delivering identity-related development artifacts (such as authorizations and roles) as an integral part of the solution and centralizing the management of this data by integrating with SAP NetWeaver Identity Management.

Microsoft .NET Security

SAP verifies interoperability with Microsoft .NET by testing specific scenarios. The following scenarios between SAP NetWeaver Process Integration 7.1 EHP1 and the Microsoft .NET Framework 3.5 have been tested:

- Synchronous and asynchronous communication (WS-RM 1.1, SOAP 1.1) with non-addressable clients with:

    - Security on communication transport level using HTTPS and authentication methods

        - X.509 SSL Client Certificate (Transport Channel Authentication)

        - User ID/Password (Message Authentication)

        - X.509 Certificate (Message Authentication)

---

6   SAP NetWeaver Identity Management can be downloaded from the Service Marketplace (http://service.sap.com); a temporary license is available for software evaluation.

¤   Security on message level using symmetric/asymmetric message signature/encryption and authentication methods

·   User ID/Password (Message Authentication)

·   X.509 Certificate (Message Authentication)

Further, WS-SecureConversation can be used to build a security context. SAP is currently leveraging WS-SecureConversation primarily to allow WS-ReliableMessaging to reuse a security context.

To Learn More

SAP and .NET security interoperability:
http://www.sdn.sap.com/irj/scn/articles-dotnet-all

Security Zones, Security Infrastructure, and Transport Security

When considering security domains, the innermost area is typically the corporate internal network. The internal security domain, or intranet, is where the core SAP Business Suite components run. ISVs with tightly integrated applications may also run in this security zone.

The outermost security layer is the boundary between a customer's datacenter network and external networks, especially the Internet. Enterprises often create a demilitarized zone (DMZ) just outside their data center "fortress" (see Figure 9-3).

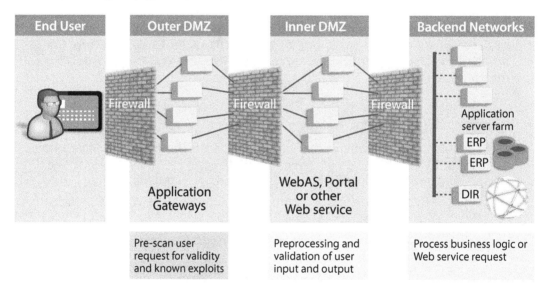

Figure 9-3. Security Zones

The DMZ typically contains network firewalls and other network edge services (NES) that provide security features such as defense against malicious access of application systems in the inner security zones of a company.[7]   However,

---

7   For a presentation on Network Edge Services by Richard Probst and Joerg Nalik, see http://tinyurl.com/nes-presentation.

DMZ security functions are not limited to network technologies; certain application components may also be placed in a DMZ. Examples include the SAP NetWeaver Portal, through which traffic going to backend applications in inner security zones might be channeled, and SAP NetWeaver Process Integration, which, when placed in the DMZ, can serve as a security layer for messaging traffic.

Even composite application components may be put in a DMZ, especially if they are designed to selectively provide business information from tightly secured backend systems to remote users without allowing general access to all data in the backend system. An example of such a composite might be an application that allows a company to communicate with its suppliers without revealing company secrets.

Moving further away from the corporate data center, some applications that integrate with the SAP Business Suite might be running outside the customer's data center. An increasingly popular example would be integration with a software as a service (SaaS) offering such as SAP Business ByDesign.

SEC-ZONE-1. SAP recommends that ISVs advise customers about which security zone is most appropriate for deploying the ISV's application.

Encryption

Another aspect of security is encryption, which may be needed at multiple layers. First of all, transport security entails encrypting network traffic to and from your application. For a typical SAP business application, all traffic should be encrypted, even if only handled within a company's internal network, because all transaction steps, user screens, and messages may contain company confidential business data. This requirement is different from online stores where most information is catalog and advertisement content and only a few data elements need to be encrypted, for example, credit card numbers during the checkout process. Sometimes stored business data is also highly confidential; in this case, encryption might also be used for storing data, whether in databases or in other storage mechanisms.

Conclusion

The most important security guidance for an SAP partner is that the partner should deliver clear guidelines to their customers regarding security best practices for their products. All points mentioned earlier in this chapter are potential touch points of security features that are built into the SAP Business Suite and that can be built into an SAP partner's solution.

To Learn More

SDN Security and Identity Management:
http://www.sdn.sap.com/irj/sdn/security

Chapter 10

NetWeaver Gateway Guidelines for Best-Built Applications

This sneak preview of the NetWeaver Gateway chapter provides only an initial overview of the topic. Guidelines and additional content are being prepared for the full version of this chapter. Visit http://bestbuiltapps.sap.com *for updates.*

Introduction

SAP NetWeaver Gateway is a product from SAP that provides access to SAP Business Suite data for lightweight, people-centric applications that can run on a variety of devices and application platforms.

To understand the importance of SAP NetWeaver Gateway, it's important to understand the larger context into which it is being introduced. The SAP Business Suite supports the comprehensive business needs of enterprise customers in a way that is flexible and meets the needs of large companies in a wide variety of industries. SAP has always allowed extensions, modifications, and add-ons to the Business Suite and a large global community of ABAP developers is involved in supporting SAP's customer and partner base by producing changes and additions to tailor or complement SAP software. In addition to these more substantive modifications, SAP customers increasingly need lightweight applications that can be developed and deployed in a very short time and that can leverage multiple large developer communities for many different application and device platforms.

Here a bridge between the traditional environment of the SAP Business Suite and lightweight applications is needed. SAP NetWeaver Gateway functions as such a bridge:

- **A bridge to non-ABAP platforms.** Gateway makes data persisted in SAP Business Suite components easily accessible by lightweight applications running on non-ABAP platforms

- **A bridge to new developer communities.** Gateway offers a framework for providing simple REST-based APIs to non-ABAP developer communities, exposing content from RFCs, BAPIs, and ABAP Dynpro screens as well as other data from the SAP Business Suite

- **A bridge that simplifies complex data structures to make them more lightweight.** The multifaceted, comprehensive business objects of the SAP Business Suite can be reduced to simpler data structures

- **A bridge that can provide agility for deploying lightweight applications.** Because of its key role in business processes, many companies follow application lifecycle management best practices for the SAP Business Suite (see Chapter 3). Lightweight applications can follow a more agile development and deployment model, compared with methodologies such as creating ABAP Add-Ons, for example

The following chapter describes the lightweight approach Gateway offers, the technology it is built on, deployment options, and how to create and consume Gateway services.

OData and REST Support

SAP NetWeaver Gateway supports the Open Data Protocol (OData). This protocol builds upon and extends open standards like RSS and the Atom Publishing Protocol that offer simple REST services. SAP leverages the extensibility of the OData protocol to provide additional annotations tailored for consuming SAP Business Suite data.

OData

OData is a web protocol for querying and updating data. OData is released by Microsoft under the Open Specification Promise to allow anyone to freely interoperate with OData implementations.

SAP endorses OData and has incorporated some extensions. These extensions have been submitted for inclusion in a future update of the OData protocol. The extensions enable human-readable labels for properties, free-text search (via OpenSearch), semantic annotations (especially for mobile devices that need integration with contacts, for example), and capability discovery, so that clients don't attempt something they can't do via a Gateway service.

REST

Representational State Transfer or REST is an architectural style that makes it possible to consume data easily over the Web using a URL.[1] Because of its simplicity and lightweight nature, many developers today prefer a RESTful approach to consumption. REST services are especially easy to consume if they are designed to use just HTTP verbs and a URL to access data from or update data in backend systems. REST services are stateless, which means that all transaction-specific information is contained in the URL and not kept on the server, making them more efficient for high-volume, low-intensity use cases.

RESTful services are widely used by popular websites such as Twitter, Twilio, Amazon, Facebook, eBay, YouTube, and Yahoo! REST makes it possible to consume data easily using a URL, performing Create, Read, Update, and Delete (CRUD) operations via the corresponding HTTP verbs POST, GET, PUT, and DELETE.

In the wake of developer popularity of REST, SAP chose to launch SAP NetWeaver Gateway to offer support for a RESTful approach to services, complementing its large collection of existing enterprise services already in use by many customers. Gateway is an evolutionary step to support an expanding range of services and offer them via lightweight application and user interface technologies that are intended for consumption by end users. As such, it complements the web service based SOA and RFC/BAPI approaches for heavier weight application-to-application (A2A) and business-to-business (B2B) integration scenarios (see Chapter 4 for details about these approaches).

To Learn More

REST: http://en.wikipedia.org/wiki/Representational_State_Transfer

The OData web site: http://www.odata.org

"SAP NetWeaver Gateway Speaks OData with SAP Annotations:" http://tinyurl.com/odata-blog

Atom Publishing Protocol: http://atompub.org/

Broader Than Mobility

Gateway and mobility are often discussed in the same breath. However, they are separate topics (and will be covered in separate chapters in this book).

Mobile devices are driving a proliferation of lightweight applications. Many companies now offer iPad/iPhone, Android, and Blackberry apps, as well as apps for other types of devices. Because mobile application proliferation is occurring at an unprecedented rate, it is easy to conflate the ease of consumption of Gateway services with their use in mobile apps. In fact, however, any type of app can consume Gateway services. Gateway's openness is key.

---

1   Representational State Transfer or REST was first described in a PhD dissertation written by Roy Fielding in 2000. Earlier, Fielding helped write the specification for HTTP.

Here are some examples of Gateway application scenarios:

- Any external office or collaboration application (like Duet Enterprise for Microsoft SharePoint and SAP)

- Desktop machines using web-based applications running PHP, Java, Ruby, or any other programming or scripting language

- Native applications on mobile devices

- Embedded devices such as manufacturing robots or route planning software in satellite navigation systems

- Any other business scenario you can think of involving some programmable device that can speak HTTP

Architecture

Figure 10-1 provides an overview of Gateway's architecture, including the consumption of OData with SAP Annotations, and a variety of Data Source Providers. This architecture is explained in detail in the SAP NetWeaver Gateway Master Guide, which is part of SAP Help.

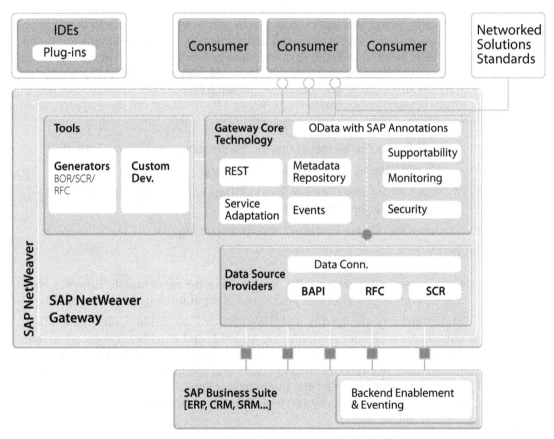

Figure 10-1. Gateway Architecture

To Learn More

SAP NetWeaver Master Guide: http://tinyurl.com/gw-master-guide

Deployment Options

SAP NetWeaver Gateway can be deployed in one of two ways in an SAP landscape:

* Standalone, shown on the left in Figure 10-2, in which SAP NetWeaver Gateway is deployed on a dedicated server

* Embedded, shown on the right. Gateway is installed as an ABAP Add-on and runs on the same system as the SAP Business Suite, so no dedicated server is required to run Gateway

Please note that SAP NetWeaver 7.02 is required to support deployment of SAP NetWeaver Gateway.

SAP NetWeaver Gateway is installed on a dedicated system

SAP NetWeaver Gateway is installed on the same system as the SAP Business Suite

Gateway Server

SAP NetWeaver Gateway Server

SAP Business Suite

SAP Business Suite

SAP Business Suite

Gateway Backend

SAP NetWeaver Gateway as ABAP Add-On

SAP Business Suite

Figure 10-2. A Simple Depiction of SAP NetWeaver Gateway Deployment Options: Standalone and Embedded

By deploying Gateway on a separate server, a single instance can provide connectivity for and content aggregation across multiple backend systems, which may be running different releases of the SAP Business Suite. It is also used for groupware such as Duet Enterprise. Standalone deployment works well for companies that want to start using SAP NetWeaver Gateway but that may have policy restrictions about when they can make changes to their SAP Business Suite system landscape.

Table 10-1 describes some of the differences between standalone and embedded deployment for Gateway.

Table 10-1. Features of Standard and Embedded Deployment for Gateway

	Standalone	Embedded
Deployment Type	Remote (in relationship to the SAP Business Suite, running on one or more separate servers)	Local (installed on the same computer as the SAP Business Suite)
Installation	Installed on a dedicated server	Installed as an ABAP Add-on
Deployment Landscape	Support for multiple backend systems, potentially running different versions of the SAP Business Suite. Content aggregation across multiple systems. Can be deployed in a DMZ for improved security	Single backend system (add-on to that system)
Duet Enterprise Support	Yes	No
Special Requirements	None	Reliant on the Backend Enablement component
Other Characteristics	Content generators, dedicated developer tools and content aggregation across multiple backends	Minimal development and runtime overhead: no dedicated server required

To Learn More

SAP NetWeaver Gateway Master Guide:
http://tinyurl.com/gw-master-guide

SAP Help on remote versus local deployment:
http://tinyurl.com/remote-local

Service Provisioning

SAP provides a growing number of ready-to-use Gateway services. However, in many situations different Gateway services may be needed for a given use case. In that case there are two ways to approach service provisioning for Gateway. First is a lightweight approach that involves taking existing SAP objects and generating a service from them. A second and more scalable approach is coding a Gateway service from scratch.

In either case, service provisioning for Gateway requires SAP skills, both technical and business skills. For coding Gateway services from scratch in addition ABAP skills are required. Services can be made available by SAP, by a partner, or by any developer with ABAP skills.

Techniques for Rapid Prototyping and Simple Scenarios

An easy no-code way to begin using Gateway is to use the ABAP Developer Workbench to generate a Gateway service based on one of the following:

- A Remote Function Call (RFC)
- An business object API (BAPI) in the Business Object Repository (BOR)
- Screen Scraping of an ABAP Dynpro transaction

Generated Gateway services consume slightly more resources at runtime than manually coded services do, making them ideal for small and medium volume use cases as well as for prototype implementations.

Note, however, that standalone deployment is required in order to generate Gateway services.

To Learn More

How To Create CRUD Operations in Gateway Services Based on Remote Function Modules: http://tinyurl.com/gw-from-rfc

How To Create CRUD Operations in Gateway Services Based on BOR Objects: http://tinyurl.com/gw-from-bor

How To Create CRUD Operations in Gateway Services Based on Screen Scraping: http://tinyurl.com/gw-from-scr

Service Consumption

SAP NetWeaver Gateway was designed to open the door to allow many types of developers to create solutions connecting to SAP Business Suite data. The fact is that since SAP NetWeaver Gateway is based on open standards, developers can use existing REST and OData libraries and APIs to consume Gateway services.

Tools for Accelerating Coding to Consume Gateway Services

While tools are not needed to write code to consume Gateway services, SAP provides some tools and plug-ins to help accelerate development for most popular development environments. For the current list of tools, please refer to the SAP NetWeaver Gateway section of SDN (http://www.sdn.sap.com/irj/sdn/gateway).

Gateway Demo System

To help interested customers and ISVs get started with Gateway, SAP has provided a demo system that is freely available via SDN. The demo system offers sample services so that developers can begin experimenting right away with Gateway.

The End . . . For Now

This concludes a very brief introduction to NetWeaver Gateway. A more complete chapter with guidelines is under development. Please visit http://bestbuiltapps.sap.com for the latest version.

To Learn More

SDN page on Gateway: http://www.sdn.sap.com/irj/sdn/gateway

SAP NetWeaver Gateway Documentation:
http://tinyurl.com/gw-documentation

Chapter 11

Mobility Guidelines for Best-Built Applications

This sneak preview of the Mobility chapter provides only a brief overview of the topic. Guidelines and additional content are being formulated for the full version of this chapter. Visit http://bestbuiltapps.sap.com *for updates.*

Introduction

Mobility is becoming the norm for corporate end-user computing devices. While people still say to one another, "I have to go to work," the fact is that many of us work from a variety of locations using mobile devices from laptops to tablets to smartphones. One could argue that mobility means that we can be at work anywhere (and unfortunately anytime).

This new milieu has not made life simpler for IT professionals. While once companies could specify which devices users would have and which IT would support, few companies take this approach now. Yet the challenges that corporate IT faces are much the same as they have always been, if not in fact exacerbated by mobility. The following questions highlight some of the challenges related to mobility:

- How can we keep corporate data secure but accessible while providing reliable performance to authorized mobile workers?

- How can we ensure that data on devices and in application backend systems remains synchronized?

- How can we support a wide variety of devices?

- How can we make sure that the software used on the devices is up to date?

- What happens if devices of corporate users are lost or stolen?

Despite the challenges, however, mobility is compelling technology, and companies are not slowing down their adoption of mobile applications.

Mobility is far from a new technology but one can argue that it has recently reached critical mass. We've moved from a few executives with Blackberries to almost everyone in the company having at least one mobile device and executives and knowledge workers sporting as many as three, with smartphones, iPads, and laptops in tow.

SAP made a strategic decision to base the interaction between the SAP Business Suite and mobile devices on the Sybase SUP and Afaria products. SAP's recent acquisition of Sybase provides partners and customers with full-featured support for enterprise mobility. The Sybase Unwired Platform (SUP) is a mobile application platform that enables developers to build applications that connect mobile workers with business data on any device, at any time.

Enterprises need to manage and secure mobile applications and devices as well. Afaria provides flexible mobile device management and security to help organizations control their mobile application portfolio.

As developers of applications for customers and partners, it's important to know the best approaches to take. This chapter will cover the following topics:

- Current mobile architecture, with an emphasis on online and offline applications and details about what those mean
- Lifecycle management considerations for mobile applications
- Device management for mobile applications
- Security guidance for mobile applications
- An inventory of SAP mobile technologies, past and present, with guidance on the best approaches to take for various use cases

Note

A full chapter on mobility is under development. Please visit http://bestbuiltapps.sap.com for the latest version.

To Learn More

SDN page on mobility: http://www.sdn.sap.com/irj/sdn/mobile

More Guidance for Best-Built Applications

Additional chapters will be added to the online version. You can always find the latest and authoritative version of this document at:

bestbuiltapps.sap.com

Please visit this site to learn more about the SAP guidelines for best-built applications that integrate with SAP Business Suite.

www.ingramcontent.com/pod-product-compliance
Lightning Source LLC
Chambersburg PA
CBHW080405060326
40689CB00019B/4138